Personal Transformation Help:

A Call to Magic

The Artful Science of
Transforming Self and World

Mitch Williams

Mitch Williams Magic Productions
665 South First Avenue
Canton, IL 61520
www.mitchinspires.com

ISBN-13:
978-1479320349

ISBN-10:
147932034X

Cover Photography by Tracey Frugoli
Edited by Marilyn Wilzbach
Foreword by George Catlin, Ph.D.
Quotation from *Esoteric Psychology Vol. II*, by Alice A. Bailey, quoted with the
permission of Lucis Trust.
Quotation from *Joy of Sports*, by Michael Novak, Madison Books, used with
permission.
Quotation from *Windows into Waldorf: An Introduction to Waldorf Education*, by David
Mitchell, © AWSNA Publications, used with permission of the author.

DEDICATION

To Richard Wayne Clark
1944—2012
Our artful and creative friend, who left us far too soon.
I just know you would have loved arguing about
the contents of this book.

ACKNOWLEDGMENTS

My profound gratitude and appreciation goes out to my editor, Marilyn Wilzbach, to George Catlin for writing the Foreword (and for coming up with the great title idea), and to my wife, Kathi, who inspires and enables me to be more than I am on a virtually daily basis.

Foreword

Magic has always fascinated me. I don't like to be fooled and think I'm clever enough to know when someone is pulling the proverbial wool over my eyes. Yet when I go to a magic show—including those of Mitch Williams—I am astounded that things are clearly happening before my eyes that are not at all possible.

It's wonderful to be so fascinated with life, with the unexpected, the seemingly impossible. And that's what this book is all about: the magic of living that we may not be noticing. Or practicing.

Mitch Williams has a message for us all. It's nicely summed up in an experience he recalls near the end of the book. It comes down to "open your eyes and change the world." But how? And is that possible? Who would dare to suggest that we could change this vast and troubled planet simply by opening our eyes? Maybe this isn't magic at all but a mere fantasy, an afternoon's entertainment but not the real philosopher's stone that will change this lead into gold.

That's the challenge of this book: Is it real? Can this man's story and all his insight possibly transform the world itself and our perception of it? I assure you, I would not be writing this *Foreword* if I were not convinced the answer is "yes."

Yes, Mitch Williams is a modern day magician, but to my eye he is also a practitioner of an equally ancient practice we associate more with the east, jnana yoga. This approach to yoga or union or realization is often characterized as the way of knowledge. But "knowledge" is a poor summation of the art of jnana yoga. It is more a process of transforming oneself through insight into the nature of consciousness.

This has been traditionally achieved through long years of meditation on such fundamental questions as "Who am I?" And "Who am I?" might be a good lens through which to view this book. It is one set of answers to this question, and I might add, an incredibly insightful set of answers drawn equally from Mitch's own life experience and his clear mastery of much of the best current teaching on the matter.

Mitch would claim that you and I are magicians also; that we are here to participate in his fairly unconventional view of magic as bringing illusion to reality. There are illusions all around us. That much is certainly clear, and every one of us does plenty to sustain their existence. As Mitch so rightly points out, the primary illusion presently plaguing our world is that of separation—that we're all here pretty much alone with the foremost responsibility being to take care of oneself. This is a belief based on plenty of experience, but is it reality? How would we know for sure?

Clear insight into the ways our minds work, or jnanayoga, is one means of answering this question, and most of this book provides just that. Page after page is filled with insight into the nature of our lives: observations of things we all do every day followed by suggestions for new ways of looking at it all.

Of course the reader still must do the work of asking him-or-herself if it's all true, what one actually believes. Mitch is well aware of this—continually posing questions and gently folding himself into the process he invites the reader to undertake. But the beauty of this book is that so much of it is so obviously well thought out that one can safely relax as if listening to a wise and trusted friend and let the ideas settle for a night or two. Then see how they look in the morning, and more importantly, see how the world looks.

We are all engaged in the age-old practice of seeing anew, paradoxically trying to develop fresh eyes, new ways of seeing that are undistorted by all our conditioning. To truly see the world as it actually is would be a wonderful thing. Sages have done so and their universal report is that it is beautiful beyond belief, that we are connected in ways we cannot imagine, and that love is the actual substance of being.

Obviously no one gets to all this in a single step. One book, one practice, one experience at a time we make our ways toward it. What is wonderful about this book is that we both experience much of the author's journey and have the opportunity to make real progress ourselves.

In many ways that is my favorite aspect of this book. What a privilege it is really get to know one other pilgrim on the path, one other serious human being who has applied himself to understanding the very steps most of us are trying to take. As we get to know Mitch, as we come to understand his magical perspective of transformation, we inevitably see ourselves and our world that much more clearly. And as we do this, we do, in fact, bring illusion to reality. Magic.

—George Catlin, Ph.D.
Author of *The Way to Happiness.*

CONTENTS

Dedication   iii

Acknowledgements   iv

Foreword   v

Introduction   1

PART ONE: Magical Principles   **3**

Chapter One
  The Power of Mystery   4

Chapter Two
  Magical Moments   7

Chapter Three
  Perception   12

Chapter Four
  It's About Time   17

Chapter Five
  The Magic of the Self   22

Chapter Six
  Cause and Effect   36

Chapter Seven
  The Levels of Awareness   44

Chapter Eight
  The Power of Magic   57

Chapter Nine
  The Global Brain   87

Chapter Ten
  The Magician   98

Chapter Eleven
  The Magic of Balance   106

PART TWO: The Big Picture   **132**

Chapter Twelve
  The World   133

Chapter Thirteen
  The Problem of Religion   152

Chapter Fourteen
  The Children   171

Chapter Fifteen
  The Magic of Art   192

Chapter Sixteen
  The Media and Technology   196

Chapter Seventeen
  Practices   204

Chapter Eighteen
  A Call to Magic   231

INTRODUCTION

I am a magician.

There are many ways we could interpret that. Yes, it's true, for most of my adult life, I've earned my living performing sleight of hand and other theatrical magic, both on stage and in more intimate situations.

But let's take a deeper look at what it means to be a "magician". A real magician would be someone who could envision an outcome in his or her imagination, and then elicit a corresponding transformation of *outer* reality. Of course, many would say that isn't possible. But wait a minute, we all know of people who can actually do this.

Martin Luther King "had a dream". He envisioned the world as it might be. Many said it wasn't possible. But his dream lead to a radical transformation of *outer* reality. But in that sense, aren't we all magicians? Don't we all have the ability to envision an outcome, and transform outer circumstance based on that vision?

But, "Oh," the skeptic in us might reply, "that isn't magic. That's just life."

My point exactly.

That *is* life. And life is *magic*. All too easy to forget.

This is a book on a philosophy of "magic". It is a result of a lifetime of study, contemplation, and real life experience. The ideas I present here are ones that I have used successfully to help me lead a more fulfilling and inspired life. They have worked for me on many occasions in many ways that have allowed me to be more successful at what I do.

By "successful" I don't mean just in terms of financial or material success, though that has sometimes been the case. I mean that they have helped to bring a richness of joy, peace of mind, and love into my life in ways that I don't believe would have been possible without the understandings that these ideas represent. I offer them in the hope that they may have value for you as well.

In order for that to happen, however, it's important to understand that these ideas are not important in and of themselves. As mere ideas, they may be interesting at best. But their only true value lies in their ability to help lead you to a personal *experience* of insight or awareness or enlightenment.

I offer this magical philosophy and the strategies herein not because I feel in any sense that I have mastered them, but in fact, because I have not. I still struggle daily to more consistently apply many of these principles in my life. It is my belief that by sharing them with you in this way I will further reinforce them for myself, learn more about them, and hopefully be better able to implement them more and more effectively, both for myself as well as for others with whom I interact.

I am both gladdened and humbled that you choose to spend time with me here and now. In your choice is magic born. For in your choice these lines of text upon this printed page take life. What sprang forth from my mind as a call to some seemingly unknown, unnamed soul, only to be concretized in these symbols of ink, now begins to take on meaning in your mind.

In your simple choice, a miracle manifests itself. For in this act of choice, of curiosity, of interest and attention, your mind and mine are joined in a moment of communion. A moment which transcends the gap of time and space and all that seems to lie between us. I say "seems" because that distance may not be so great at all in truth. That gulf that lies between your mind and mine may be naught but an illusion of misperception, as we shall see, if you continue to make this choice of spending time with me, and thus of leaving time itself behind.

If you choose to join me on this journey, I'd like very much to share my thoughts and dreams, and tell you of my world: a world of magic and wonder, of creation and mystery, of innocence and grace. But then, it is my belief that *all* our worlds are fashioned thus; that magic is all around us and permeates the very essence of all things seen and unseen, and we but choose to see it not. But we can always and ever choose again, in any moment.

What is your choice?

PART ONE

Magical Principles

Chapter One

THE POWER OF MYSTERY

"The most beautiful thing we can experience is the mysterious."
—Albert Einstein

Did you ever wonder? My good friend and fellow professional magician, Andrew Dakota, is fond of asking that question. Did you ever *wonder*? The experience of wonder is something that can take us to another place entirely. It can bring about complete and radical transformations of our perceptions. It can take us out of the limitations of time-bound awareness and into the experience of the eternal Now. So, *did you ever wonder?*

Whenever we find ourselves in awe—of *anything*—whether it's the magnificence of nature, or a piece of art, or a performance that moves us, or even a magician on stage doing something that seems impossible, in that moment we leave behind our normal concerns and worries and all of our limited perceptions of ourselves and our everyday world, and we have an experience of pure inspiration—*inspirutus*— being "in the spirit". The experience of awe or wonder is the true source of all inspiration and of all aspiration, of being motivated to reach beyond and rise above.

For as long as I can remember I've always had an innate need to understand how things work. I think it's one of the things that drew me to magic as a child; I wanted to unravel the mystery. It's also inspired a lifelong interest in science. Some of my earliest memories involved being outside, and simply watching ants move in and out of an ant hill, or examining the various plants in our yard, or watching the clouds move across the sky, or staring up at the stars at night. I'd be completely in awe of these things, and an hour would go by in what seemed like a moment.

And I wondered what made it happen.

It's also led me to increasingly bigger questions. One of the big mysteries with so much room for exploration is how people work.

Why do we do the things we do? Which, of course, led to an interest in a study of psychology and human behavior.

In addition to magic, one of my other early passions came when I was introduced to Judo and other martial arts. Since I had aspirations to excel; in Judo, at magic, and in other areas as well, I also became interested in the peak performance aspects of human behavior. As a young adult, I was invited to the Olympic Training Center in Colorado to train with the U.S. men's Judo team, where I experienced a variety of peak performers, in Judo and in other sports, first hand.

I became immersed in a study of various self-help literature and in certain aspects of transformative psychology. How is it that some people can achieve beyond the norm? What are the obstacles that prevent us from doing so? And how can we overcome those obstacles?

I've also continued to question—to wonder—about the even bigger mysteries. What does it all mean? How does it all fit together?

One point of intense curiosity for me has always been in finding apparent contradictions or paradoxes. In fact, I consistently find paradoxes to be some of the most fertile ground for exploration, discovery, and insight.

How is it that bumblebees shouldn't be able to fly, yet they do? Why is it that the less patience we have and the more we hurry, the longer everything takes? How can an atom be both a "wave of energy" and a "particle of matter"? How can it be that the way to discover who we really are as individuals comes from giving up the need to "be someone". In the words of musical artist Tracy Chapman, "Why are the missiles called peacekeepers when they're aimed to kill?" If God is infinite Love, how could He (She?) allow destruction and suffering? Magic itself is the paradoxical representation of both the great illusion, and infinite possibility.

It's in searching for resolutions to such apparent contradictions that we so often find meaning in life. It's certainly been fertile ground for me in my own exploration.

The other area of insight for me, perhaps paradoxically, is in finding the connections between things. This is so often an even bigger area of wonder and mystery. Seemingly unrelated aspects of life suddenly reveal themselves to be governed by the exact same principles.

An example of this in my own life came when I met Channing Pollock, a famous magician and movie actor who became a good friend and mentor. Through Channing's influence, I began to see that seemingly unrelated areas of my own life—my interests in magic and performing, artistic self-expression, psychology and peak performance, Judo and the martial arts, and Eastern philosophy, to name just a few—were really all interconnected aspects of my own unified sense of personal purpose.

There followed a period of time when serendipity, synchronicity, and what for me at the time were absolutely uncanny, often mind blowing and even seemingly magical coincidences became daily, regular events in my life. They became so common in fact that I eventually stopped being shocked by them and began to simply accept them as a natural phenomenon to be expected.

And of course the theme for me is and has always been magic. I do believe in magic. I believe the very essence and nature of life is magical. And we forget it at our peril. A life devoid of magic and wonder is to my mind little more than mere existing. There is magic all around us all the time, and the key is to simply remember to look for it.

Chapter Two

MAGICAL MOMENTS

"The most fortunate are those who have a wonderful capacity to appreciate again and again, freshly and naively, the basic goods of life, with awe, pleasure, wonder, and even ecstasy."
—Abraham Maslow

Having performed magic professionally for a wide variety of people for my entire adult life, both in this country and in several others, I've come to have a deep fascination and respect for the impact that the experience of magic can often have on individuals, apparently across all cultural and social boundaries. Why are so many people seemingly so profoundly affected by the experience of something that merely *appears* to be outside the bounds of physical possibility?

I've come to believe that there is in fact something truly magical that is taking place in these interactions when I perform magic. Of course, the *real magic* is not in what I'm doing, at least not in any physical, technical sense. It lies somewhere deeper, in the perceptions, the emotional and psychological responses, and the human interactions of the people present during these magical encounters.

Somehow we experience—and I say "we" because when the real magic happens, I experience it right along with the audience—we experience something that seems to transcend our normal, everyday perceptions to something more extraordinary. Of course, I am only the initiator of these experiences. The members of the audience and I are co-creators of these, what I like to call, "magical moments".

But these magical moments are by no means exclusive to magicians and their performances. They happen to everyone in many different ways. In fact, it can begin with anything. It can be any situation that inspires that experience of wonder, of awe, of a momentary, unbridled sense of joy.

7

One of my all time favorite quotations comes from Albert Einstein:

"The most beautiful and deepest experience we can have is the sense of the mysterious. It is the source of all true art and all science. He to whom this emotion is a stranger, who can no longer pause to wonder and stand rapt in awe, is as good as dead: his eyes are closed."
—Albert Einstein

The experience of wonder does indeed take us to another place —to a place outside our normal level of perceptions: to a place where, for a moment, we see things differently, we see the world through new eyes, and we step briefly outside of time. As Einstein implies, it leads to inspiration, the source of artistic endeavor, and of scientific exploration, and of the experience of true discovery.

Maslow's Peak Experiences

What's more, these wondrous, joyous, magical moments, while they might seem at first to be merely pleasant but fleeting breaks from our normal mode of experience, can often have much longer lasting and deeper consequences. Abraham Maslow, who is considered by many to be the Father of American Psychology, found that these transcendent moments of wonder have profound implications for how we live our lives.

Unlike his predecessors in psychology, who focussed almost exclusively in the area of pathology, i.e., in what goes wrong with human psychology, Maslow was more interested in exploring what goes right; in fact, in what goes very right with human behavior. His research concentrated on those individuals who had reached what he called "self-actualization", the very highest points of human achievement and beyond.

He found that these highest achieving individuals had many traits in common, one of which was that nearly all of them reported having these experiences that I call magical moments, and that Maslow referred to as "peak experiences".

Maslow described these peak experiences as moments of exceeding joy and well-being that often included a sense of interconnectedness, of awe, and of perceiving the world from a higher perspective beyond that of the normal, individual "ego" self. They were often profoundly life changing and even transcendent in nature, and could lead to the release of great pools of creative energy and to a higher sense of purpose in life.

Athletes often speak of these experiences as "being in the zone". This state can sometimes arise when we are totally absorbed in an activity that requires complete concentration, such as sports or mountain climbing, for example. There is a sense of time standing still. Our senses become super heightened. And there may be an altered state of awareness, sometimes perceived as an effortless moment of perfection.

Of course we all have magical moments of one kind or another on occasion. It might even begin with something simple. We stop to look at a beautiful flower and suddenly it becomes something entirely new, something we've never seen before. And the beauty, for an instant, fills up our entire experience in a moment of profound joy and discovery. We lose all sense of self and are absorbed in the beauty and feel completely connected and 'at one' with it.

The problem is that most of us dismiss these magical moments as insignificant, or take them for granted, or even resist and suppress them. If we think of them at all when they happen, we simply consider them to be random, pleasant, but largely irrelevant events with little or no relation to our normal lives.

A Greater Potential

To the contrary, however, I believe that these magical moments go to the heart of what life is, and they whisper of what life could, and perhaps should be, for each and all of us on a regular basis.

As we shall see, in many ways we experience life mainly through a self-imposed illusion of reality. We perceive things not as they are, but through the lens of our preconceived ideas of past and future. We filter our perceptions of the world around us through these preconceptions so that we are literally creating a veil of illusion rather than seeing the world as it actually is.

Because we spend our moments yearning for or feeling guilty over a past that never in fact happened as we remember, or hoping for or dreading an anticipated future, we miss the only thing we ever really have, which is this present moment. Magical moments change all that. They bring us distinctly and unquestionably into an awareness of NOW.

For an instant they allow the veil of illusion to be lifted so that we see clearly. This seems extraordinary, in part, simply because it is so radically different from how we normally perceive things.

"But what's this got to do with life?", you may ask.

What if these magical moments became the norm? What if they were common, the way we tended to be? How would it effect the way in which we live our lives?

At first, you may be inclined to think, "Well, I'd never get anything done, because I'd be 'lost' in every little moment." But is that really true?

One form of magical moment can come when we are totally immersed in meaningful work. Have you ever gotten so caught up in an activity that it seemed as though an hour went by in the blink of an eye? Your focus was complete and there was a sense of rightness about it? In these experiences we are actually far more effective than normal. We're not talking about 'zoning out', but truly 'tuning in'. It's about tuning in to the power of the present moment with a heightened sense of awareness.

What's more, if the experience of these magical moments became the norm and each moment became a moment of wonder, of beauty, of appreciation, what would that do to the way in which we interact with one another?

The innate sense of interconnectedness that is an essential element of the experience of magical moments tends strongly towards a completely compassionate and harmonious approach to other humans. Wouldn't that make conflict infinitely less likely? Wouldn't we be more inclined to cooperation and to looking out for one another's needs?

Feelings such as hatred and prejudice are incompatible with the experience of these magical moments, and vice versa. You literally can't experience them simultaneously.

Maslow called these sustained, longer lasting peak experiences "plateau experiences", and he found that they were characteristic of individuals who had attained the higher levels of self-actualization. He believed that peak experiences and plateau experiences should be studied and cultivated as a means for personal growth, integration, and fulfillment in life.

There are in fact ways to induce these magical moments and to learn to live more fully in the moment. The first and simplest way is by giving them our attention and becoming more and more aware of those moments. Look for the magical and the extraordinary around you. Pay attention when something beautiful catches your attention. Rather than ignoring these moments, or taking them for granted, give them your full and undivided attention. Because the more you think about these magical moments and reinforce them in your conscious (and subconscious) mind, the more they will begin to become a regular part of your experience.

Another way to induce magical moments is by practicing the process of stepping out of time-based perception, into living fully in the present moment. And that's one of the ideas we'll be exploring together—a little later[1].

Chapter Three

PERCEPTION

"If the doors of perception were cleansed every thing would appear to man as it is, Infinite. For man has closed himself up, till he sees all things thro' narrow chinks of his cavern."
—William Blake

One of the great things for me about being a professional magician is that I literally get to play around with people's perceptions. Of course if you're good at this, it's a big responsibility. Cult leaders and charismatic politicians use this ability to twist people's beliefs to get them to follow them and their selfish aims.

But getting people to voluntarily and willingly suspend their disbelief, urging them to question their normal perceptions, can actually be a very good thing indeed. We tend to think that our perceptions of the world actually reflect reality, that how we see things is how they actually are. But nothing could be further from the truth.

We all perceive things a little bit differently, and it's never completely accurate. If you go to the scene of a car accident and ask four or five people what happened, you'll inevitably get four or five different answers. If you take this a step further and compare those answers, for example with video footage of the same accident, it becomes apparent that none of them had it completely right.

Our sensory perceptions, which we use to interpret the world around us, are actually nothing more than electrical impulses of one kind or another. Our sensory organs of sight, hearing, taste, touch, and smell all receive different types of input and translate them into electrical signals that are transmitted through the nervous system to the brain. Then we interpret those signals and assign meaning to them.

Of course that's where the process breaks down. Our *interpretations* of the information are imperfect at best. Furthermore, the sensory data that we can collect at any given moment is only partial and never complete (for example, you can't see all sides of an object simultaneously). So if we interpret it as being "the whole picture", which more often than not we do, our perception immediately becomes *mis*perception—what nearly all perception is in reality.

The problem is, we base our beliefs about the world around us *on those perceptions*. This wouldn't be a problem if we always remembered that our perceptions were inaccurate, and therefore those beliefs should always be kept open to reinterpretation. Unfortunately, most often we do not.

"I saw it with my own eyes," is typically meant to imply that I "know" that it's true. But it isn't. As a sleight of hand artist who deals in creating experiences that seem to twist the laws of physical reality, I can attest to this.

If we begin to understand that everything we perceive of the world around us is really just an illusion, it opens doors that we may not have imagined previously. In the words of a bumper sticker I once saw:

"If you can't change your mind, are you sure you still have one?"

Unfortunately, we most often tend to staunchly defend our beliefs as "true" even if it means living a life of conflict and hatred.

If I *identify* with my beliefs, *i.e.*, if I have consciously or unconsciously begun to internalize my beliefs as an essential part of myself, and if my beliefs also seem to be in direct conflict with yours, I will then automatically interpret your beliefs as threatening since, if they contradict mine, they threaten my sense of "self". They threaten "who I am". Now your beliefs are dangerous *to me personally*, and I must therefore do everything I can to prove them to be false or to annihilate them.

But what if you're doing the same thing? Now we're in big trouble.

And this is the essence of all religious, political, and any other type of ideological warfare.

Of course we don't do this consciously. We don't realize that we've chosen beliefs based on misperceptions and then made them a part of "who we are". In fact if we realized this consciously, we'd no longer be able to continue justifying the process, and it would unravel. And that's our way out. We must *make* this process conscious. We must begin to *realize* that our perceptions, and the beliefs that are based on those perceptions, are inaccurate and therefore should always remain open to reinterpretation.

In a very real sense, all our perceptions are selective, and in that sense, we create our own version of our personal illusion. In any given moment, we choose where to direct our awareness and which sensory information to pay attention to. We also choose how to interpret that information and how to assign meaning to it. But usually we "choose" to not be aware that we are making these choices. We must begin to take conscious responsibility for these choices.

Deeper Still

Let's look a little more closely at this idea of perception and what it really is, and what it really means about the nature of illusion and reality.

Scientists have discovered that everything in the material universe is actually made up of fluctuations of energy and information. The actual nature of matter is not at all what our senses tell us that it is. What seems to be solid only appears that way because that's how our sensory organs interpret the information. At the atomic or quantum level, it's a very different story.

The atoms and molecules that make up an object are often thought of as particles of matter, as if they were infinitely tiny pieces of the object. But this actually isn't true. In reality they are infinitesimally tiny bits of energy. The only reason they are called "particles" in fact, is that sometimes these tiny bits of energy can *seem* to exist at one particular point in space at one particular point in time. But they can also exist as waves of energy with no particular precise location but with movement, direction, and "momentum".

These tiny fluctuations of energy within a physical object all interact continuously with one another in an endless dance. And they do so in just such a way that, at our level, in the precise manner that our senses interpret the information of the energy fluctuations, they *seem* to be solid. But it's really all just a clever illusion.

In Sanskrit the word for illusion is *"maya"*. According to Hindu philosophy the entire world is actually *maya*, or an illusion. Literally translated, maya means "not that". The implication is that reality is "not that" which we perceive with our senses. Long before scientists had discovered the laws of quantum physics, the ancient sages understood that this was the case. The entire world, and everything beyond it that we see, is an illusion.

Welcome to the Grand Illusion.

But if our perceptions are just illusions, what does that mean? Does it mean we can never count on anything to be real? And if our perceptions are false, how do we determine what is true? What about our beliefs about life—must we throw them away completely and suffer the culture shock of having no foundation for how to live our lives?

What if rather than regarding our beliefs as some absolute truth, we thought of them instead as working hypotheses? In other words, we continue to believe what we believe so long as those beliefs serve us well, and at the same time we remain ever open to something more.

For example, I believe in the ultimate and inevitable higher potential of the human spirit because, by doing so, I tend to consistently work towards its manifestation, both in myself and in others. I believe that we all have the ability to become more, and therefore I act on that belief by working to become more myself, and to do my best to urge and inspire others to become more as well. And so this belief serves me.

I can acknowledge that it may or may not be ultimately true. But in pursuing it as a working hypothesis, so far at least, everything I have experienced in regard to this belief has continued to uphold it as true. I also realize that that could in fact be because I'm filtering my experience *through* the belief. It might seem to be true only because I may consciously or unconsciously ignore or rationalize away those experiences that seem in conflict with the belief. So I do my best to remain open.

It seems to me that the only true constant in life, in the entire universe in fact, is change. In every moment everything is in a continuing dance of transformation. Of course, transformation is the essence of 'magic'.

If change is the only constant and is therefore unavoidable, then we are either growing and becoming more, or we are simply beginning the process of dying. In fact, death is seen in many cultures as the "Great Transformation". More to the point, in terms of our beliefs and our thinking, it seems crucial that, as the philosopher and teacher J. Krishnamurti indicated, we take care to never "reach a conclusion". When you come to a *conclusion* in your thinking, that implies that you've *stopped*.

If you've stopped growing and changing, the force of nature will take over, and the inevitable change will be towards dying, in your thinking at least, but also perhaps in your outer life as well.

If you take a moment to think about it, youth is about learning, discovery, becoming more of the person you will be when you're an adult. Children are these wide open vessels of discovery and exploration, and that's how they learn. But what if we continued that attitude throughout life? What if we remained open and flexible in our thinking? Isn't that the essence of a youthful attitude?

In that sense, I think it's essential that we not reach *conclusions* with our beliefs, but instead be constantly in a state of inquiry. Discovery and growth are about asking—they're about wonder. Did you ever wonder? I hope so!

This takes us back to the experience of wonder inherent in the magical moment. We need to remain open to those moments of wonder, of inspiration, of discovery, so that we're always curious and wanting to learn more about everything, including even our own beliefs.

As long as we're asking, we're moving forward. Is this belief true? Does it serve me? Does it reflect reality as near as I can currently tell, or is there something I'm missing or avoiding? Having the inquisitiveness and curiosity of youth is about moving forward and becoming more. Reaching a conclusion is about stopping, it's about ending, about... *dying.* I want to choose life. What will you choose?

Chapter Four

IT'S ABOUT TIME

"When you are courting a nice girl an hour seems like a second. When you sit on a red-hot cinder a second seems like an hour. That's relativity."
—Albert Einstein

L et's take a moment (or three or four) to talk about time. Like the physical world, time too is an illusion. In fact time, as we measure it, is simply a function of physical change, so if the physical world is not as we see it then neither is time. A second, a minute, and an hour are all increments of the physical change of the earth and its relation to the sun.

The Science of Timelessness

Einstein showed us that even how we perceive time is not a constant, but is simply relative to our point of reference. Speed of light is always measured as a constant: 186,282 miles per second. He realized therefore that if you were somehow able to travel at velocities approaching the speed of light, since light is coming to you at a constant rate regardless of whether it's coming from the direction you're traveling in or the direction you're coming from, and since we perceive everything based on light waves and energy patterns, how you perceive and experience time would be vastly different from how it is experienced by someone who was simultaneously *not* moving at those same speeds.

What?

Exactly.

But let's use a quick example to clarify. Let's say I'm in a train moving at 60 miles per hour. You're standing on the ground next to the train tracks and, as the train approaches, you throw a ball toward me at a speed of about 5 mph. Since I'm on the train moving 60 mph and the ball is coming from the opposite direction at 5 mph, from my perspective it would appear that the ball is moving towards me at 65 mph. To you, it's moving away at 5 mph.

The weird thing is, if instead of throwing a ball, you shine a flashlight towards me as I approach, and if we could both measure the speed of the light from the flashlight as it moved towards me and away from you, it would be measured as the same for *both* of us, even if I were moving really, *really* fast.

And since speed is measured as a function of distance traveled per a given amount of time passing, and since time passing is just a function of physical change, (and all of our perceptions of physical change come from our senses, which are simply how our brains register light and other energy patterns), the only thing that can be different for each of us, is... time!

If you didn't get any or all of that, don't worry. There are other ways to think about this.

Now Is All There Is

Remember what happened yesterday? No you don't. Yesterday doesn't exist, except as a thought in your mind. Therefore it's only imaginary. Can you experience yesterday right now? For that matter, can you experience any past time right now? *Only in your imagination!*

And what about the future? No such thing. Only in your imagination.

So what does that leave us?

"Yesterday is history. Tomorrow is a mystery. And today? Today is a gift. That's why we call it the present."
—Alice Morse Earle.

Now is all there is. What time is it? Now. It always is. If past and future are an illusion, then so is time.

Sadly, as I mentioned before, most of us waste the overwhelming majority of our present moments obsessed with thinking about the past or worried about the future, neither of which actually exist.

In his book *The Power of Now,* and in his talks on the subject, Eckhart Tolle makes this problem quite clear. He points out that even in simple things we're caught up in "mind chatter" about the past and future which is geared to prevent us from fully experiencing each present moment.

He gives the example of picking up a glass of water to have a drink. As the glass is traveling up towards our mouth, we already want it to be there. As we begin to drink it, we already want it to be in our stomach, quenching our thirst. Once we're done with it, we already want the glass to be out of our hand, even before we put it down.

And as a result, we've never really experienced this simple activity. In fact, we've never really experienced *water!* If we had, we would have noticed immediately what a wondrous and miraculous substance it is. Tolle suggests that we must learn to really immerse ourselves in each moment. As you pick up a glass of water, how does it feel in your hand? As you lift it, what do you see? How does the water move and refract light? As it approaches your lips, how does it smell? As you take some into your mouth, what does that sensation feel like? How does the water taste?

But don't make the further mistake of trying to answer these questions, because then you're turning them into a judgement *about* water, rather than simply being fully in the experience of it. The abstract experience itself, if you're truly and fully in it, can't really be described in thought or in words. It simply is. It is vivid and multi-sensory and magical and miraculous in its own right. And that is the magic of NOW!

It's important to get out of the mind chatter *about* our experiences, the judgement and analysis and interpretation of them, and instead practice simply being fully in those experiences in each moment. To the extent that we're able to do this, each moment becomes a magical moment.

Of course, that's easier said than done because we've become so attached to our mind chatter and judgements and our emotional guilt and fear and blame about things that have happened to us, (or more accurately, that we *think* have happened to us.) In fact, we've become so attached to these emotionally-based judgements about our experience, that in most cases we've come to think that *we are them!*

At an unconscious level, we've come to identify with these illusory perceptions of past and future until we unconsciously believe that they are a part of who we are! And so to give them up feels like self destruction, and we feel threatened by the very idea of letting go of these perceptions.

Resisting them is not the answer either, since we only tend to further empower anything that we resist. The answer is to simply remind ourselves to be fully in the moment. As soon as we notice that we're taking part in the mind chatter and all the convoluted judgmental thoughts, we need merely use that as a reminder to instead merely *pay attention* to the present moment.

In fact, we can simply choose to pay attention to the judgmental mind chatter itself. Rather than resisting it, as soon as we notice it we can choose to step back mentally and just observe what's going on. And that simple shift can help bring us back into an awareness of the present.

Of course it's important when we notice these judgmental thoughts to not make the further mistake of judging the thoughts themselves as wrong or bad. That just amounts to 'resisting the resistance', and it only reinforces the problem. Just observe the thoughts without judgment, as you would watch a cloud in the sky.

"Trying" to let go of something is like having a death grip on something with your right hand and trying with all your might to pry your fingers loose with your left hand. That which you resist only becomes stronger.

To truly let go—of an attitude, of tension in your body, of a self-defeating belief system, or any other unhealthy habit—you need simply *pay attention* to what you are doing. Most of the destructive habits that we hold on to are mainly being chosen at an unconscious level.

When you truly pay attention, you bring your ongoing unconscious choices to a level of conscious awareness. You simply notice, take note of what you are in fact doing. You see it clearly. With this conscious, present moment awareness, the active choice to continue holding onto the behavior (for that is what it in fact is), simply falls away.

So much of the time when we're doing one task, we're wishing we were somewhere else, doing something else. We miss our present moments by resisting them, or judging them as insignificant or valueless. But if you use each moment as an opportunity to practice being present, even the seemingly unpleasant activities become filled with the potential for experiencing true magic.

The next time you're sitting stuck in traffic, instead of judging it, remind yourself to become fully aware of the entire experience. Notice your breathing and the sensation as the air moves slowly in and out of your lungs. Pay attention to the sunlight, and the colors and shapes of the other cars. What is there to notice that you've never truly seen before? What is there to discover?

Even common moments can be filled with beauty and meaning if we simply choose to let go of our endless judging and resistance of them. If you think you know what something is, you've come to a *conclusion*. You've stopped. You've stopped truly experiencing.

We think we know what a glass of water is, or a car, or a person. And by continually prejudging them, we no longer actually experience them. We've relegated the present experience of them to some past perception, that was also probably based on a previous prejudgment, and almost certainly inaccurate in any case. If change is the only constant, then those things are also changing, and so each moment is a totally new experience with them. *If* we're open to seeing it.

As we've already ascertained, learning to be present in each moment is one of the keys to having magical moments filled with wonder and joy and discovery and inspiration. It is possible for us to live our lives in a state of continual appreciation and enjoyment rather than one of judgment, resistance and denial.

But in order to do so, as the Bible says, we have to become as little children. Children are wide open to the world around them. And they're totally immersed in each present moment. We must remind ourselves to allow ourselves to once again become immersed in the wonder that is around us. We've become habitually immune to it, and it takes willingness to break that habit in order to become truly open once more.

Chapter Five

THE MAGIC OF THE SELF

"The reason I talk to myself is because I'm the only one whose answers I accept."
—George Carlin

Who am I? When asked that question, most of us tend to come up with a variety of answers that are role related. I am an entertainer. I am a husband. I am an artist. I am a Christian. We often define ourselves by our careers or our relationships or our beliefs.

But don't those things have more to do with what we do (and perhaps even what we think) than with who we are? It may be true that what we do, in some cases at least, may reveal something of who we are as unique individuals. But I think the real question hints at something much more fundamental. We might look instead at what might be called 'accidents of birth'—our race, our nationality, our social status. However these, too, are still superficial and say nothing of our true identity.

Behind all the externals, the titles and roles and even the psychological conditioning, lies something more. What if we were to strip all of these away. Then we ask, "Who am I?"

The problem is that, just as with the world around us, we tend to think of our own identity based on beliefs and perceptions *about* ourselves, rather than on the moment to moment *experience* of who we are. And as we've already determined, perceptions are always inaccurate.

Ironically, in an odd 'chicken-and-the-egg' syndrome, one reason that our perceptions are faulty and little more than a 'clever illusion', is that we perceive the world through the filter of this false sense of who we are. Whatever our idea of who we are, *that* becomes the basis by which we judge everything else.

What's more, this mostly unconscious idea of who we are also determines how we behave and how we respond to each and every situation that we encounter in each and every moment of our lives. Before we can begin to look into the nature of our true identity behind this facade, I think it's important to understand just how all encompassing this *sense* of self truly is. It really does effect everything else, for good or ill.

A Brief Overview of Self-Image Psychology

In his classic self-help book, *Psycho-Cybernetics*,[2] Dr. Maxwell Maltz describes how he found that this sense of identity had literally everything to do with how we live our lives, and that it was in fact malleable. Dr. Maltz was a plastic surgeon who became fascinated when he began to notice that some patients, upon having corrections of their facial features, underwent radical transformations of their *personalities*. And their entire lives changed. Why did this happen? Further, why didn't it happen to *all* of the patients?

Maltz found that the patients who had transformations of personality did so because they changed how they saw themselves. He found that this transformation of self-image lead to truly magical transformations in every aspect of the person's life. (One of Malz's later books was even entitled *The Magic Power of Self-image Psychology*.)

Malz also found that the human mind works as an automatic goal-seeking device, so that, like a programmed guided missile, whatever is held in the conscious and unconscious mind becomes a "programmed goal" that the subconscious mind immediately goes about achieving. And the *prime* goal is always the person's idea of who they are, or their "self-image". So whoever we believe ourselves to be becomes the primary self-fulfilling prophecy in our lives. All of the power of our creative energy goes into making it true. Or to quote the Bible, *"As a man thinketh, so is he."*[3]

What is possible or not possible for us as individuals is almost entirely determined by this all encompassing self-image.

Of course, the good news is that our self-image is open to change. In fact the majority of our self-image is developed by our conditioning, especially in childhood, but to varying degrees by what happens to us and how we interpret it throughout our entire lives. The problem is that much of that conditioning is at a totally unconscious level.

A Few Definitions

It might be helpful at this point to clarify a few of the terms commonly used in the study of self-image psychology so we're clear about what is meant:

- *The conscious mind* is that part of the mind which has the thoughts, images, and beliefs of which we are consciously aware. It's also the level of conscious choice.
- *The unconscious mind* is that part of the mind which has the thoughts, images, feelings, and beliefs which we have repressed or in some other way pushed out of our consciousness and of which we are therefore no longer consciously aware.
- *The subconscious mind* is that part of the mind which Malz identified as functioning as an impersonal, goal seeking, cybernetic, "servo-mechanism". It simply does what it's told by both the conscious and the unconscious mind.
- *Self-image* is the '*picture*' we have of who we are.
- *Self-ideal* is the ideal picture of who we most want to be.
- *Self-esteem* refers to how much we like ourselves and value our worth as an individual.
- *Self-concept* is the overall idea of 'who we are', consisting of self ideal, self-image, and self esteem.

The goal, of course, is to begin to transform our self-image so that it becomes more and more in line with our self-ideal, or the self we'd most like to be. Since it is the unconsciously held limitations and negative aspects of our self-image that restrict us from being successful and moving closer to a state of self-actualization, the key is to bring those unconscious limitations up to a conscious level and transform them to something more positive.

Since the subconscious mind acts to move unerringly towards whatever is 'programmed' into it by the conscious mind, one way to do this is to deliberately hold the new goal, (in this case a set of more positive and helpful beliefs about oneself), consistently in the conscious mind. This is why so many self-improvement systems utilize the power of tools such as affirmations and visualization, since they help to program the new image into the mind.

The False Ego Self

As valuable as this process is, it is all nonetheless still at the level of belief and perception. Which is, of course, why it works. Since our perceptions, including those about ourselves, are never completely true or accurate, the important question is simply, "are they helpful?" Do they serve us to move towards being all that we can be? If not, we can choose to change them.

While this process can be quite effective in many cases, in some areas it does in fact have definite drawbacks, in my experience. For example, when the new goal image that you wish to hold is in sharp contradiction to what is held unconsciously, it can set up a state of internal conflict. The unconscious "self" may even take actions of its own to prevent us from effectively transforming our self-image to a more positive and healthy goal image.

Since the self-image is actually based on these more-or-less false perceptions, we actually all have what might be called a "false self". This is the self at the personality level, and it is often referred to as the "ego". The ego is built of all these false beliefs and perceptions about ourselves, and for all practical purposes, becomes who we think we are.

Unfortunately, these false beliefs are mainly built on fear and other related negative, emotionally-based misperceptions. Further, because of the overwhelming creative power of our minds, the ego, even though it is based on false assumptions, actually takes on a life of its own and sets up a complex system of self-defense and self-preservation.

Herein lies the internal conflict and the difficulty which can often arise in improving our self-image. In my view, the problem is that the nature of the misperceptions of our false ego self lies mainly in seeing ourselves as separate from all that is around us. This is what Alan Watts called the "skin encapsulated ego". Albert Einstein (yes, I do love quoting him) described the problem in this way:

"A human being is a part of the whole called by us 'Universe', a part limited in time and space. He experiences himself, his thoughts and feelings as something separated from the rest. - A kind of optical delusion of his consciousness. This delusion is a kind of prison for us, restricting us to our personal desires and to affection for a few persons

nearest us. Our task must be to free ourselves from this prison by widening our circle of compassion to embrace all living creatures and the whole of nature in its beauty."
—Albert Einstein

Who Are We Really?

But behind all the perceptions, what is the *reality* of who we are?

Am I what I do? Am I my beliefs? Am I my emotions and emotional conditioning? Am I the thoughts that I think? Perhaps a better question is who is this person who is doing, who is believing, who is emoting and thinking? Who am I behind and beyond all that? Am I simply this individual, separate, finite-in-time-and-space, human physical/emotional/mental structure? Or am I something more?

One of the further insights gained from quantum physics, the study of matter at the atomic and subatomic level, is that there seems to be no real separation between *anything*. Atoms, photons, and other subatomic "particles" can all interact with one another instantaneously even over vast distances in space, without regard to the apparent limitations of distance, time, or the speed of light.

Since science has shown that nothing can move faster than the speed of light, the implication is that there is no real separation between matter at the quantum level. It is, in potential, infinitely interconnected.

Further, if we think of life even at our everyday level, how do we really separate anyone or anything from its environment? How can we even think of an individual person as separate from the environment of the Earth in which we live? Physical life is impossible without the nurturing resources of our environment; of oxygen and water and plant life, for example.

Even to think of ourselves as somehow separate from the human kingdom itself is at its root impossible to do. Yes, we can choose to move into a remote cabin in the mountains and live alone as a hermit. But our conditioning and the way we think and function all comes from our human interactions. Even if we choose to isolate ourselves, doesn't our very absence in some way effect the other people around us?

If we have a complex artistic mosaic made of hundreds of individual tiles, and remove just one tile from it, isn't that where our eye immediately goes?

The science of Chaos Theory has shown that even a butterfly flapping its wings has a nearly infinite and indeterminate effect on its environment. The effect of the butterfly's wings on the surrounding air interacts with the rest of the air around it and spreads out from there in an unpredictable but significant chain reaction, forever altering even the weather patterns in other parts of the world!

The fact is that everything, and everyone, affects everything else. We all interact with our environment in ways that make us inseparable from it.

If this is true, how can even the most seemingly insignificant human life be seen as separate from all the other people on the planet? We tend to think of ourselves as separate individuals, but perhaps this too is an illusion, and the reality may be something completely different.

I would also contend that it is this false sense of separateness that allows us to continue to justify and rationalize all kinds of destructive behavior towards others. If you believe that you are separate from others, then selfish behavior and 'win-lose' scenarios, can be rationalized as being appropriate. But if we are not in fact separate at all, simple self interest would demand that we act always and only for the benefit of everyone.

I believe that our true identity as human beings lies somewhere deeper than our outer individual forms, at a level that is in no way separate from that which surrounds us. It is who we are in the moments of stillness *between* our random thoughts, between one emotional feeling and the next, between even one breath or one heartbeat and the next. It is this Authentic Self that we experience in the Magical Moment. And it may be far more real than all the physical and other appearances on which we base our "normal" day-to-day existences.

And the experience of Self at this level is in sharp contrast to our normal, ego-based sense of self.

The Ego and the Authentic Self

Because it is a false self based upon the illusion of separateness, and because at some level it realizes this, the ego lives in a constant state of terror that we will discover its secret and that it will be annihilated as a result. Of course this is more or less true, in the sense that as soon as we see any false perception clearly, it fades away and is corrected and replaced with a more accurate perception.

The ego's greatest enemies therefore are inner stillness, and the experience of the present moment, because it is in these experiences that we see truly clearly, and see through the false premises of the ego. When we still our cluttered, clamorous thoughts and simply allow ourselves to be in a state of alert presence, in that moment the fear and anxiety and guilt and resentment and all other aspects of the ego go away, as does the ego itself, in fact.

In order to maintain and uphold its illusion of separateness, the ego must always see enemies; those 'others' who threaten its existence and happiness. Whether these enemies are other people, or outside situations, or past suffering, or possible threatening future events, they must be resisted at all costs.

But it is this very resistance that creates the perception of the 'enemy other' and upholds the ego's illusions. Of all the ego's various complex strategies for self-preservation, one of the most common and most insidious is its ability to perceive its own faults as 'out there' in the people and situations around itself. In psychological terms, this tactic is called "projection".

This is a particular form of self-delusion, or deliberate though largely unconscious misperception. Essentially, the ego realizes at some level that it has unhealthy and self-destructive issues, tendencies, attitudes, and other habits that if we saw clearly we would find intolerable in ourselves and we would act to get rid of them. So in order to hold on to them and keep them out of our conscious awareness, the ego 'projects' them onto the outside world, and most commonly onto the people around us.

One clue into what form our own projections may take is to make note of those things that we find the most objectionable, annoying, distasteful, and intolerable in other people. These are usually traits that we ourselves have in some form or other, that we can't stand to look at in ourselves, and so we project them onto others.

"Everything that irritates us about others can lead us to an understanding of ourselves."
—C.G. Jung

Have you ever noticed, for example, that really pushy, controlling people tend to be completely unforgiving and intolerant of other people who are also pushy and intolerant, and yet they seem oblivious of the same traits in themselves? This is projection. And it is the ego's main tactic for upholding and justifying unforgiveness. When we begin to realize that the traits that "make" us angry and resentful towards others are ones that we also have ourselves, it becomes much more difficult to maintain our unforgiving feelings towards them.

Projection is a form of seeing ourselves as separate from others, whereas seeing *through* the projection allows us to join with them and understand that we're not that different. Blame, anger, resentfulness, intolerance, annoyance, and hatred are all results of projection, and they all also serve to reinforce and justify its continued existence. The ego needs to be "right", and to make others "wrong", and projection is its favorite tool for doing so. Allowing ourselves to become aware of the tactic in ourselves makes room for acceptance and compassion.

There's an old saying that whenever two people meet, there are actually six people present: each person as he sees him or herself, each person as the other person sees them, and each person as they actually are. How each person sees themselves is the ego, how each person sees the other person is ego projection, and each person as they actually are would be the Authentic Self.

Striving

The ego cannot afford to be at ease or content with anything, at least not for very long. So it keeps us chasing after the *one thing* that it claims will make us happy. But its real point is not to *have* the one thing but to always be yearning for it. This way it can maintain the sense of incompleteness that is the essence of ego existence.

In those cases where the ego actually gets whatever it is that it claims to want so desperately, it will quickly discover that this isn't what it wanted after all; it will soon find fault with it, and blame it for 'betraying me' by not being fulfilling after all. We see this in so-called "love" relationships. We seek after that "one person", that one woman or man that will be our heart's desire, and we "fall in love". Of course what the ego calls love is really just an emotional attachment based on neediness and not real love at all.

We seek someone who will fill that empty place inside. But then rather quickly, "the honeymoon is over", and the person disappoints us by not being the perfect mate that they represented themselves as being. They 'tricked' us into loving them by pretending to be our one true love.

And in every other area of life, the ego frantically seeks after that which it assures us will bring fulfillment, and then blames these outside situations when they don't. In order to justify this endless pursuit, it must always judge the current situation, and the present moment, as completely intolerable.

The Authentic Self does not judge at all. It simply observes and accepts everything exactly as it is. The Authentic Self doesn't seek fulfillment for it is already complete and whole and has no need to add anything to Itself in order to be fulfilled. It has no enemies since it doesn't perceive Itself as separate from anyone or anything else, and therefore sees no conflict between "other" and "self".

The Authentic Self is also beyond the level of physical perception which is always faulty to some varying degree. The Self simply is. The ego identifies completely with the body and believes that the body is "who I am". It also identifies with it's own tumultuous thoughts and emotions, but they too tend to be centered around body identification and the defense of its various vulnerabilities. Faulty perception is the ego's world and its very foundation.

The ego glorifies the body and sees the body (and to a lesser extent the emotional and mental 'forms') as the ultimate "me". We see this clearly in the pursuit of bodily and form-based perfection in the media images that bombard us daily. We all want the perfect body, and our self-worth seems diminished when we fail at having it.

The True Self lies beyond the forms of body, emotions, and thoughts, but can work *through* them as extensions, or vehicles, or expressions of Itself. Do I believe that I *am* my body? Or do I believe that I *have* a body? If I believe that I am my body, then when things happen to it, when it becomes sick or injured or grows old, I will believe that who I am is lessened. If I realize that Who I Am is not the body but something more, then my sense of Self will in no way be diminished when my body is no longer at its peak.

The ego is all about "look at me", look at how wonderful I am.

Of course since it doesn't really believe this, it struggles constantly to uphold the lie, and lives in terror that someone will see through the lie and realize that I'm not so wonderful after all. The ego constantly builds itself up and, conversely, it will do everything it can to tear others down in contrast. The ego is all about comparisons and competitiveness, in an endless attempt to "prove" that it is better than... all the while fearing deep down that it isn't.

The ego lives in a state of continual competition, defensiveness, and attack, which it sees as completely justified in order to protect itself from all the outer threats. Since it is separate from all else, and at odds with all else, it must compete against these outside forces in order to defeat them and therefore avoid being destroyed by them.

The Authentic Self never opposes—it merely waits patiently while the ego runs around frantically defending itself and trying to attain some golden key of fulfillment which always remains just out of reach. Eventually, because the ego is acting consistently on false premises and the results of those actions therefore become more and more unbearable, the ego simply tires us out to the point that it becomes more and more difficult to uphold its constant state of resistance. Then when we let down our defenses and become still for even a moment, in that moment the Authentic Self can be experienced.

Transcending the Ego

The question is not whether we *have* an ego, a false self, since virtually everyone does. Those individuals who have completely relinquished the ego are incredibly rare indeed. And the question is also not whether we *are* a deeper and truer Self than the ego, since this cannot be proved, but only experienced. The real question is which do we identify with most of the time. And for nearly all of us, it is unquestionably the ego.

But to the degree that we can begin to release our attachment to and identification with the ego, and spend moments of stillness where we step back from ego identification into the realm of the Authentic Self, to that degree will we begin to find true peace and fulfillment—not as something to be pursued but as Who we really are. This process of releasing ego identification in favor of the experience of the Authentic Self is the entire process of moving towards self-actualization.

We release the ego not by opposing it, however, because we actually empower whatever we resist. Remember in fact that "resistance causes persistence."[4] When we resist something, we are choosing to perceive it as powerful and threatening, and by so doing we are programming the subconscious mind to give us that result, and therefore literally using the power of our creative imagination to strengthen that which we would fight against.

We release the ego by simply observing its various false premises. We shine the light of our awareness into all the ego's darkest corners, and by simply seeing it for what it is, we begin to release our attachment to it.

At first, when we notice ourselves acting in hateful, resentful, or other destructive ways, when we notice ourselves acting as the ego in other words, we will be inclined to want to annihilate and eradicate these tendencies in ourselves. But attempting to destroy the ego and its various devices is actually an ego approach to ego relinquishment, and it is one of the ego's favorite defense mechanisms, since it further reinforces the belief in conflict that is its very basis of existence.

What we can do instead is to simply notice the various ego tendencies when they arise. Normally, the ego unconsciously acts out these tendencies, and in fact that's how it maintains them. If we could see clearly that we are acting destructively, we'd simply choose not to do that. So by simply noticing the behaviors when they arise, without judging them as either "bad" or "good", we can then see them clearly and choose to leave them behind if we wish.

Over time, through this simple act of observation, which is actually a choice to be more and more consciously aware in the present moment rather than living in the ego's realm of past and future, we slowly begin to weaken the hold that the ego has over us, and we open the door to a more consistent experience of our Authentic Self.

Moving Into the Realm of Authentic Self

As we experience the Self more and become more familiar with its nature and its various aspects such as peacefulness, acceptance, and compassion, we can also begin to include these into our overall self-image, so that they become programmed into our subconscious mind as our primary "goal image". This brings the creative energies into play to assist in our becoming more identified with Who we truly are, in place of the false self of the ego. (However, while it might seem contradictory, we inevitably need to give up all forms of identification, or self-image whatsoever, as we'll discuss in just a moment.)

At first we may have just a glimpse of our deepest Self. It might happen during a moment of intense emotional pain, when we finally can't take it any more and simply surrender—give up and stop resisting. Or it might come in some experience of wonder or intense focus where we let down our defenses. But in that instant of stillness which we enter by giving up resistance lies the Magical Moment. And the Authentic Self.

It may be quite fleeting, and our ego mind will tend to dismiss it as meaningless. "Oh, that was just a nice experience, but it's not important." Then we may find that these glimpses become more common, until we begin to realize that we can actually go into them intentionally by becoming still.

From there the process becomes one of having these experiences more and more often, until we learn little by little to experience them not only during contemplative moments of solitude, but to actually bring them into our day-to-day activities. Once we begin to develop the ability to bring this "in the moment" sense of presence into our daily lives, we begin to shift from having the ego run our lives to a state in which more and more, we actually function as the Authentic Self, rather than as the ego, and life begins to magically transform itself in ways we could never previously have imagined.

The great paradox, though, is that true self-actualization is ultimately about giving up *images* or *ideas* of the self altogether. The actual experience of the Authentic Self is in fact beyond concepts, beyond what can be conceived at all. It simply is. Therefore, to the degree that we still identify with a 'self-image', we won't be *fully* experiencing and expressing Who We Really Are.

Making the choice to have a more positive self-image is a tool which is inevitably aimed at transcending itself. We use a healthy, positive self-image to move out of ego identification and towards Self identification, which is ultimately beyond all *concepts* or *images* of the self.

In those magical moments where we actually experience the Authentic Self, we aren't 'seeing' ourselves as anything, we simply experience life fully, and ideas of who we are fall away completely. In that sense, it's even a bit pointless to try to describe the experience, as I've been attempting to do here, since it ultimately defies definition. These ideas *about* the Authentic Self are simply signposts at best, geared to help us move towards the actual experience.

The moment-to-moment *experience* is the real point. I suppose the great paradox of self-image psychology is that while the self-image is the most powerful goal image and it determines so much about our lives, ultimately the goal is to use it to go beyond itself, to a moment-to-moment experience of our True Self, which actually transcends images and forms of any kind. When we begin to function as the Authentic Self, to the degree that we do so we no longer need 'ideas' of who we are at all. We simply Are.

Discovering Our Uniqueness

Another aspect of experiencing our Authentic Self is that we often begin to discover our own uniqueness. Our unique talents, predispositions, characteristics, and our perspective on life as distinct individuals often begin to come shining through. In the entire history of the world, there's never been another person exactly like… you, or… me, or any one of the other seven billion infinitely unique human miracles on our planet. And there never will be again.

Just as this present moment is a one of a kind, never to be repeated event, so too are you! And this uniqueness is your gift, both to yourself and to the world. As we reveal, demonstrate, and express our uniqueness, we often find the channel through which we can make our greatest contribution in life.

What is it that drives you? What are you most passionate about? And what do you value the most? Not just in the purely emotionally-based 'what can I get for me' ways of the ego, but at the much deeper 'heart level' of Who you truly are. For it is here that we will most often find the path in life that will bring the most meaning and purpose to our lives. Finding our uniqueness can help us to develop a true sense of mission.

Perhaps paradoxically, as we discover our uniqueness and find our true place in the world, it deepens our connections with others. The ego would have us believe that being unique is about being separate from others. But in truth, it is our uniqueness that brings us together. As they say, if you and I saw everything the exact same way, one of us would be redundant.

It is this infinitely diverse spectrum of unique individuals that makes up the magical mosaic that is humanity. In experiencing the Authentic Self, we discover both our own uniqueness and our own place in this magical work of art that is the human race.

Chapter Six

CAUSE AND EFFECT

"Shallow men believe in luck or in circumstance.
Strong men believe in cause and effect."
—Ralph Waldo Emerson

"**W**hat goes around comes around." "Whatever you sow, you shall also reap." "For every action there is an equal and opposite reaction." Science, religion, and popular culture all acknowledge the significance of what might be called "cause and effect" as it applies to both nature and human experience. In the East, this principle is often referred to as *karma.*

It could be rightly said that "cause and effect" is one of the great universal laws of nature. On a personal level, we say that in life we get back whatever we put out. And this is very true. But it's also very difficult if not impossible for the ego to admit.

At the level of perceptions, one way to see it is that since all our perceptions are selective, what we are "getting back" in the form of our perceptions of the world around us is actually based on what we are "putting out", in the form of our intentions, beliefs, and choices, both conscious and unconscious, of how to perceive the world. Science has also discovered that our choices of how to perceive outer reality actually effects and to some degree determines its actual *objective existence*!

According to quantum physics, a subatomic particle such as an electron or a photon cannot exist simultaneously as both a wave and a particle. The more specifically you measure its position as a particle, the less you can know about its momentum and energy as a wave. Since different instruments are used to measure each, how a scientist chooses to observe a quantum event at a particular moment in time literally *determines the nature of that event* at that moment in time.

There can be no objective observation of subatomic events, because the act of observation (perception) actually effects the nature of the event itself. This is true even if, for example, the event we are observing is the condition of a photon (particle) of light as it passed around a galaxy thousands of years ago on its way to us, since the galaxy is so distant that it took thousands of years for the photon to reach us and for us to observe it. Spooky, huh?

It's uncertain how far we can take this since, at our normal scale of everyday life, the effects an observer has on quantum events are so infinitesimally small as to be unnoticeable. More to the point, we can, in fact, observe cause and effect as it works out in every area of life, even at our human scale. Every choice that we make in every moment of our lives works out as an 'effect' in the form of results that will then make up the conditions of our lives, for good or ill.

If I treat everyone around me with anger and aggression, it's almost certain that I'm not going to get harmonious responses from most of them. Conversely, if I treat everyone around me with kindness and consideration, my life will be filled with people who treat me well in return.

If we take this even further and choose to take conscious responsibility for all the results we receive from life, based on the belief that we are at some level simply getting back what we put out, blame and resentment become impossible. If all perceptions are selective, and we are in fact choosing how to see the world around us regardless of whether that choice is conscious or unconscious, then the world that we see, in a sense, is merely a projection from within our own minds.

If we see hatred and conflict around us in our external world, perhaps it's simply a reflection of what we have within at some level. In that sense, the outer world as we perceive it could be seen as a mirror of our inner world; a reflection, if we so choose to realize it, that can help us to see what we have repressed within ourselves.

To my mind, from a human perspective, one of the main purposes of cause and effect is as a teaching device geared to help us to see more clearly and to choose more wisely. If we continuously make destructive choices in life, the results of those choices will bring us destructive and painful consequences, until the pain becomes so intense that we eventually choose to give up the destructive patterns of behavior. Einstein once defined insanity as: *"doing the same thing over and over again and expecting different results."*

Of course that's exactly what the ego does. The ego immediately rejects the idea that painful effects are caused by its own actions. That's why it projects the destructiveness onto the outside world and sees enemies all around itself. If we take responsibility for everything that happens to us, all of the ego's constructs begin to crumble.

This becomes much more challenging to apply when truly horrendous things happen to people who apparently did nothing to cause them. The point is not that we should accept guilt for such situations, since guilt is just another ego distortion geared to keep us in a state of separation and conflict. It's rather that even if there seems to be no way that we could have chosen or caused painful situations, to the degree that we can simply choose to take full responsibility for the conditions in which we find ourselves, to that extent will we be empowered to move forward and be free from the continued limitation of resentment, fear, and justified anger.

As we now know from modern medical science, holding chronic destructive emotions such as anger and resentment over time inevitably turns inward, causing a variety of illnesses. The ego wants desperately to see itself as a victim to outside circumstance, and it continually refuses to accept responsibility for the painful things that happen to us. As we choose to accept full responsibility for literally all the causes and effects that make up our lives, the ego limitations begin to fall away, and we experience ourselves more and more as the Authentic Self.

As our sense of self expands to include the world around ourselves, rather than just the "skin-encapsulated ego", we naturally begin to recognize and accept a much wider circle of responsibility, and our sphere of influence also expands. Like the butterfly affecting distant weather patterns, we begin to realize that the effects of our thoughts and actions are virtually infinite in their reach. Every small act of compassion forever alters the world in which it is performed.

How we choose to perceive the world around us is also a 'cause' that can actually affect our outer environment. In the words of Dr. Wayne Dyer, *"When you change the way you see the world, the world you see changes."*

For example, one way that we can begin to overcome our own ego's tendency towards projection that we discussed in the previous chapter is by choosing how we will perceive other people. Do we see others as egos, or as unique expressions of Who We Truly Are as human beings? Do we focus our own attention on their ego-based faults and tendencies or do we look deeper, beyond the defenses of the ego to Who they are at a more fundamental level?

In any moment, we can choose whether we will see a person based solely on their outer, ego behavior, or we can look beyond it to the Real Person within. If someone seems to be attacking me in some way, for example, I can choose to feel threatened or irritated or offended by it. In which case I will no doubt act in a way that will, in one way or another, tend to reinforce that person's own need to attack and defend. I've 'bought into' the person's perception of him or herself as weak and angry and aggressive.

Or I can instead recognize that his or her actions are based on fear, which is in turn based on the false perception that the person is separate and vulnerable and incapable of being 'OK'. I can choose to look beyond this perception and instead see the person as connected to me, as capable and as whole. The ego *separates* by *projecting* its own inadequacies onto others. The Authentic Self *includes* by *extending* Its own sense of wholeness to others.

By seeing another person as an ego, I reinforce both my own sense of ego identification as well as that of the other person. And by seeing him or her instead through the eyes of the Authentic Self— not separate from Who I am but as complete and whole—I reinforce the sense of self-actualized Identity for both of us.

Generosity Reflected

Several years ago when I was living in Los Angeles, long before the movie *Pay It Forward* popularized the concept, I was filling my car up one day at a gas station. As was fairly common, while there I was approached by a young man asking for money. He was stooped over, with his shoulders hunched, a guilty expression on his face, and his eyes downcast, never looking directly at me. He said, in a somewhat whiny, almost pathetic tone, "Could you help me out? I'm stranded and I need money to take the bus to get home."

I said, "Sure, what do you need, a couple dollars?"

He replied, "Yea,… I guess so," still not looking up at me.

As I handed him some money, I said, "I want you to consider this a loan…"

He immediately interrupted me, with even more guilt in his voice, "Yea, allright," still not able to look at me.

I continued, "But I don't want you to pay it back to me, I want you to pay it back to someone else who needs it someday the way you do now."

He immediately looked up at me, making direct eye contact for the first time, and he underwent an amazing, almost magical transformation. He stood up straight, his face and shoulders relaxed, and his face lit up in a bright smile. He said, this time with conviction and sincerity, "OK. I will!" And his enthusiastic "Thank you!" was filled with all the confidence and appreciation that he'd been lacking before.

I was really astounded by the metamorphosis he underwent, in his bearing, body language, and facial expressions, going in an instant from neediness and despair to seeming truly empowered and sincerely grateful. It was literally almost as though a huge burden had been lifted from his shoulders. It seemed to me that his outlook shifted instantaneously from "I'm not OK, not deserving, and not capable," to a contrasting attitude of "Yea. I'm OK, and *I can do that!*"

I don't know whether this was a momentary lifting of his spirits or whether it had any long term effect, and I have no idea whether he ever returned the favor to someone else, but just having that opportunity to witness his dramatic transformation before my eyes was worth far more to me than the small amount of money that I gave him. In that moment, he gave back to me in a way I'll certainly never forget.

Because I decided to see beyond this young man's apparent neediness and powerlessness, and instead chose to perceive him as capable and generous beyond the boundaries of his current situation, he apparently was able to see himself that way as well, at least for that moment. In return, I got to see my small act of generosity reflected in a definite and memorable way.

In a very real sense the law of cause and effect is actually the governing principle that determines all that we receive in life, all that we achieve and all that we experience in any way. Even our thoughts have an effect not only on our own inner experience, but perhaps even upon the world around us, and certainly on the world as far as we perceive it to be. Amazing transformations can occur when we open ourselves to the possibility of perceiving things differently.

Numerous studies have indicated, for example, that prayer has a statistically verifiable effect on healing. In studies where groups of people prayed for others who were ill, even when the patients did not know they were being prayed for, their recovery went significantly better in a number of specific areas. In one such study, coronary care patients with similar conditions and symptoms were split into two groups, one of which was prayed for and one which was not. Neither the patients nor their doctors and care givers knew which group they were in. Those in the group who received intercessory prayers on their behalf were significantly less likely to have a heart attack, need antibiotics, or require intervention such as ventilation or intubation.

These types of results are also apparently unrelated to the specific religious affiliation of either the patients or of those doing the praying, or to the form or type of prayer used, so long as it involves either asking for or visualizing specific positive outcomes such as a quick, easy recovery, free from complications.

Though the idea that there would be a cause for every situation we encounter seems to be obvious, the ego mind nonetheless distorts this understanding at every turn, often reversing true cause and effect in its perception. For example, the ego consistently tends to shift responsibility for all negative results outward onto other people or situations. "It's the government's fault, the economy, or the rampant immorality in society." Some people even blame God. On the other hand, the ego also tries to take credit for anything positive in an attempt at self-aggrandizement.

If something is going wrong, the ego looks for someone to blame. In a relationship, it's always the other person's fault if things go wrong. "It certainly wasn't anything *I* did!" says the ego. "She *made* me angry!" As though someone else had total control of our emotions.

A significant aspect of moving towards self-actualization, however, lies in how much responsibility we take for the circumstances of our lives. This is true at the collective level, within groups, as well as at the individual level. The collective ego looks for blame and enemies in people who are 'different'. 'Those others', whether they are of another religious background, another race, another political perspective, or another nationality, are seen as the cause of our problems.

The ego tends to interpret cause and effect strictly in terms of guilt and blame, which in its eyes demands retribution. Our criminal justice system, for example, tends to be not so much about justice, in the sense of uncovering the truth and holding people responsible for their actions, as it is about guilt, blame, vengeance, and punishment. What if, in courts of law throughout the land, rather than finding people "guilty" or "not guilty", we found them "*responsible*"?

True cause and effect is always impersonal. (It is neither good nor bad. It simply brings back whatever we put out, in some form, sooner or later, but inevitably.) As we begin to understand this great law, it has profound implications for how we live our lives. First, we learn that harmlessness is an absolute necessity, a fundamental starting point, and minimum requirement for living with any measure of personal peace. And compassion becomes simple pragmatic self-interest.

Freedom of choice is also essential, because it's only by having the freedom to make mistakes, sometimes extreme ones, that we can in turn experience the effects of those mistakes. Since these are inevitably painful in some way, they thereby teach us to choose more beneficial actions. This is how we learn and grow and begin to move beyond identification with the ego.

When we attempt to control another person's behavior, even 'for their own good', we are interfering with the flow of cause and effect in their life, and robbing them of the valuable lessons which come about from making mistakes. This is one of the greatest challenges of parenthood, in that it's necessary to find a balance between guiding a child and simply staying out of the way and allowing them to 'skin their knees' once in a while so that they can learn for themselves the valuable lessons of life.

One of the great responsibilities we have in life, both as individuals and in the collective which we call society, is when we are in the position to act as the vehicle through which cause and effect works out. As parents we sometimes must act to artificially create the 'effects' which teach children to alter their behavior in less destructive and selfish directions.

As a society we are sometimes placed in the position of needing to act as the agents of cause and effect for others, as when we imprison someone who habitually harms other people to prevent him from continuing to do so. This is an enormous responsibility, however, never to be taken lightly. Ideally it should always be undertaken with clear-minded detachment and not through the egotistical, emotional framework of anger, resentment, and retribution.

It's also helpful to keep in mind that many of the choices that we make which act as causes for the results we get back in life are made largely unconsciously. We *react* to situations, without conscious awareness of the choices we make, rather than *responding* with awareness to situations. You could think of a "reaction" in terms of chemical reactions: they happen automatically without any (conscious) thought. In practical terms it's also like the body's automatic, involuntary nervous reflexes, as in a 'knee-jerk reaction'.

That's not to say that we're not choosing these reactions, simply that we're not consciously aware of the choices we make, and therefore we're also unaware of their causal relationship to the effects that we generate from them. It's only when we become more aware of our choices that we are able to respond rather than react, and that we then experience true freedom of choice. It's only then that we begin to have the conscious ability to direct and choose the causes that generate the effects in our lives.

Again, while it might seem obvious, cause and effect is so fundamental to every aspect of our experience at every level and, because of the ego, so prone to misinterpretation, that it warrants careful, open-minded, impartial consideration. Simply put, if we don't like what we're getting back from life, we need to take a closer look at what we're putting out.

If we want to experience more abundance, we need to be generous. If we want to be inspired, we need to do whatever we can to inspire others. If we want freedom in our lives, we must act to set others free. And of course this applies to pretty much everything else we're exploring here, as will become even more obvious as we proceed.

Chapter Seven

THE LEVELS OF AWARENESS

"Problems cannot be solved at the same level of
awareness that created them."
—Albert Einstein

If we're exploring human awareness, consciousness, and human behavior in general, it might be helpful to take a look at the various levels at which we experience life. Understanding these various levels and the role they each play in our experience can be enormously useful in our own self development. Here they are as I currently understand them:

- *Physical Level:* Survival and reproduction.
- *Emotional Level:* Desire.
- *Mental Level:* Thought, truth.
- *Intuitive Level:* Spiritual, unity, oneness.[5]

Physical

At the 'bottom' is the physical level. In terms of consciousness, this is the level that's concerned mainly with survival and reproduction, our basic biological imperatives. At the purely physical level we're simply looking for gratification. For nearly everyone, so long as things are working correctly, this level remains largely unconscious and automatic. We're not really aware of it for the most part, nor do we need to be unless something goes wrong.

Emotional

The next level is that of our emotions. This level can be boiled down mainly to the quality of *desire*, and of it's flip side (really just an aspect of desire), fear. At this level the overriding question is: "What can I get for me?" We're driven by what we want personally and by the fear of not having it. All emotions can be seen simply as various aspects of desire.

This is also the level at which most of our problems arise, since the purely emotional consciousness is focussed mainly on the gratification of the ego. It's all about "me". The emotional level always has some degree of distortion, sometimes greater, sometimes less, and at this level no true clarity is possible.

Interestingly, at this level confusion about physical needs also comes into play. When the physical level remains unconscious, it tends to take care of itself. Unfortunately, we tend to fixate emotionally on many of our physical needs and make them *emotional* problems. We become emotionally attached to unhealthy food choices and eating habits, sexuality, and other physical comforts and gratification. As a result, they, too, become distorted and unhealthy.

Most of the problems in the world stem from the fact that most people have their consciousness centered mainly in the emotions most of the time. This is true on a personal level as well as on the group level. Most problems in human relations come down to people relentlessly pursuing their own selfish desires to the exclusion of the needs of others. We may *believe* in being altruistic as an intellectual ideal, but when we are allowing ourselves to be run mainly by our emotional urges, we tend to fall far short of any real altruism in our actual behavior.

I think it's also important to make the distinction between emotions and qualities such as love, joy, and bliss. Strictly speaking, in this context, these are actually not emotions, but much higher states of being and consciousness. What passes for love, for example, on the emotional level is really just an emotional attachment to another person. It's more about possessiveness than love. True love is unconditional and concerned only with the welfare of others, with no selfish motivation or regard for one's own personal desires whatsoever.

The other problem with this level is that we tend to repress many of the more disturbing emotions. By doing so, they move to an unconscious level, where they become even more distorted and build up what might be called "emotional pressure". Since they are trapped inside rather than being expressed in a healthy manner, the pressure is released either through distorted outbursts here and there, or by building to a point of explosion, or by becoming internalized to the point of self-destructiveness.

The ideal, healthy use of emotions should be, like the physical level, largely automatic. You can also think of this as "e-motion", where "e" equals "energy". "E-motion" is *energy in motion*. So long as there is a healthy flow, keeping things moving, we're good. The problem arises when we either fixate on something emotionally, or repress our emotions to avoid experiencing emotional pain.

Mental

Above the emotions is the mental level. This is the level of thought, of the mind. It's at this level that for the first time we can begin to gain actual understanding of both ourselves and our environment. For the first time we can begin to look beyond ourselves and our own personal desires to what might in fact work for everyone. The mental level is about discerning what is true.

When we begin to center our consciousness on the mental level, to the degree that we are honest with ourselves we can start to make a distinction between what is a merely selfish desire and what might, in fact, be a more healthy choice, both for ourselves and for others who might be influenced by our choices.

At first, because we are still mainly centered in the emotions, we often tend to use the mind simply to rationalize and justify our various selfish emotional desires. And we can become quite skillful at this. But we can also use the mind to look beyond this to what is not possible at the purely emotional level, namely, finding the truth. On the emotional level there is always distortion and inaccuracy. But with clear, open-minded thinking that is relatively free of any purely emotional bias, we can begin to distinguish the true from the false and move towards a clearer understanding of the world around us and the part we play in it.

This mental level search for the truth is, of course, the basis of science. Science, at its best, is about objective observation and using a clear, intelligent line of reasoning to discover the secrets of the world around us. That's not to say that the sciences are always without personal bias; far from it. But that is the objective. And the scientific approach to exploration is actually a fairly good way to learn in our lives in general. The proper balance of open minded curiosity, healthy skepticism, and a careful testing of working hypotheses will usually serve us quite well in most areas of life.

Intuitive

Above the mental level is what could be called the intuitive level, or perhaps the spiritual level, or what some psychologist refer to as the "superconscious level". This is the level of the magical moment —the peak experience. I believe it is also the level of our "Authentic Self", who we *truly are* at our deepest and most essential level.

I call this the intuitive level because it is from the intuition that we get those seemingly magical bursts of insight that often turn out to be the perfect solution to some given problem. This is one of the main foundations for the creative process, as we'll be discussing later.

This is also the level of wholeness and 'connectedness'. When we have an experience at this level, however fleeting it may be, for that moment we leave behind our normal perspective as the time-bound, "skin-encapsulated ego", and no longer see ourselves as separate from that which surrounds us.

While I sometimes hesitate to use the term "spiritual" since it has taken on what is for many a somewhat controversial connotation (much like the term "religion"), it does nonetheless describe what we're talking about in the sense that these experiences go beyond our normal 'form-bound' level of perception. And they are truly magical in that sense since they allow us to step out of the normal limitations of physical, emotional, and mental forms.

Keep in mind however, that any attempt to describe these experiences will always be limited and inaccurate, since the very experience of this level literally defies explanation. The very fact that they are "beyond form" means that they cannot be adequately expressed in 'forms' such as language. They are also magical in the sense that they affect and transform us in what are often quite profound ways. In fact, the word "trans-form-ation" literally means to "go beyond form".

Ironically, I believe it is in this realm of the intuitive level that our true Identity also lies. I say "ironically" because for most of us experiences of this level tend to be the exception rather than the norm. Nonetheless, in contrast to the limited, largely emotionally-based, false self of the ego, experiences of ourselves at the intuitive level are infinitely more expansive, all inclusive, and simply feel 'true' in unarguably profound ways that are difficult to put into words.

'Who we truly are' is one of the great mysteries of life. If we are not merely our physical bodies, or our emotions, or even our thoughts, but something more, what is this "something more"? When we have experiences of the intuitive level, of a magical moment or peak experience, even though they may be in every way in sharp contrast to our normal level of perceptive awareness, they also tend to be more real in our experience than anything else we have encountered. It is here that we are truly 'at home'.

We often tend to think of only the physical level as real. The thought is that if we can't see, hear, smell, taste, or touch it, it doesn't exist. But perhaps we need to reverse that thinking. Since even these physical senses are only relatively real and are, in fact, only electrical impulses registered in the brain, perhaps the truth is 'not that'... but something *more*. I believe that it lies in this intuitive level of experience.

Experiences of this level almost universally enhance life at the other levels. They bring more joy, wonder, and a deeper capacity for love and compassion.

The Hierarchy of Our Experience

In any given day our awareness may touch any or all of these levels at various moments, and in some cases we may even have at least some awareness on more than one, or perhaps even on all the levels simultaneously. But the important question is, "Where is our awareness *centered* most consistently?" As I've already indicated, for most of us our awareness tends to be most centered on the emotional level the greatest amount of the time.

It's easy to see this both on a personal level and in greater spheres of influence. Rather than behaving in a detached and rational manner, and responding to situations based on the true needs of those situations, we often *react* to circumstances, particularly ones in which we have even the tiniest bit of emotional investment (and often even to those in which we seemingly don't!), in 'knee-jerk', emotionally reactive ways.

This, of course, is the realm of the ego—the false self that sees itself as potentially threatened by nearly everything and everyone around itself. It is therefore constantly in a state of defending itself from these various "threats", often in a rather *offensive* manner.

In the world at large, this often plays out in ideological warfare. Through the lens of the egocentric framework, "my belief system", whether political, religious, or concerning literally anything else, no matter how seemingly significant or insignificant, is the only one that has any real validity. You only have to look at the political spectrum to see how blatantly true this is. Modern politics is not about solving the needs of the people. It's about approaching every problem as a potential threat to 'my ideology' and a potential opportunity for me to demolish any other seemingly conflicting ideology.

What we need to do, first on an individual basis which then will lead eventually to a collective one, is to begin practicing holding our awareness at higher levels than the purely emotional. We do this first by simply observing open-mindedly and clearly what is going on around us. This in itself is challenging, of course, since we tend to observe things through the filter of our emotional biases. And we also have to remind ourselves that our perceptions are only relatively accurate at best.

But practicing detached observation of situations is a good first step in moving towards actually *thinking* clearly about them rather than simply *reacting emotionally* to them. We also need to remind ourselves that clear thinking is more about asking, about inquiry, than it is about 'reaching a conclusion'.

Whenever possible, it is perhaps even more crucial to look for and induce experiences at the intuitive level, to move out of the ego framework altogether, however briefly, into the realm of the Authentic Self.

I'm not making the case for being unemotional, or for repressing emotional expression. That is just the other side of the same coin of emotional "polarization". Healthy emotional expression is an important aspect of being fully human. But we do need to move towards allowing the emotions to be a natural extension and expression of the higher, mentally and intuitionally focussed consciousness, rather than allowing ourselves to be completely run *by* our emotions and fears and desires.

We need to learn to think, clearly and objectively. And little by little, we also need to move beyond thought itself to a place of stillness, which is the realm of the superconscious and the intuition, which then begins to inform and become the foundation of our thoughts and emotions.

Maslow's Perspective

In his studies of human development, Abraham Maslow discovered that humans move up through various stages of what he called a "hierarchy of needs" which, in my view, has direct correlations to these levels of awareness we're exploring. He found that we are motivated first by very basic physical and then emotional needs, and they must be met first before we can move beyond them to higher level needs of influence and personal development.

Maslow originally listed his hierarchy of needs as follows:

1. ***Biological and Physiological needs*** - air, food, drink, shelter, warmth, sex, sleep, etc.
2. ***Safety needs*** - protection from elements, security, order, law, limits, stability, etc.
3. ***Belongingness and Love needs*** - work group, family, affection, relationships, etc.
4. ***Esteem needs*** - self-esteem, achievement, mastery, independence, dominance, status, prestige, managerial responsibility, etc.
5. ***Self-Actualization needs*** - realizing personal potential, self-fulfillment, seeking personal growth and peak experiences.

He also later added a higher need which he called "Transcendence", which is another way to refer to the superconscious or spiritual level. One aspect of the transcendent state that he identified is that individuals at that level are motivated to help others to move towards self-actualization.

Maslow's hierarchy of needs is a very well known theory that most college students become familiar with in basic psychology classes. While there is some cross-over between the levels, I find that they directly mirror the rise in consciousness from physical to emotional to mental to spiritual.

As I explored these levels myself, both in my studies as well as in my own personal experience, I also came to hold the belief that at some point in the journey of self-development, this hierarchy of needs would invert itself, so that the higher needs for self-actualization and transcendence became the most essential ones to an individual. I eventually discovered that this is precisely what Maslow himself had found later in his work.

Growing Up

We can also see this process of moving to higher levels of consciousness in the natural development of a child. As infants, the awareness is almost purely physical. Babies are completely dependant upon their parents and caretakers for their basic physical needs, and this instinctual level of awareness pretty much encompasses all their experience.

As toddlers, children become almost purely emotional. They can move from anger to glee to sadness in seconds, with no attachment to any one of these. From the age of about 7 onward, children begin to finely-tune their emotions and develop a true emotional identity.

Then around age 13 or 14, adolescents gradually become more intellectual and rational in their perspective of the world around them. They begin to learn to think for themselves (which any parent of a teenager can tell you can be a trying time indeed!)

Eventually, in healthy individuals, as we move into the maturity of adulthood we also tend to look beyond these to something more. For some people this may be in passionate creative pursuits, for others it might manifest in a religious or spiritual interest, or as a simple need for solitude and reflection.

These stages can be different for different individuals, but most of us do have at least some experience on each of these levels at various points in our lives. They also have some significant implications for the process of education, as we'll explore later. What becomes more important as we develop further, as I mentioned previously, is where we center our awareness the majority of the time, and in striving to spend more and more of our focus at increasingly higher levels.

Honesty, Sincerity, and Detachment

One way to move more consistently into the higher levels of awareness and functioning is to practice a simple discipline of honesty, sincerity, and detachment. In any situation, to the degree that we can apply these three traits, we can be fairly certain that we're on track. Of course while they are quite simple, as with anything worthwhile, expressing them consistently is often easier said than done.

Honesty refers to much more than just speaking the truth and not telling lies. What we're really talking about is honesty of mind. It's when all our thoughts, words, and actions are consistent and not at all in conflict with one another. There is no deception or denial of any kind. How many of us can say that we are always free from self-deception of one kind or another in each and every situation?

For example, if you have a strong belief in the importance of protecting our environment, and yet you occasionally throw a piece of litter on the ground without thinking about it, or you turn on the air conditioning higher than you need it, or make other similar choices without giving it much thought, then you're not being completely honest with yourself. Of course we may in fact have beliefs that are seemingly in conflict, such as a belief in protecting the environment, and a desire to keep our family comfortable and warm in the winter. The point is to pay attention to the choices we are making, and to do so as honestly as possible, even if that means we decide to make compromises at times.

Sincerity is the equivalent of honesty, but on the emotional level. It's coming from your heart, connecting 'heart to heart' with another person. It's about being genuine, and not emotionally false in any way. The emotions are then simply an expression of a deeper level of Self, of our compassionate, spiritual, Authentic Self.

Detachment means that we're not holding on to things. It doesn't mean that we have no connections to other people or situations, it simply means we're always willing and able to let go if it is appropriate. We can often become attached (emotionally and otherwise) to possessions, to people, and to ideas. As my wife, Kathi, once wrote, "There's a lot to be said for letting go."

Detachment also means that we're not attached to specific outcomes or to having things our way. Ghandi wrote:

"By detachment I mean that you must not worry whether the desired results follow from your action or not, so long as your motive is pure,

*your means correct. Really, it means that things will come right in the
end if you take care of the means and leave the rest to (God)."*
    —Mahatma Gandhi

Or to quote the Chinese philosopher, Jianzhi Sengcan:

"The Great Way is not difficult for those who have no preferences."

Detached Involvement

Attachment and denial are the two extremes that create
imbalances in life. A detached involvement in the circumstances of life
is the desirable, balanced state that answers them both.

Attachment comes from the belief that material experiences of
any kind, which can include material possessions, but also more
abstract 'form' experiences including our thoughts and emotions, are
of importance *in and of themselves*. Here we see the craving of material
possessions, self-centered behavior, mindless adherence to beliefs,
emotional attachments, possessive relationships, and compulsions such
as addictions and over-indulgences.

Denial is the belief that you can simply ignore your life
circumstance. This is the refusal to deal with one's situation in the
delusional hope that it will go away. And denial is, of course, really
just the flip-side of attachment, since it's yet another way of holding
onto or keeping whatever is being denied by not dealing with it.

Having a detached involvement in life is the more balanced
approach in which you are, to quote a popular phrase, "in the world
but not of it". Detached involvement means being open to
experiencing everything in the material reality, while at the same time
realizing that those 'form experiences' whether physical, emotional, or
mental, are not important *in and of themselves*, but *only* in that they are
learning tools in the form of feedback.

To my mind the importance of the experiences in our life lies in
the meaning *behind* the experiences. It's about the connections we
make—with other human beings, with our creativity, and with the
experience of life itself. We needn't be attached to the forms that the
experiences take, but simply be in them, appreciate them, enjoy them,
and learn from them.

The seeming paradox is that they have no *literal* importance of their own, and yet they must be experienced, because to deny their experience is to deny one's own thoughts, feelings, sensory experience, and state of mind. Which brings us back to honesty, sincerity, and detachment. It's really about accepting things as they truly are, rather than fixating on how we want them to be or on how we think they "should" be.

In a sense, attachment and denial are both forms of resisting the essential meaning and essence behind our outer experience, and both are used as a means of holding onto the illusion of our ego-based separativeness.

Any perception, belief, or emotional attitude we have that is in conflict with seeing ourselves as whole and loving and capable is an aspect of the limited ego illusion. And while the separative ego self-image is actually a false belief, that doesn't mean it has no power. So long as we identify with the ego as our "self", it is backed by all the power and resources of our dynamic, multi-layered creative capabilities, which are powerful indeed.

Psychic Trauma

One of the main obstacles for most of us in moving beyond the ego framework towards self-actualization lies in overcoming the unconscious emotional programming that we hold. Especially in childhood, whenever we are exposed to events in which our basic human needs are not being met, it can cause a form of psychic trauma.

If we are not able to fully accept the pain of these events and integrate it and allow ourselves to heal—which is most often the case when they occur in childhood, since we are not yet emotionally mature enough and resilient enough to endure them on our own—rather than moving through us the trauma is then pushed down to an unconscious level where we carry it with us as unresolved emotional blockages.

These emotional blocks can take a variety of forms, including self-limiting beliefs such as "I'm not loveable", "I'm not capable", "I can never have what I want", "I can't...", "I have to...", to name just a few. These blocks and limited beliefs then become 'true' for us, and we are for all practical purposes unable to move beyond them, until and unless we once again bring the blockages up to a conscious level where they can be integrated and released.

In several of his books and PBS television specials, best-selling author, John Bradshaw spells out in great detail both the psychology behind these emotional traumas as well as a number of processes for releasing them. He explains how various types of blockages can be identified, based on the fact that they take different forms, depending upon the particular stage of childhood in which they were originally formed.

He also points out that virtually all of us have these emotional wounds from childhood psychic trauma. Since none of us grew up in perfect situations (no parent is perfect and no one had all their needs perfectly met) we all experienced one kind or another of emotional trauma, and as a result we all carry some form of emotional blockage. Bradshaw's insights into the role these blocks play in our lives and his techniques for moving beyond them are ground-breaking in their implications, and I highly recommend his work, in particular his PBS series, *Bradshaw: On Homecoming*. (I also just learned that his most recent book was nominated for a Pulitzer.)

The important thing to remember about moving through our unconscious emotional blocks is that it is most likely to be an ongoing process. As one layer of emotional pain is uncovered and brought to the light of our awareness, another deeper layer is often revealed. Just as our growth and personal development is a lifelong endeavor, so too, may be our healing.

One of the problems with attempting to undo the ego is that we are doing so from within the ego perspective. The ego wants the pain to all go away right now, and feels threatened if it doesn't. But choosing to perceive this as a threatening situation, is actually one way of maintaining the ego dominance.

The entire ego framework is built on the belief that we are separate and therefore vulnerable to harm from 'outside' ourselves. And so we are also always looking outside of ourselves for our safety and gratification.

The Authentic Self, in contrast, is whole and complete in and of Itself, and is also invulnerable to harm from outside influences. It simply is. Though we can choose to push it down out of our awareness and effectively separate ourselves from it, the essence of Who We Are at our deepest and truest cannot be threatened in any way. Since this Authentic Self cannot be threatened by outside influences, it simply accepts them exactly as they are, including the painful aspects of life. This is, in fact, an aspect of the compassionate nature of the True Self. In fact, the word "com-passion" means to "suffer with". The Authentic Self is willing to suffer with another, including the 'other' of the ego "self".

The paradox is that pain is transcended not by resisting it, but by accepting it. Psychiatrist M. Scott Peck opens his best-selling book, *The Road Less Traveled,* by mentioning the Buddha's admonition that all human life is suffering, and that this is a great truth because once we truly accept it, we transcend it. In other words, once we fully accept that life is painful we are no longer trapped into experiencing it that way. (I do love paradoxes!)

Chapter Eight

THE POWER OF MAGIC

"Those who don't believe in magic will never find it."
—Roald Dahl

Magic strikes me, metaphorically speaking, as the ultimate paradox. On the one hand, it represents all that is not real: the "Great Illusion". And on the other hand, it represents ultimate potential: all capabilities reaching far beyond physical limitation.

It points out in blatant terms that our perceptions are never truly what they appear to be. No matter what our perceptions of the universe may be, they fall far short of its actual reality. Like the conjuror's prestidigitation on stage that creates the illusion of reality in the minds of the audience, so too do we manipulate our own perceptions to create a symbolic facade of reality that we believe to be true, even though it is actually no more than a projection from our mind.

And yet magic also represents our ever present but seldom acknowledged ability to go past the illusion; to stretch our perception of what is possible; to understand that reality has no limitation. Magic whispers the captivating message that we can do whatever we want; that anything is possible if we will only believe—as indeed it is! In the words of Napoleon Hill: *"Whatever the mind of Man can conceive and believe, it can achieve."*

The power of magic is the power of transformation: to transform one thing into another. As the medieval alchemists sought to transform base metals into gold, which was actually a metaphor for the transformation of the human spirit, we too have the ability to use the power of 'magic' or transformation. As I mentioned before, the word "trans-form-ation" means to "go beyond form".

Of course, the biggest transformation is within ourselves. To transform our own human expression into all that we can be, and to share that transformation with the world around us.

The Process of Magic

But there is also a *process* to 'magic'. It is a process that we can actually learn to use—consciously and practically—in our daily lives, to do things that might at first have seemed to be impossible. And isn't that the real essence of magic—the idea that the impossible is possible?

Sound like nothing more than wishful thinking? Well, let's take a closer look. If we actually could do real magic, if we could just snap our fingers and instantaneously whatever we wanted would appear magically before us, it would still involve the process of envisioning, in our mind's eye, the outcome which we desire, and then somehow causing it to become a physical reality. And that process just might sound familiar to you.

To my mind, what I'm referring to here as "magic" is actually synonymous with art, creativity, achieving a goal, and what is sometimes called "creative visualization". They are all the process of having an inspiration, putting it into a mental form, filling it with emotional energy, and bringing it into physical manifestation. The artist has an inspiration that she then brings into some specific physical form so that it can inspire other people. The magician does exactly the same thing, creating 'flashes of wonder'. And creativity is also the same process, used to fill some specific need.

As we discussed earlier, one of the core principles that Maxwell Maltz puts forth in his book *Psycho-Cybernetics*, is the idea that the human mind really functions as a "goal-seeking servo-mechanism". The word "cybernetics" comes from the Greek word *kybernētēs*—the steersman or rudder of a ship. Cybernetics is the study of systems that move towards goals by receiving feedback, comparing it with the desired outcome, and continually taking actions based on the feedback in order to continue moving towards the goal, much like the guided missile analogy.

One interesting fact to note is that a guided missile is off-course about 90 percent of the time. It finds the target by continually homing in on it, comparing its course with the direction of the target, and making continual course corrections until the target is reached. In fact, it's by *being off-course*, and then making note of the specific discrepancy and responding accordingly, that the missile actually finds its target. So *Psycho-Cybernetics* would be this process as it takes place in the human mind.

Imagination

The programming for our own internal guided missile, and the secret to magic, if you will, lies in our *imagination*. It is in our imagination that inspiration is born. And it is through the creative use of the imagination that all human accomplishment is achieved. Einstein said:

> *"Imagination is more important than knowledge. For knowledge is limited to all we now know and understand, while imagination embraces the entire world, and all there ever will be to know and understand."*
> —Albert Einstein

My friend, Andrew, likes to say that human beings are really 'creative dream machines'. To my mind, it's only through the effective use of the imagination that we truly live, because only when we create are we expressing our true identities as reflections of the Creator.

And the creative capacity exists in that 'magical land of imagination' ! Whatever you dare to dream, make it real; see it for yourself; inside yourself. No problem can stand against the power of the creative imagination. Can you imagine a better life? Can you imagine happiness, solutions, self-love, fulfillment? The only thing that keeps the 'life not lived' from being experienced as life lived to its fullest is lack of imagination and lack of belief.

In studies involving their Olympic athletes, Russian scientists discovered that those who used visualization outperformed those who used only traditional training methods. Four groups of athletes were studied, the first of which devoted 100% of their training time to physical training, the second used 25% of their time for visualization training and 75% for physical training, the third devoted 50% to each, and the fourth used 75% visualization to 25% physical. The fourth group that devoted 75% of training time to visualization performed the best of all the groups.

A few weeks before the 2000 Olympic trials, US platform diver

Laura Wilkinson broke her foot in a training injury. Everyone with any knowledge of the sport assumed it was a forgone conclusion that it would be impossible for her to compete at that year's Olympic Games. For weeks she was unable to even get in the water, much less actually do any diving. But each day she visualized her dives over and over in her imagination, completing her entire training regimen in her mind. And she also saw herself at the Olympics receiving the Gold Medal. She did qualify and compete at the Olympics, and though she started the competition in 8th place, behind the highly favored Chinese team, she came from behind to win the Gold.

The reason the imagination is so powerful is that the goal-seeking subconscious mind cannot tell the difference, and literally makes no distinction between an actual experience and one that is vividly imagined. And unlike actual practice, when we visualize we can always imagine *perfect* performance, so we are practicing the perfect outcome. By using visualization we are literally programming the goals into our subconscious mind, and it then goes to work impersonally to achieve whatever goal it is. It doesn't judge the goals as either good or bad, it simply homes in on them and works to bring them about.

This is also why people who continually worry, or put themselves down, or have a generally negative perspective, tend to get exactly the results and experiences that "prove" their fears to be warranted. They are literally programming their lives for disappointing experiences and outcomes.

My point is that this creative power, which for my purposes I'm calling the "process of magic", works for *everyone all the time*, regardless of whether we use it consciously and deliberately, or whether we simply allow our minds to focus on whatever fearful, anxious, or other self defeating thoughts may arise. I truly believe that creativity is our birthright, that humans are creative by their very nature, and we either learn to use that creativity consciously, purposefully, and mindfully, or we are 'used by it', in the form of whatever random images we hold in our minds.

The Process

Let's take a closer look at what this "process of magic" actually entails. As I mentioned before, I think of this as the same process as art or creative accomplishment. There are essentially four steps to the process, which relate directly to the four levels of awareness or experience which we discussed earlier. In contrast to the hierarchy of needs, this process begins from the top, down. Or you could also think of it as from the innermost, outward.

Keep in mind that this process applies to any creative activity, in literally any area of life. It could be actually creating some fabulous and complex work of art, it could be overcoming a seemingly insurmountable personal crisis, it could be attaining some specific goal, or it could simply be saying the right words to the right person at the right time because you feel inspired to do so. The entire process could take years to complete, or it could all happen in an instant. In any of these cases, the same basic principles apply.

Inspiration

We begin with the intuition. That place of wholeness and connectedness deep within each of us is also the source of all true inspiration. When we create, it is important that we begin from this place of intuitive awareness so that our sense of purpose and direction will be sound. If you've ever had an experience of pondering on a problem and, in a moment of relaxation when you least expected it, you had the perfect solution suddenly flash into your mind, then you'll understand how powerful this can be.

Mental Form

Once we have an intuitive sense for what we want to create, the next step is to create a vivid mental picture of it in our mind's eye. The more clearly we can experience it in our imagination, utilizing all five senses, the more real it will become in our experience until it's attainment becomes second nature. We are literally creating a form in 'mental matter' which is sometimes referred to as a "thought form". This mental form is like the blueprint for our magical work of art. It also becomes the goal target of our subconscious mind.

Emotional Energy

Once we have a vivid mental image of what we want, we must then fill that image with the energy of our emotions in the form of a burning desire. It's not desire, however, in the normal ego perspective of "I want", but more in the sense of a strong intention. This is the energy that fills the form and breathes life into it. It gives color and depth to the mental image. It is also the magnetic attractive energy that draws our creation to us, and us to it. This makes the mental image vibrant and attractive and sets all the wheels in motion. This is the true purpose of emotional energy when used in healthy ways.

Physical Manifestation

Lastly, we realize the desired outcome in some specific, concrete physical manifestation. Usually this means that we simply take whatever physical action or actions are required to achieve our goal and create our "work of art" in physical form. The specific form will of course depend upon the nature of the creation. It may be a more harmonious work or home environment. It may be a beautiful painting. It may be a personal goal. Or it may be literally any other outcome of any kind that you can think of as desirable.

Imagination

Again, the secret to the entire process lies in our imagination. On the intuitive level we stretch our imagination to a new idea; on the mental level we focus our imagination on the detailed image of our goal; on the emotional level we enflame the imagination with a burning desire; and on the physical level we realize our imagination in some concrete form.

Many people will say that they aren't creative and they don't *have* a good imagination. This simply isn't true. We are all creative by nature. It is an essential and fundamental aspect of who we are as human beings. When we say things like, "I don't have a good imagination", or "I'm just not creative", what we're really doing is telling our creative imagination, and programming our subconscious mind, to NOT give us good ideas! We're literally using the powerful mechanisms of creativity to block our own creative abilities.

The creative process and the subconscious mind are completely impersonal, and they will do whatever we ask them to do. It doesn't mean we're not creative, it simply means we're not thinking creatively —and that is always a choice!

In fact, several years ago a major oil company became concerned that some of the people in their research and development department weren't nearly as creative as some of the others in the department. They hired an entire team of psychologists to study the problem, and they conducted extensive interviews with the people in the department, asking a wide range of questions, from personal preferences to educational background to childhood experiences, and everything else they could think of.

After conducting literally months of research and examining the data from every possible angle, they were able to determine only *one factor* that set the "creatives" apart from the "non-creatives". The creative people thought of themselves as creative, and the uncreative people didn't.[6]

The Importance of Beginning With Intuition

One of the main issues that I take with many of the recent popular books, seminars, and other information on using visualization, goal setting, and similar techniques to create the life you want, is that they often give little if any emphasis to the necessity of always beginning and centering the process at the intuitive level. The problem is, we don't *have* to begin at the intuitive level in order to use the process to get things that we want. The power of the mental/emotional focus combined with the willingness to do whatever we must to attain our desires can and will bring them about.

But how we *choose* those desires is not without consequence. Goals that come from figuring it out intellectually are often still at the individual ego level, and they can therefore be selfish, counterproductive, or even destructive in one way or another. If our focus is still in the emotional ego perspective of "what can I get for me?", what we desire more often than not will in some way be detrimental to others, and ultimately to ourselves as well. To put it simply, sometimes what we think we want isn't what we really ought to have.

We see evidence of this in those individuals who accumulate huge fortunes by trampling on the needs and rights of others. These are often charismatic, powerful personalities who use their creativity to relentlessly achieve their desires, with little or no consideration of how their actions effect others. Or they rationalize their destructive actions as being somehow for the greater good. But at what cost?

The great universal law of cause and effect ensures that every destructive act *will* have its consequence. Whenever we act in a way that is harmful to others, the effects will ultimately return to us in one way or another, at some time or another. Like a branch snapping back in our face, eventually but inevitably we *will* reap what we sow.

When I look at the lives of those who have gained fame and fortune by following a path of selfishness and greed, while they may live seemingly glamorous lives on the outside, they nonetheless never strike me as truly happy people. More money doesn't bring happiness; it just amplifies whatever you have inside. If you are essentially unhappy, lots of money will make you lots more unhappy and unfulfilled.

Intuitive solutions to problems, on the other hand, always have a sense of perfection about them. One of the essential attributes of experience at the intuitive level is that of harmlessness. Intuitively directed goals always turn out to be for the highest and greatest benefit of everyone that they affect in any way. And given that we are all infinitely interconnected, "who" our actions effect is always *everyone!*

Tapping Into the Power of Intuition

When we have experiences at the intuitive level, our sense of separateness dissolves. The defining lines between our individual selves and 'other' are no longer distinct. It therefore becomes impossible to act from the normal, ego-based win-lose scenario. If I am not truly separate from others, if they are simply aspects of my greater sense of Self, to take any action that would be harmful to another person would also be harmful to myself.

In this sense, the popular, competitive win-lose approach to life is simply another example of an aspect of the false ego perspective.

But it's not even a consideration at the level of intuition. Selfish desires, and harmful actions, are the antithesis of the intuitive state, and they cannot be experienced simultaneously.

Beginning the creative process at the intuitive level, and using it as the basis for inspiration, guidance, and direction, ensures that our sense of purpose is always sound and of the greatest possible benefit to all whom it touches. And more often than not, intuitive direction offers solutions to our problems that are incredibly comprehensive and productive in ways we never could have imagined by simply trying to figure them out.

So, how do we receive these intuitive inspirations? How do we recognize them when they arise? At first glance this might seem like a rather unreliable way of ordering one's life. But being open to and tapping into intuitive direction is actually a skill that can be learned and developed and that can be counted on more and more consistently.

If you've ever had the experience of choosing to do something that turned out to be a huge mistake, it may give you one clue into the intuition. Often what happens in these situations is we make choices based on what seems to be logical and even well thought out reasoning, but somewhere inside it just feels wrong somehow. When we act on it anyway and it turns out disastrously, we say that we knew something wasn't right about it.

That inner feeling telling us to beware is the "still small voice" of the intuition. Unfortunately, we most often tend to ignore it or push it down or drown it out with our ongoing mind chatter. Of course we do so to our own misfortune.

In its separative need to be in control, the ego wants to figure things out on its own. Since listening to the intuition means letting go and giving up that control to some degree, the ego will resist the voice of the intuition and do its best to rationalize it away. "That's not logical", "It's impractical", "It doesn't make any sense", and "What a bunch of idealistic nonsense... just give me the 'facts'!", are all ego-based excuses for why using the intuition is a bad idea. The ego perspective would argue that practical, reasonable people don't rely on anything so vague and irrational as this. Of course that simply isn't true.

If we make a careful study of the greatest men and women in all areas of human affairs, one of the common threads is that they learned to rely on this type of intuitive guidance. In the world of business, Andrew Carnegie, John D. Rockefeller, and Conrad Hilton are three famous examples of people who all regularly depended on intuition when making business decisions. More recent examples include Bill Gates and Steve Jobs.

One well known story from Conrad Hilton's life is an example of what many called "Connie's Hunches". Hilton was submitting a sealed bid for a New York property which he'd evaluated as being worth $159,000, and he put together a bid in that amount. That night he went to sleep, and when he woke, the figure $174,000 stood out in his mind, so the next morning he changed the bid to that amount. He won the bid, and afterwards it was revealed that the next highest bid had been for $173,000. Later he sold the property for several million dollars.

The work of well known scientists is filled with examples of the importance of intuition as well. Here are a few quotes:

"Intuition will tell the thinking mind where to look next."
 —Jonas Salk

"It is always with excitement that I wake up in the morning wondering what my intuition will toss up to me, like gifts from the sea. I work with it and rely on it. It's my partner."
 —Jonas Salk

"The intellect has little to do on the road to discovery. There comes a leap in consciousness, call it intuition or what you will, and the solution comes to you and you don't know how or why."
 —Albert Einstein

"There is no logical way to the discovery of these elemental laws. There is only the way of intuition, which is helped by a feeling for the order lying behind the appearance."
 —Albert Einstein

"All great achievements of science must start from intuitive knowledge. I believe in intuition and inspiration.... At times I feel certain I am right while not knowing the reason."
 —Albert Einstein

"It is through science that we prove, but through intuition that we discover."
—Henri Poincare

One well documented story of the role that intuition plays in scientific exploration involves Friedrich August Kekulé and his discovery of the structure of the benzene molecule. He wrote in his diary:

"I was sitting writing on my textbook, but the work did not progress; my thoughts were elsewhere. I turned my chair to the fire and dozed. Again the atoms were jumbling before my eyes. This time the smaller groups kept modestly in the background. My mental eye, rendered more acute by the repeated visions of the kind, could now distinguish larger structures of manifold conformation; long rows sometimes more closely fitted together all twining and twisting in snake-like motion. But look! What was that? One of the snakes had seized hold of its own tail, and the form whirled mockingly before my eyes. As if by a flash of lightning I awoke..."

Upon awaking, he suddenly realized that the benzene molecule was formed by a ring of carbon atoms, much like the snake in his dream. His discovery paved the way for the theories of modern organic chemistry.

Finding Our Intuitive Voice

While many people stumble upon the process of using intuition by accident, there are common patterns in how it occurs, and in the nature of the intuition itself which, if we begin to understand and follow, will allow us to learn to depend upon the intuition more and more reliably. First, it's important to understand that the intuition is indeed the "still small voice". We have to listen for it and be open to it. Rarely will it jump in where it isn't first welcomed. The intuition will never speak more loudly than the ego, so we have to still the tumultuous emotions and erratic thoughts of the ego mind in order to hear it.

Generally, in order for intuitive insights to arise, there are two conditions which must be present: what I would call "seeking" and "receptivity". By *seeking* I mean that we are looking for something, asking for an answer to something, that our attention is actively focussed on solving a problem or filling a specific need. With intuitive insights, "ask and it shall be given, seek and you shall find" definitely applies. In this sense, asking has an 'invocative' quality, and it sets the process in motion, so to speak.

What I'm calling "asking", in this context, can be taken quite broadly. It can also include a form of focussed contemplation combined with open-minded curiosity. We ponder on a situation, perhaps visualizing possible responses or solutions or outcomes, but without reaching any specific conclusions: simply remaining open and curious. Whatever we hold in our conscious mind clearly and consistently, along with a sense of inquisitiveness and interest, plants the seed in the subconscious mind and sets the wheels in motion.

Secondly, we have to be in a condition of open receptivity to actually receive intuitive solutions. Usually this means some form of relaxed state. Again, it's necessary to still the noise and commotion of the ego mind. One way that this process often works out is that we spend a period where we are actively focussed on trying to solve a problem, and then when we have let it go completely, and aren't even thinking about, especially if we're doing something relaxing or fun, the correct answer just pops into our mind when we least expect it.

This focussed seeking followed by relaxed receptivity can take many, many different forms, and the process can take place over extended periods of time or it can happen instantaneously. But when an intuitive solution presents itself, these two qualities are nearly always present in some way, even if they are totally subliminal and we aren't really even consciously aware of the process.

Intuitive inspiration can take the form of a solution to a problem, large or small, or it can sometimes come as a greater sense of purpose. We may feel inspired to create something new, or to take action on some issue or cause. There is often an element of service involved, of sharing something worthwhile with others. Artists often experience this as a compelling vision for what they wish to express and create: an idea that almost takes on a life of its own and which they feel passionate about pursuing.

Sometimes these intuitive inspirations come as a sudden flash of insight, but they can also come in many other forms as well. At times they may arrive in the form of some kind of uncanny coincidence, in an experience of what is often called synchronicity or serendipity. In fact, several years ago I had one of these occur when I was doing a series of lectures in which I talked about this very topic.

My wife, Kathi, and I were travelling through the southwestern United States on a lecture tour I was conducting in various cities. If you're like me, at one time or another you'll have had the experience of not being able to remember a particular word that you need to express a certain idea. For some reason, for about three days in a row, I couldn't think of the word "serendipity". It was annoying me a bit, since it expressed this idea of experiencing meaningful coincidences that I talk about in my programs.

After trying and trying to think of it for what seemed like days on end, I finally just gave up and decided it would come to me eventually, as is almost always the case. Later that day we drove into Flagstaff, Arizona, where I was to do a talk the next day. Minutes after arriving in town, as we were driving to our hotel, I happened to look up and noticed that we were driving right past a little shop called the "Serendipity Bookstore". It certainly was for me.

Intuitive impulses can also come as an inner urge to do one thing or another, without necessarily having any rational reason as to why we should do it. It just feels right, like the 'thing to do'. There are many well-documented cases of people whose lives have been saved by taking action on these intuitive hunches.

I just read a story about a tornado that roared through Tuscaloosa, Alabama on April 27, 2011. As reported on CNN, Tillman Merrit, a young resident, was huddled in a hallway of his house with three friends when he suddenly had the urge to jump into the closet. He later said that he heard a voice in his head saying, "Go to the closet, go to the closet." He did so, and moments later, he was the sole survivor. When it was over, there was just a small hole left for him to crawl out, and, except for the closet he was in, the entire house had been thrown to the other side of the street.

We can also learn to use intuitive guidance when trying to decide whether to do one thing or another. If we focus on the decision, then allow our mind to become quiet, we can often sense the right choice. It's an experience of 'knowing-at-a-heart' level. One way is to envision each choice in turn, and in doing so we can often sense if one of them "just feels right in my heart".

In this sense, we can in fact also come up with consciously-conceived solutions in the normal way, and we can use all the resources of our creativity and our conscious, analytical mind to do so, but the key point is that any solution that we decide upon must pass the test of whether it feels appropriate at this intuitive, *heart level* of the Authentic Self. If we are truly honest with ourselves, we will generally always know deep down whether something is right or not.

While this may seem at first to be somewhat obscure and intangible, tapping into the intuition is like any other skill in that the more we practice using it, the better we become at receiving intuitive insights and inspiration, and the more reliable the ability will become.

I believe wholeheartedly that it's essential that this be the foundation and the starting point for all creative endeavor. Beginning with intuitive guidance means that what we create will be truly beneficial and of true value for all. If we ignore intuitive direction, we are doomed to act from the ego perspective, which is inevitably destructive and self-defeating. And since the ego can become quite skilled at rationalizing and justifying reasons to have its way, it's crucial that we learn to distinguish between the selfish desires of the ego and the benevolent guidance of the intuitive Authentic Self.

One key that can often be helpful in discerning the difference between an intuitive impulse and one that springs from the emotionally-based ego perspective lies in how and where you 'feel' it in your body. Emotional impulses are generally felt in the area of the solar plexus, just below the diaphragm; whereas intuitive impulses tend to be experienced as a sensation in the chest at the level of the heart. "I knew it in my heart," can often be literally true. How and why this is so isn't necessarily important in and of itself, but for some people, it can often be a useful indicator of experience.

Another clue is that ego desires are nearly always accompanied by underlying feelings of fear, anxiousness, or a general sense of uneasiness, even if they are sometimes kept just below the surface of our awareness. Intuitive solutions, however, consistently have a sense of wholeness and rightness about them. Regardless of whether they embody a long term, grand, inspiring vision, or an immediate, simple, practical course of action, we can always count on intuitive direction to be the right answer at the right time.

Creating the Mental Form

Once we've gotten an intuitive inspiration—which establishes our goal: our vision for our "magical work of art"—we must then be able to see it clearly in our mind's eye. The ability to create a clear, vivid, detailed image of an objective in our imagination is one of the most powerful and practical skills that we can develop. The more clearly we can see our intended creative outcome, the more it will become an absolute reality in our consciousness, and consequently the more substantially it will be programmed into our goal-seeking subconscious mind. Once this happens, our subconscious mind will go to work tirelessly and unerringly to bring it about.

Of course, when I say we need to "see" the objective, I'm not just talking about what it looks like visually. I mean that we experience it in vivid detail, using all five senses, in our imagination. We experience it as though it were already an established fact, existing right now in our physical world.

Exactly how would it look? What would it sound like? Are there specific tastes, smells, or physical or tactile feelings associated with the experience of the goal?

For example, if my own goal were to present an inspiring, entertaining magic show at some specific high profile event, I would envision myself in the situation, actually performing at the event. I can see the entire environment in the auditorium, down to the most minute of details: the lights, the scratches on the stage floor, the smiling faces of the individual audience members, the types of clothing they are wearing. I can hear their laughter and applause as well as my own footsteps on stage, the music that accompanies my performance, and my voice as I deliver my lines. When I interact with individual audience members I may be able to smell their cologne. Perhaps I can still taste the toothpaste that I used before the show. I can feel the clothes I wear, and the various sensations in my body as it moves across the stage, as well as the form, weight and texture of the props that I use. I might imagine the audience giving me a standing ovation at the end of my performance, and feel the overwhelming energy of their appreciation pouring out to me, as well as my own sense of satisfaction at having delivered something worthwhile to them.

The more distinctly and specifically we can paint this mental picture the more potent it will become.

We can also further concretize the image in our minds eye by writing it out as though it were already an accomplished fact. Written goals have a powerful effect on the subconscious mind. It's most effective to write them out using present tense, positive language. For example, *"On September 5, I present an outstanding and inspiring one man stage show at the civic auditorium, for which I am paid $XXXX and to which the large audience responds with extreme enthusiasm."* Taking this a step further, an additional highly effective habit to develop is to write the goal out each morning, and carry it with you throughout the day.

This process of using written goals and affirmations has been written about extensively and described in great detail in many books and other sources of information on goal setting, success, and self improvement, including the all time classic, *Think and Grow Rich*, by Napoleon Hill.

Creating visual representations of the goal can also be useful in this regard. Many people find that making drawings of their objectives can help affirm the image. Others search through magazines and cut out relevant images to create a collage that represents the desired outcome. Anything that we can do to make the images of our chosen goal more substantial, distinct, and *real* in our imagination will help tremendously in moving towards its accomplishment.

One additional, very powerful technique is to use a combination of deep relaxation along with vivid visualization. One form of this is a process called "autogenic conditioning". It's one of the techniques used by Olympic athletes for deeply and potently programming their subconscious minds for success. When we can create a state of deep relaxation, the subconscious mind becomes exponentially more receptive to the images that we program into it while in this state.

Briefly, the process uses a combination of inner affirmations and visualizations focussed on each part of the body in turn, imagining them to be limp and heavy, or heavy and warm. You'd repeat to yourself, "My arms are limp and heavy", and then vividly imagine them to be so for a certain period, before moving on to the next part of the body. Once you've gone through the entire body in this way, and you are in a deeply relaxed state, you then clearly envision your current goal in distinct detail.

Given that it takes a great deal of practice to prevent the mind from continually wandering during this process, it's helpful to use a guided recording to help stay on track through each step. You can create one yourself by recording yourself saying each affirmation, with a space between each one. (I also offer an audio CD program which has a guided version of this process that I produced several years ago, and which can be read about on my website.[7])

The True Purpose of the Emotions

Once we've created the mental blueprint, we need to fill that image with the energy of the emotions, generally in the form of a burning desire. However, given our tendency to become attached to and to fixate on emotional experiences and desires, it's probably helpful to think of it as simple energy, rather than pure "wanting". As I explained before, the emotions serve as the magnetic, attractive energy, and they breathe life into our mental image and give it a depth of feeling and vitality.

As we discussed previously, the emotions are essentially the energy of desire. The difference being in this case, that they serve the greater, intuitively-based vision, rather than being the point in and of themselves. The emotions as well as the mind and body become the tools we use in service of the intuitive Authentic Self. Rather than identifying with the emotions, and believing (consciously or unconsciously) that they are "who we are", they instead simply become one means of how we express Who we *truly* are. They become one of the devices which we use to create the magical work of art that is our life. This also allows us to have a certain amount of detachment from the desire itself so that it doesn't become a more unhealthy, and ego-based, obsession.

When we are centered mainly in the emotions, our desires are in the selfish ego framework. But when we allow ourselves to be guided and directed from the intuitive level, the emotions can simply serve their appropriate purpose rather than being the *center* of our experience. In this sense, emotions such as affection, humor, and satisfaction can actually become lower reflections and expressions of the higher, spiritual-level attributes of true love, compassion, joy, and inner peace.

Rather than functioning selfishly from the ego, we allow ourselves to be motivated by the altruism and compassion of our intuitive, spiritual Authentic Self. And of course, our emotions have an important role to play in this process. They are what move us to action. In fact, the word "emotion" is very closely related to such ideas as *movement, motion, motive,* and *motivation.* Our emotions supply us with the energy we need to move forward on our chosen path.

Essentially, we learn to direct our emotions in service to our greater sense of purpose, rather than allowing ourselves to be run and controlled *by* our emotions. When we make this shift, we can and will still experience the full range of emotional expression, and we can even enjoy them and appreciate them for the vital, human experience that they are. They're just no longer the whole point.

As we begin to make this shift, we most often find that our emotions also become less erratic and reactive. There is a sense of calmness and peacefulness that begins to take hold, and we begin to have fewer and fewer experiences of the negative, fear-based emotions such as anger, anxiety, hatred, resentment, and guilt.

We become much more detached from our emotions rather than needing to cling to them mindlessly. Paradoxically, with greater detachment comes a much greater sense of humor. Learning to laugh at ourselves, especially at the things that once caused intense emotional upset, is a true sign of a healthy psychological state. Our emotional responses to the world around us become more reflective of the higher states of joy and compassion. Ironically, by letting go of our *attachment* to our emotions, our capacity for leading joyful, lighthearted, and deeply compassionate lives deepens considerably.

Simply put, our emotions begin to *serve* us, and the people we meet, rather than leading our lives as slaves to our each and every erratic and arbitrary emotional impulse.

The emotional realm of experience and expression provide the colors and the vibrancy and the magnetic, energetic, dynamic, kaleidoscope of *feeling* and desire. When we're trapped in complete *polarization* in this whirlwind of "wanting" energy, and when we *identify* with our personal experience of it as *"who we are"*, the seemingly powerful realm of the false ego rules over our life.

When, however, this vibrant rainbow of feeling is not *who we are* but instead merely a tool of expression, a paintbrush used to breathe life into the picture we as the Authentic Self wish to paint in our perceptual reality and manifest into physical form, then we can become truly Masterful at what we do and what we create. We learn first to bring the tumultuous storm of emotions to a point of stillness. Then when we do use them they are directed by and in service to our higher impulses, rather than being the central focus of our life experience.

But it is only in giving up our attachment to this emotional self-image that we enable ourselves to *use* the emotions truly dexterously, creatively, and beneficially by transcending the ego and acting and creating under the guidance and perspective of our true Authentic Self.

It doesn't matter if we're not yet functioning in consistent, moment to moment awareness of and immersion in the Authentic Self. So long as we connect with it whenever possible, pay attention to the intuitive impulses it reveals to us, and remember to simply take note when we are functioning from more ego-based reactions, while at the same time having the intention to act from the perspective of the Authentic Self whenever possible, we will begin to develop the ability to use the mind, the emotions, and the body as valuable tools for the magical, artistic expression of Who We Really Are.

In practical terms we can also include emotional experience as an aspect of our mental visualization. As you clearly and vividly imagine your goal as already accomplished, what positive emotions accompany the experience? Make this one more aspect of your visualization.

Make It So

Finally we express our magical, artistic creation in some specific physical form. Sometimes how this is to come about will be obvious and even inherent in the nature of whatever it is we are creating. In other cases, we may at first have absolutely no idea how to accomplish the chosen goal. Sometimes as soon as we are clear about the outcome, we can immediately take action to bring it about. Other times we wait for further intuitive inspiration on what actions to take.

In some situations, we may find ourselves experiencing a magical moment in the form of one of those uncanny coincidences that can sometimes arise in response to our "seeking". Sometimes, seemingly almost like magic itself, the right opportunity can simply spring forth at the right moment. The intense focus that we generate by clearly visualizing our objective helps create a sensitivity to opportunities designed to move us toward its accomplishment.

The main thing is that so long as we maintain our mental/emotional focus on the creative outcome and remain willing to take whatever action or actions seem most intuitively appropriate to manifest it, while at the same time remaining open to further intuitive guidance, our goal-seeking subconscious mind will take care of the rest, and take us unerringly to the target of its accomplishment.

The Whole Process

Although I've described this process of "magic" as consisting of these four individual, sequential steps, keep in mind that in actual application, there may often be a great deal of overlap. Sometimes one or more of the stages can occur simultaneously, and there may not even be a clear distinction between them. Sometimes the entire process happens instantly and more-or-less subliminally. There are two important things to keep in mind though.

First is that the intuitive level must always be the foundation for every aspect of the process. The intuition is always the beginning point, the point of initial inspiration, and it is also the place to which we return consistently throughout the process, to confirm the appropriateness of any given action, as well as for further guidance and inspiration.

Secondly, it is important that we not leave out any of the four steps. If we don't begin at the intuitive level, our goal is likely to be ego driven and destructive. If we don't create a clear, vivid mental image of the objective, it will remain murky and uncertain, and it's accomplishment will be difficult or even unlikely. If we don't fill the mental "thought form" with the energy of emotion, it will eventually become lifeless and wither away before it is accomplished. And if we aren't willing to take whatever actions are necessary to achieve the goal, it won't come about.

One interesting point is that if we look at each of these steps individually, we find that the process moves from abstract to concrete to abstract to concrete. It begins at the abstract level of the intuition, then moves into the more specific, concrete details inherent in the mental vision, to the purely abstract level of emotional energy, and finally to the concrete level of physical manifestation. In this sense there is a definite aspect of balance to the whole process.

And lastly, this process of magic has…

…One Final Step

Once the process is on its way and the creation has begun to take form, the last step is that we must sever our connection to what we have created. This might at first sound odd. Why create something that we want if we're just going to cut it loose? However, if our magical, creative, artistic creations are ever to reach their true potential, they must be allowed to take on a life of their own. In order for that to happen, we must learn to 'set them free'.

The creative act is analogous to raising a child. Actually, it's more than just a good analogy since conceiving, birthing, and raising a child is, in point of fact, the ultimate human creative act. All the same elements apply quite literally. The seed of inspiration is an act of conception. Allowing the specifics of our creation to become real in the mind's eye is its gestation. Taking action to build the work of art is its birth. Shaping and forming it into what it will eventually become is guiding it through its "childhood", where it is necessary to protect and nurture the vision as the work progresses. And once it has become completely formed and has reached its "adulthood", we must set our creative offspring free to allow it to be what it will.

If, for example, I write a book but never publish it and allow it to be distributed, in the fear that it won't be good enough, how does it help anyone else? I have to "let it out into the world". If I create an inspiring and uplifting magic show but never perform it before an audience, it was largely a waste of time. While as a performance artist, my act may be a continual work in progress, in any given performance I must release it in its current form and allow it to stand on its own.

If I feel inspired to say a few kind words to someone in some specific situation, but then try to control the outcome and the person's response to my words, I will minimize or even completely prevent their potential beneficial effect. I must release my attachment to the outcomes and results of what I have created.

If we have created purely, our creations will live or die based on their own merits. If they are to have any chance whatsoever of reaching their potential, we must be willing to allow this to take place, without our continual need to oversee the outcomes.

Keep in mind that not all creations will reach their intended potential. But that doesn't mean they are without effect and influence in the world. And it doesn't mean that they were inappropriate or uninspired. Some of our creations may be "ahead of their time" in the sense that the people they are meant to serve simply aren't ready to accept them fully. It doesn't mean they aren't valuable. They will be as beneficial as they can be in the world in which they exist, given the current circumstances of their environment.

Similarly, it's also important to always be aware that the main point of focussing on a goal is ultimately *not* achieving the goal itself. You may think this sounds contradictory.

It might even seem to fly in the face of all I've said up until now. Why have a goal if the point isn't to reach it? In real terms, whether a future goal is achieved or not is completely irrelevant. What's truly important is what we do *here and now.*

The true power of a goal lies in its ability to give us a sense of purpose and direction here and now, in this present moment, so that our thoughts and actions *in the moment* will be the most effective and beneficial that they can be. Paradoxically, the more unattached to outcomes we can be, the more effective we'll be in taking positive action in any given moment.

Sometimes though, the absolute best thing that can happen is that we fail to reach a chosen goal, because in the process we learn valuable lessons that then enable us to choose even better directions. Failure to reach a goal isn't a true failure unless we perceive it to be so. Seen clearly, it is actually a valuable step forward on our path to self-actualization and service to humanity. It teaches us and thereby enhances our abilities to act even more effectively from that point forward.

The point is to always have a sense of purpose and direction *right now.* The "future" will take care of itself, and we may end up choosing a totally different direction and a totally different goal in that present moment yet to come. So long as we are focussed and purposeful in each present moment, we can have faith that the best possible outcomes will inevitably manifest themselves, even if they end up being dramatically different than what we imagined.

For this and many other reasons, it's crucial to have a balance of both passion and commitment towards our intended magical creations, while also maintaining an appropriate measure of detachment from their actual outcomes. We have to let them go.

Once we release our creations, it's no longer up to us what effect they have. It may be great or small. It may be completely imperceptible from our perspective. They may in some cases seem to have no effect whatsoever. But the fact of the matter is that we as individuals can never know for certain what specific effects our creations and our actions have on the world around us. We must simply create them and be willing to release them into the world.

In a sense this is an act of faith. By this I don't mean "blind faith", where we believe something just because we're told that we should. I mean faith in the sense of it having the power to move mountains. I think it's important to remember, that:

"All acts of love are maximal"
   —A Course in Miracles

Much as the butterfly's wings can effect distant weather patterns, each act of creative kindness has the potential to spread out in an infinite chain reaction, the details of which we will never and can never know. But we don't need to know. We simply need to trust that if we create from intuitive inspiration, and release our creations to do their work, that they will do so in the most appropriate and the most potent form possible in the moment.

This is the creative act. This is true art. This is the process of magic. Magic is the ability to do the "impossible". Can you do magic? Of course you can!

Creating Versus Attaining

One thing to keep in mind is that there is a diametrically opposite difference between attaining and creating. The ego, or what Eckhart Tolle calls the "little me", constantly seeks to attain. It runs after material possessions, the perfect relationship, even non-material "things", such as more knowledge or more understanding, in order to feed its sense of self-importance. The ego is continuously craving more. What can I get for me? It's always looking for something outside of itself that it wants to attain or possess in the delusional belief that whatever it is will finally bring the satisfaction and fulfillment that it craves.

And that's how most people tend to use their creative, goal-seeking abilities.

True creating, and the proper use of our "process of magic", or art, is something different. It doesn't spring forth from the emptiness and incompleteness of the ego trying to fill and gratify itself. It begins at the level of intuitive inspiration, of the Authentic Self, which is already whole and complete in of itself. It doesn't "need" anything else in order to be complete. It already is. The true creative act springs forth from an experience of Self, of Reality, and it then expresses itself into the world in some form. It is an inspired expression of the perfection within.

It may take any form as it is expressed, but it isn't running after anything. It's not motivated by craving or by desire in the normal sense. In that regard it tends to be more about filling the needs of those in the world around it than about filling the needs of the individual personality from which (or more accurately, *through* which) it arose.

As we experience inspiration, we feel a need to share the experience with others, so that they too can transcend the ego in their own magical moment experience. This is the true purpose of art. True inspiration, when we have an experience of the wholeness and clarity of the magical moment, also inspires us to want to share the experience in some way so that others may be similarly inspired. To quote Tolstoy:

"Art is a human activity having for its purpose the transmission to others of the highest and best feelings to which men have risen."
—Leo Tolstoy

In this sense, our process of magic, of art, or inspired creativity, is essentially an act of service. Just as Maslow discovered that those who reached self-actualization and higher levels were moved to assist others to reach self-actualization, we discover that selfishness and inspiration are incompatible. Inspiration needs to be shared in some way, even if it is only by simply exhibiting the qualities of compassion and peacefulness that arise from it when we interact with others.

Here's a great description of this process of intuitive, "superconscious" inspiration and the need to express it:

> *"A flash of light breaks through to the aspiring mind; a sense of unveiled splendour for a moment sweeps through the aspirant, tensed for revelation; a sudden realisation of a colour, a beauty, a wisdom and a glory beyond words breaks out before the attuned consciousness of the artist, in a high moment of applied attention, and life is then seen for a second as it essentially is. But the vision is gone and the fervour departs and the beauty fades out. The man is left with a sense of bereavement, of loss, and yet with a certainty of knowledge and a desire to express that which he has contacted, such as he has never experienced before. He must recover that which he has seen; he must discover it to those who have not had his secret moment of revelation; he must express it in some form, and reveal to others the realised significance behind the phenomenal appearance."*
> —Alice A. Bailey[8]

Putting It Into Practice

The more we use our magical creative abilities and apply this process to all the situations of our lives, the more it becomes a habit. It's important to develop the habit of applying the process to *all* areas of our lives, not just the big important choices, but even to the small, seemingly insignificant ones as well. By checking in regularly with our intuitive voice, and aligning our outer selves along the path which it sets forth, there is a subtle but steady and definite shift away from what Eckhart Tolle calls the "problematic story" of the ego life and, little by little, more and more into the moment-to-moment realm of the Authentic Self.

As we apply the process more and more consistently in every area of our lives, our lives can begin to take on a certain aesthetic flow where there is a sense of rightness and perfection, even in the midst of the more difficult or painful experiences. Our lives can literally become our own magical works of art which we create and transform at will, according to our inspired vision.

When I say there is a sense of perfection about our lives, I don't mean that everything turns out according to some perfect, idealistic dream world. That is what the ego endlessly struggles to attain. "If I only had... *that!* I'd be OK." The sense of perfection I'm referring to isn't about the absence of challenge or difficulty or even pain. But even in the midst of these experiences, there is a sense of grace, and poise, and rightness. We begin to develop a deep sense of acceptance for things as they are right now. And yet we also continue to create anew, transforming our lives ever towards a more perfect manifestation of our greater potential.

When difficulties arise, we no longer tend to view them as "wrong" or "bad", but instead see them as valuable lessons sent at exactly the right time in exactly the right way to help us further along our path of discovery and creative unfoldment. We recognize that it is actually these more difficult and challenging situations that bring a sense of beauty and depth to our lives that would have been impossible without them.

Fascinating Beauty

This particular lesson was brought home to me in a rather unique and pointed way several years ago on one of our visits to the Ancient Bristlecone Pine Forest in the Inyo National Forest in California. At about 10,000 feet up in the White Mountains, the forest is home to the oldest living trees on the planet, several of which are over 4,000 years old. These ancient trees are like nothing you've ever seen; like something straight from the world of a J. R. R. Tolkien novel. It is a truly magical and sacred place.

I'd find myself transfixed in awe at the intricate and beautiful twists, turns, and textures of the trunks of these amazing, primeval life-forms. As we began hiking up through the four mile mountain trail that runs through the ancient grove, I'd stop to look at one of the trees that was so unique and odd and striking in its vivid colors, forms, and intricately gnarled grains, and find myself caught up in fascination for several minutes. Then I'd glance up and see another tree that was completely different and yet every bit as odd and fascinating, and I'd end up fixated on it for several more minutes.

Then I looked up and suddenly realized that that *entire side of the mountain*, for what seemed like miles around, was literally covered with equally amazing trees, each of which was completely unique from all the others and yet totally wondrous and mind blowing in its bizarre otherworldliness and strange beauty. And it slowly began to dawn on me that these ancient trees, that were literally clinging to the side of a mountain in what seemed to be the most inhospitable environment imaginable, were a testament to a profound form of patient, persistent survival and endurance. You could often see the history of their individual struggle in the form of each tree.

Some trees had been struck by lightening at some point and had huge holes burned completely through them. Others had been knocked over by huge boulders from higher above, and had been pushed sideways. In the case of those that had been burned by lightening or had part of the tree die, the remaining living part of the tree had slowly grown around the burned part and used it as an anchor to hold it in place on the mountain.

If a tree had been struck by a huge rock, it slowly grew around the rock and formed itself to the shape of the boulder, using it to stabilize itself. I remember two trees in particular where one had fallen over and died, right on top of the other one, and the second tree had grown around the fallen tree so that it looked like some strange Hercules, lifting the weight of the other tree with its "arms".

As I became aware of the various histories of the trees, I began to realize that the trees that had suffered the most hardship were by far the most fascinating and beautiful in appearance. I realized that those trees that hadn't endured as many challenges, that grew on less steeply inclined terrain and that hadn't suffered any apparent traumas, simply grew straight up and looked more-or-less like normal trees, and seemed far less unique and interesting by contrast.

Even thinking about it now, I'm still in awe at the quiet, simple wisdom, inherent in nature, which these trees express so profoundly. The Bristlecone Pines don't judge their harsh environment as "bad". They don't think it shouldn't be the way it is, or that it's somehow unfair or evil or even intolerable. They simply accept it for exactly what it is and work with it in complete harmony, and it is the source of their unique, otherworldly beauty.

Making the Process a Habit

When I was a teenager and was teaching myself sleight-of-hand magic, and teaching myself to play guitar, and exploring my talents with drawing, painting, and other visual arts, at some point I realized that the experience of any artistic endeavor had an inherently spiritual quality to it. While I couldn't necessarily have put it into words at the time, I felt a deep sense of rightness and wholeness in creative disciplines. I also began to realize that literally *anything* we do could be an artistic endeavor if we simply approached it in that way.

I believe that the more we bring this process of magic—of artistic discovery, of creative responsiveness to life's challenges—into everything that we do, the more we will begin to develop a natural, harmonious, artful synchronicity to all areas of our lives. Life then begins to become artistically and creatively fulfilling, rather than drudgery. Even what were once tedious, monotonous, and distasteful tasks and activities become an essential and valuable opportunity to practice and experience our creative Self expression.

This magical, artistic, intuitive flow that we develop is difficult to describe, since it lies in the abstract realm of the magical moment. But there is a subtle but definite shift in how we perceive the events of our lives. They all begin to fit together in often serendipitous ways to form a mosaic of simple harmony. Not only do we see our life as a magical work of art in itself, but we begin to view it as an essential part of the greater Work of Art that is the world in which we "live and move and have our being".

As any one of us takes even a small step to shift away from the ego framework of problematic, competitive, fear-based yearning and fixation on past and future, towards the intuitively founded framework of responsive, cooperative, purposeful poise in each present moment, we all begin to move inexorably toward a world in which this process becomes common experience rather than extraordinary exception to the rule.

What if it became the norm for people to deal with life's challenges in intuitively directed, creatively integrated, compassionate ways that were inevitably of service to any and all that they touched? I truly believe that this is not only possible, but it is where humanity is ultimately headed. I believe that it is the next great step in our collective human evolution.

Oh sure, you might think I'm just an idealistic dreamer...

Or as John said:

"You may say I'm a dreamer, But I'm not the only one,
"I hope someday you'll join us,

"And the world will live as one."
—J. Lennon

But isn't it the idealists who are also the visionaries? What were Martin Luther King and Mahatma Ghandi but idealists? We often think of idealists simply as those who are unrealistic, with their heads in the clouds. But aren't they also the ones who dare to dream as realistic and practical that which others dismiss as impossible and unattainable?

There is a theory in both biology and psychology that states that whenever a particular experience is shared by a significant enough number of members of a given species that it reaches a certain critical mass, the experience then becomes common to the entire species. Famed psychologist, Carl Jung, postulated the existence of a "collective unconscious" which, while similar to our individual, personal unconscious mind, is common to all of humanity. He theorized that this was an explanation for what he called "archetypes", those common symbols and images that arise again and again in the mythologies and religions of nearly all cultures, even those with little or no direct relation to one another.

In biology there are also many cases that illustrate this principle. One example is of experiments with rats in mazes: once rats in one part of the world learn to navigate a particular maze, rats elsewhere are then able to learn to navigate the same maze more quickly and easily.

In psychology and education, this has been advanced as a possible explanation for why average scores on IQ tests rise over time. The more people there are that have taken the tests, the easier they become for other people. On a practical level, as more of humanity develops any given skill, the more easily it is taught, learned, and attained by any particular individual, until it begins to become the norm.

It seems to me that, in our natural development and evolution as human beings, the more people there are who begin consciously and deliberately learning to use their innate creative abilities in the same manner as those extraordinary, self-actualized leaders in science, the arts, and every other field of human endeavor, rather than using them unconsciously in the normal, destructive ego framework, the more humanity as a whole will begin to move towards a state of "group self-actualization".

So let's do our part, shall we?

Chapter Nine

THE GLOBAL BRAIN

"group mind: (noun)
"1: the beliefs and desires common to a social
group as a whole.
"2: a hypothetical psychic unity or collective
consciousness of a group of individuals."
—Merriam-Webster Dictionary

With the widespread proliferation and use of the internet and mobile communication devices, humanity is now interconnected in ways and to an extent which was never before possible in history. What we now accept as normal, the ability to instantly and effortlessly connect and communicate with one another all over the globe, would have been considered magic only a generation or two ago. Advances in computer technology are making possible and even commonplace what previously was only a far distant dream in our collective fantasies.

The human race has always been interconnected with one another, through our common origins and nature. However we are now literally seeing and experiencing our connectivity and interdependence directly on a daily basis. Major world events are instantaneously broadcast and communicated everywhere, immediately, as they occur.

Unfortunately we still behave as though we're entirely separate from one another. In the process, we threaten our own future survival. Thanks to the immediacy of our media, the uber-wealthy parade their riches before the faces of those living in abject poverty in more blatant and consistent ways than ever before. Technological advances have also given us the ability to kill more people, more effortlessly, over greater distances, than ever before.

Shortsightedness and greed have motivated us to use technology in ways that are slowly but utterly poisoning the very planet on which we depend for our survival.

Unless we begin to acknowledge and recognize our oneness and interdependence, and act accordingly, the separative ego approach could turn the magic of our technology to the tragedy of our own inevitable downfall and destruction.

Fortunately, there appears to be a trend arising towards shifting this approach. Early in 2011, rising from grassroots levels, protests which began in Tunisia and then spread to Egypt and throughout the Middle East, demonstrated to the astounded eyes of the world the truly magical transformations that are possible through cooperative, peaceful, public passive resistance.

During the protests in Egypt, amazing stories of solidarity and unity began to emerge. Groups of Christians joined hands forming human barriers to protect Muslims as they knelt for daily prayers. In similar cases, Muslims protected Coptic Christians as they prayed. The symbol of a Muslim crescent embracing a Christian cross began to spring up everywhere. In cases where police and military offered no protection from chaos and looting, ordinary citizens stepped forward and joined together to protect not only their own neighborhoods, but also such public assets as the historic library in Alexandria.

Amazingly, this was an uprising with no definite leaders, no central charismatic personalities around which others rallied. It was a movement where the voice of the people spoke forth clearly as a true power of its own.

Another shortcoming I see with many if not most of the popular information on success strategies, self development, and goal setting, is that it is focussed almost exclusively on *individual* goals and achievement. Most of these systems recommend focussing our creative imagination on getting the perfect job, a new car, our dream home, or other financial or personal achievements.

While this can in fact work as a means of personal advancement, this approach barely scratches the surface of what is truly possible with our "process of magic". We need to move beyond this to the framework of group level integration and collaboration. Our process of magic is actually best utilized as a group process rather than merely another personally focussed way of 'getting what I want for me'. The unified nature of the superconscious and intuitive experiences tends towards cooperation and collaboration.

In our western society, and in the United States in particular, we aggrandize and glorify the individual and personal accomplishment of all kinds. We idolize our media and sports figures, giving them nearly deified status, and falsely elevate them to heroic and mythical proportions. We worship celebrity, personal success, and rugged individualism, and tend to place far less emphasis and importance on cooperation and group integration. Even in our political systems, we often value personal freedoms above the collective group good.

Admittedly, my own career is at least somewhat based on this approach as well. As an entertainer and potential media figure, a good deal of my success has relied upon promoting myself as a unique personality with attractive and appealing qualities and talents. But I also recognize the need to move towards a more integrated approach.

Whenever I'm involved in projects or activities where I'm part of a group effort, working in cooperation with others, I frequently find myself completely immersed in the rapport that develops, and a new energy and awareness comes into play. There can often be a very powerful sense of group identity and group abilities that transcends the capabilities of the individual people involved. As with so many areas of the natural world, the whole is far more than just the sum of its parts.

This process of group integration has profound implications for our process of inspired magical, artistic creativity. When used as a group process, for the group good, rather than simply as a means for attaining personal objectives, the process becomes not only more integrated and altruistic, but exponentially more effective. In *Think and Grow Rich* and several of his other books, Napoleon Hill wrote extensively about what he called the "Mastermind Principle". He defined it as:

> *"The coordination of knowledge and effort of two or more people, who work toward a definite purpose, in the spirit of harmony... No two minds ever come together without thereby creating a third, invisible intangible force, which may be likened to a third mind."*
> —Napoleon Hill[9]

If you've ever been part of a truly integrated group of people working together for a common purpose, you'll know what a profound and stimulating process it can often be. It can be a magical moment experience in its own right. This is occasionally experienced with sports teams:

> *"When a collection of individuals first jells as a team, truly begins to react as a five-headed or eleven-headed unit, rather than as an aggregate of five or eleven individuals, you can almost hear the click: a new kind of reality comes into existence at a new level of human development. A basketball team, for example, can click into and out of this reality many times during the same game; and each player, as well as the coach and the fans, can detect the difference.... For those who have participated on a team that has known the click of communality, the experience is unforgettable, like that of having attained, for a while at least, a higher level of existence: existence as it ought to be."*
> —Michael Novak[10]

One quality of the intuitive level experience is that, since it dissolves the separateness of the ego and allows us a taste of our interconnectedness, it generally inspires us to more consistently work with others in cooperative effort. Similarly, allowing our unique individuality to become absorbed in the teamwork and synergy of a group purpose can actually be yet another way of tapping into the intuitive experience itself. Paradoxically, as we deliberately immerse ourselves in the group, rather than our uniqueness being repressed or diluted by it, it is actually enhanced.

Another well-documented example of the power and effectiveness of group purpose was the Apollo space program. In 1961 President Kennedy announced the inspiring and ambitious goal of sending an American to the moon before the end of the decade. In a careful study of the individuals who made up the various team members working towards this goal, it was found that in almost every case, they each performed at far higher levels of effectiveness, efficiency, and ingenuity than they did at any other period in their lives, either before or after the Apollo program.

The sense of group purpose and an inspiring vision made each person work better than they ever could have done on their own. Each person's unique talents and abilities shone forth in ways they never had before. And the result was a shining moment in history when Neil Armstrong took the "giant leap for mankind" on July 20, 1969.

Joining Together to Change the World

As we begin to take even the smallest of steps out of the ego framework and into the moment-to-moment experience of intuitive awareness, we are inspired naturally to be of service to others in some way. When we seek out and join with others who are similarly so inspired, we can literally begin to change the world.

"Never doubt that a small group of thoughtful, committed citizens can change the world. Indeed, it is the only thing that ever has."
—Margaret Mead

The title of this chapter is borrowed from a video presentation by author, Peter Russell, entitled *The Global Brain*. In it, he speculates that the interconnectivity that's currently being facilitated by the global communications revolution may be assisting to move us inexorably towards a new stage of human evolution.

He points out that at each stage in the formation of life and consciousness, there is a process of the merging of billions of individual components that join together to form a greater whole. Billions of atoms make up a single cell, billions of cells form a human brain. Now there are billions of humans on the planet beginning to connect consciously with one another. Russell surmises that the next stage will be the emerging of an even greater *group intelligence and awareness* formed from the collective that is humanity. The whole is always greater than the sum of its parts.

If we look at this a bit more closely, we could say that at present much of the collective organism of the human race is out of accord with itself and acting more like a cancer than a healthy life form. When individual cells in the body attack one another, we call that cancer. A healthy society, of cells or of human beings, would be when the individual components of the organism act in cooperative harmony to ensure the continued life and well-being of the whole.

Divisiveness and separative behavior are antithetical to the harmonious and healthy functioning of society. Whenever we create boundaries between ourselves, through religious differences, political divisions, racial prejudice, separative views on economic and social status, gender bias, extreme nationalism, xenophobia, or any other form of intolerance or discrimination, we contribute to the furtherance of the "dis-ease" of humanity.

The ego loves these "other-isms" because, if it can label others as bad or evil or less worthy than itself, it can then rationalize inflating its own sense of self-importance by contrast. But the ego always ignores and denies the fact that we are not at all separate in reality, that what we do to others, we do to ourselves. And thus its actions are consistently self-destructive as well.

Each of us can have a positive impact on this process, however, by choosing to work more in groups in cooperative rapport with others. Getting involved, in community groups, in service organizations, in grassroots political movements, are all opportunities for creating and furthering the existence of group unity. Even simply making a commitment to work more harmoniously with one's coworkers is a contribution to this end.

I recently became a member of Rotary International, through the local Rotary club in my hometown. I love the Rotary motto: *"Service above self"*. It is the very essence of the principle of transcending the ego in favor of helping others. Rotary is a worldwide organization, with 33,000 clubs in over 200 countries and more than 1.2 million members.

As an organization that is "nonpolitical, nonreligious, and open to all cultures, races, and creeds", Rotary serves both the individual communities in which its clubs exist, as well as the international community as a whole. One of the prime goals of Rotary International has been the elimination of polio, and thanks to the work and donations of Rotary members throughout the world, we are literally on the brink of eradicating this tenacious disease. Appropriate to our topic here, the Rotary International theme for the 2011—2012 year is *"Reach Within to Embrace Humanity"*.

Of course, any time that any one of us chooses cooperation over competitiveness, and concern for the needs of others over their own, we help to reinforce the overall sense of unity and interconnectedness that is a necessity to our continued survival, and a prerequisite for this next step forward in human progress. We begin to join together as one humanity, and begin to actually exhibit and demonstrate the age-old ideals of goodwill and peace on Earth.

Group Consciousness, Not Mass Consciousness

This greater sense of group consciousness and unity that we seem to be moving towards as a next phase of human development is distinctly different from the largely unconscious mass consciousness that we often see today, for example, in extreme racist and nationalistic group mindsets. The very fact of our interconnectedness as human beings produces the tendency towards assimilation into groups, even when it is at the level of mindless ego attitudes.

Mass consciousness is a sort of collective ego mind, formed of the accumulation of individuals who are functioning, at least within the context of the group, within the fear-based ego framework. Ironically, and paradoxically, this type of mass consciousness is a joining together that is actually based on separativeness. We see this in displays of mob violence and mass hysteria, for example. In riots and similar types of mob-based disturbances, we often see individuals acting out in violent, aggressive, and hateful ways that they would normally never do on their own.

In a more subtle fashion, this is exactly what happens on a massive scale when we allow ourselves to be mindlessly carried along by separative trends based upon demonizing other groups and making enemies of those who hold different political or religious perspectives. It was astonishing to me how quickly after 9-11 the American public went from expressing and receiving compassion and sympathy over our losses to allowing ourselves to become swept up into a climate of hatred and a 'justified' crusade against the 'terrorists' in Afganistan and Iraq.

I'm not by any means suggesting that we not stand firm against crimes of aggression. It is absolutely appropriate and necessary to hold those who perpetrate atrocities against humanity accountable for their actions. However, the *way* in which we do so is an enormous responsibility, never to be taken lightly, and if we act from the knee-jerk, reactive framework of ego aggression, we only succeed in reinforcing the very attitudes of hatred, violence, and intolerance that we claim to be fighting against.

We also see the herd consciousness when society allows itself to become anesthetized by consumer driven media designed to entice our collective egos into wanting to "keep up with the Joneses", in a competitive materialism that only feeds upon its own sense of hopelessness. Those in power who function from selfish ego perspectives can only continue to maintain that power when they can succeed in keeping the masses of people under the spell of a competitive, "them against us" mentality.

Our true common needs are never served by these types of mass separative attitudes. Arguably, the most potent of social unrest comes in the form of collective, peaceful passive resistance, as advocated by Mahatma Ghandi and Martin Luther King, and as demonstrated so admirably by the people of Egypt recently.

A truly awakened, well-informed, unified public opinion, based on shared common experience and interests, is a force that cannot be resisted. I strongly suspect that in the coming years this harmoniously integrated form of people power will become the world's new "Superpower", against which no political or economic tyrants will be able to stand for long.

It's Not One or the Other

Of course our individual self-development is, indeed, important in its own right. As any one of us advances towards finding our own unique talents, abilities, and sense of purpose, it allows us to more fully and effectively serve others and join with others in cooperative effort. In fact, without distinct, awakened, well-developed individuals who lay claim to their own uniqueness, and courageously step out of the ego framework, the type of group consciousness of which we're speaking is impossible.

With those who are firmly rooted in the ego, only mass consciousness is possible. Mass consciousness and the collective group ego depend for their very existence upon people who are unable or unwilling to think for themselves. Individuality is repressed, and individuals are encouraged, or even forced, to "toe the line" and fit in with the masses. The collective ego fears those who are different, and represses independent thought as its most threatening enemy.

In short, I'm not suggesting we should give up our own individual development and advancement in order to merge into the group. Quite to the contrary, in fact. It's not an either/or proposition. Individual self-development and group consciousness go hand in hand and enhance one another.

As so potently demonstrated in the Apollo space program, in a fully functioning, harmonious group, the uniqueness of the individual is allowed to flourish. It is the foundation upon which the integrity and effectiveness of the group is formed. Without individuals who are capable of stepping out of the ego dynamic into moment-to-moment, intuitive presence of mind, no truly awakened, fully functioning group is possible.

With individuals who *are* capable of being intuitively present and creatively adept, the coherency and potential of the group is exponentially amplified beyond anything we can imagine. True magic, and accomplishing the impossible, becomes regularly attainable. This is what makes this type of group consciousness the leap forward in human evolution that I believe it to be.

Group Versus Self

So, the question naturally arises: "How may a person devote him or herself unequivocally only and always to the benefit of the whole, the group, without any sacrifice of one's individuality and unique view and self-expression?" We've been taught in our society, much to our credit (although the idea has come to be so widely abused), to value the individual and to protect individual rights and freedoms. The very concept has in fact, especially here in the United States, become an accepted way of life.

How are we to forego all this training to be individuals in order to submit to the greater good of the entire group, whether it be our family, state, country or, in a more holistic sense, the entire world? We are told "listen only to your heart to know what to do", and at the same time, "do only what is best for everyone involved". Both points of view, while in seeming contradiction, apparently have a great deal of validity and merit.

Is it ever appropriate to give up one's own dreams in order to further realize the salvation of one's fellow human beings? And if we do submit to such a path and truly sacrifice our personal aspirations, are we really helping anyone? It would seem the more noble and worthwhile choice to submit to the group welfare, certainly, and no one could fault such action, but the simple question is: "Is it the best and most beneficial course of action?"

Or is this entire line of reasoning simply an attachment to the idea of personal (and perhaps selfish) security? Would it not be true that anything that benefits the entire group by definition automatically benefits the individual within the group? In that sense, doesn't it seem that anything you may do to help others also helps yourself?

But what about those personal dreams and aspirations? Are they important or not? Is there a middle path that can be tread, not of compromise, but wherein both the individual expression and the service to the group whole can be realized without sacrifice of either? And if there is such a path, how can it be found? Of what does it consist? Is it simply an impossible ideal, or is there a practical way to live one's life that walks the fine line between service and group benefit on the one hand, and self-expression and self-development on the other?

The answer lies in the fact that the question of service versus self-expression, or the group versus the individual, depends entirely upon the concept of the "self" with which we are dealing. If we assume an exclusive, separate, individualistic self—the ego in other words—the actions will be selfish.

But if we assume a larger concept of the Self, a more inclusive one in which one's self is seen not merely as a separate individuality, but as also inclusive of all that surrounds the individuality, then the actions will be directed towards the good of the whole, because the whole will be seen as an extension of and not at all separate from the Self. The individual becomes a specific and unique expression of the entire whole. In such cases, when the individual follows his or her innermost aspirations, provided that they are intuitively directed and sound, those aspirations will prove to come from and to work for the benefit of the greater whole.

Of course, even when we do have those profoundly inspired experiences that transcend the ego in a flash of presence and clarity, we so often slip quickly back into "the story of the little me". How can we hope to maintain our connection with the greater sense of our Authentic Self amongst the stresses and challenges of everyday life which we've been conditioned so thoroughly to react to with fear, anxiety, guilt, and irritation?

A simple solution lies in what Dr. Wayne Dyer calls *"The Power of Intention"*. We have to understand that this is a *process,* and that part of the process is functioning through the filter of the ego mind in which we are currently enmeshed. We simply hold the intention to move beyond it whenever we notice that we're in it. In fact, noticing that we're in it is in itself an act of stepping out of it.

Just having the intention helps us to remember to be more mindful. Of course, it's important to not judge ourselves or beat ourselves up when we slip back into separative ego attitudes. In fact, this reactive judgement is yet another of the ego's clever tactics of maintaining its hold over us.

We need only hold the intention to practice being present and to see ourselves as the Authentic Self, and then simply take note of it, without judgement or emotional reaction, whenever we notice ourselves back in the ego perspective. By making that simple choice and trusting in the process, we find that perhaps slowly but nonetheless inevitably we begin to move more consistently into the habit of the presence of mind which is the realm of the Authentic Self.

And step by step we move more firmly into playing our role in group awareness as well.

Chapter Ten

THE MAGICIAN

"Only to a magician is the world forever fluid, infinitely mutable and eternally new."
—Peter S. Beagle

At the beginning of our narrative journey here together, I mentioned that I am a magician, and I hinted that it might reach a bit more deeply than just the theatrical interpretation. Now that we've explored a certain perspective on the creative and transformative process that magic represents, perhaps we should look a bit more closely at what it means to be "a magician".

Joseph Campbell was a scholar recognized by many as the foremost modern authority on world mythologies. Following up somewhat on the work of psychologist Carl Jung and his focus on archetypes (those common symbols that arise repeatedly in various cultures), Campbell discovered that the very same stories and symbols popped up again and again in the various religions and mythologies throughout the world, that they also often arise in meaningful dreams, and that these symbols and stories had direct relevance to our growth as human beings.

Campbell's book, *The Hero With a Thousand Faces*, is considered the seminal modern work on mythology, and it was George Lucas' inspiration for the plot-line of his *Star Wars* movies. Campbell found that all stories and myths are really the same story-pattern which he called the "hero's journey". He summarized this "monomyth" in the following quote from his book:

"A hero ventures forth from the world of common day into a region of supernatural wonder: fabulous forces are there encountered and a decisive victory is won: the hero comes back from this mysterious adventure with the power to bestow boons on his fellow man."
—Joseph Campbell[11]

Of course the hero comes in many different guises in the various stories (thus the title of his book), but they all share common themes which are directly relevant to our own individual journeys toward self-actualization. Further, if we find specific archetypal hero figures to which we relate strongly, we can use them as role models upon which to base our self-ideal, the 'person we'd most like to be'.

It's yet another way of giving our goal-seeking subconscious mind a positive target to seek out. This is a useful tool, keeping in mind that it is one that will inevitably be left behind once it has served its purpose; once we've transcended the ego, that is. Until then, these hero archetypes can be used to help move us in that direction. The "Magician" is one such useful achetype.

Tools That Transcend Themselves...

The paradox is that, while the archetype of the Magician is useful as a goal self-image, ultimately we must leave behind all self-concepts including this one. Like all tools that serve as signposts on our journey towards self-actualization, it's important to remember that they are signposts and not the goal itself.

Signposts give us a sense of direction and keep us moving forward, but if we obsess on them they become handicaps that hamper our further progress. The point being that we use them as tools as long as they are useful, but also remember to not become attached to them, and remain willing to leave them behind when appropriate.

With that in mind, I find that the archetype of the magician holds a great deal of potential in this regard. Not only is the magician the person who can do the impossible, who can transcend the normal order of physical laws and limitations, but the mythological magician is also the great sage—the holder of the timeless secrets of great wisdom, knowledge, and enlightenment.

In fact, the words *magician* and *wizard* both have roots that imply great wisdom. *Magician* comes from *mage*, *magi*, or *magus*, those who were the ancient priests, protectors of the mysteries. The "Wise Men" from the Bible are also sometimes called *Magi*. And of course, *wizard* means *wise one* as well.

The Magician is one who lives in the physical world but, since his awareness has evolved to superconscious or intuitive dimensions, is no longer limited by the physical laws of the world. This is what is meant to be "in the world but not of it." Here's a somewhat poetic and metaphorical short essay I wrote several years ago on...

The Magician

The Magician is the perfect combination of the warrior and the philosopher. In him is the complete balance of action and contemplation; of power and wisdom. He creates a harmonious blending of an intense air of mystery with a child-like sense of humor. He walks the narrow path of balance between the alchemical poles of Spirit and matter. To be "in the world but not of it" is the goal of the magician. Complete detached involvement is the path he strives to tread.

Unlike the common warrior, who takes the active path for personal (or "national") gain, or the mystic, who isolates himself from the world in hopes of some brief glimpse of the infinite, the magician must stand with his feet firmly set in **both** worlds; the spiritual and temporal.

It is often a lonely path he must tread; for those who live in the world cannot understand why he responds to the world as he does; and those who seek only the monastic path cannot understand his involvement in the world at all. He must constantly balance the directed drive of purpose with the care-free humor of detachment.

In faith he walks; sure of his actions, but unattached to their outcome. His inner expression meets the outer need, and the result is healing and growth.

The magician understands that our experience of the world as "reality" is ultimately an illusion. He remains aware of both the unreality of the illusion and the importance of the proper use of the **experience** of the illusion, which will inevitably transcend itself. In understanding that the illusion is not real, the magician is able to **work** with it effectively, free of the confines of its limitations.

And this is the role of the true magician: to bring the illusion back to the Truth.

When we see ourselves as magicians, our goals shift from the ego perspective of attaining more to an intuitively directed, purposefully compassionate, moment-to-moment responsiveness to life. The Magician is one who can stand firmly at the center of chaos and calmly and mindfully respond to the turmoil, inevitably transforming it by his very presence.

The Magician commands the forces of nature, not by trying to control them, but through a deep understanding of their essential qualities and by acting in harmony with them. The Magician transforms 'lead into gold'; turning the baser, heavier experiences of life into something precious and priceless. And the Magician sees through the illusion of outer appearances with the vision of deep insight into Truth.

And of course, the Magician is one who understands the Science and Art of Magic. What is the importance of magic? As we discussed previously, magic represents the ability (and the desire to experience that ability) of exhibiting a power or reality beyond the apparent limits of our physical reality. The desire to express this ability which is inherent in each of us reflects the desire to be free of the limitations (real or perceived) that keep us from expressing, experiencing, and realizing our full potential, our highest aspirations, and our true Identities.

Magic in its theatrical and literary forms is therefore an artistic and metaphorical representation of what each of us might be capable if we were to free ourselves of our self-imposed limitations and express ourselves as freely as we would truly wish to do. It is the artistic interpretation of an "Identity" that we would each very much like to embody. The Magician is the one who has mastered this ability, and thus become master of his or her own destiny. As such, the Magician has several key traits and abilities:

- Seeing Through the Illusion to Transform It

  The Magician understands that our perception of the world is nothing more than a projection from within our own minds. Thus, as we transform ourselves, we transform the world. Much like Neo in the movie *The Matrix*, the archetypal Magician begins to see through the illusion of perception and thus develops the ability to shape its form at will.

It is said that Merlin, the magician/wizard from Arthurian legend, lived life backwards, remembering the future before it had occurred. In his novel, *The Return of Merlin*, Deepak Chopra interprets this as an act of creation. By 'remembering' the future —by seeing it clearly in our imagination—we bring it into existence in the form which we have already envisioned it to be.

- Inspired by Wonder

In practical terms, when we see ourselves as real magicians, and use the archetype as a true role model, we live life in a constant state of wonder. We see that all the realms of nature embody a great sense of mystery that, if we remain even minutely open to it, inspires profound experiences of pure awe. We allow ourselves to be inspired and guided by the deep pool of natural wisdom that flows forth from within ourselves as we live in the wonder of mystery. And we create by transforming our outer reality to more closely reflect the wonder of our inner inspiration. The Magician leads life as a Magical Work of Art.

- Detachment and Humor

Detachment is one of the key traits of the Magician. Since he realizes that the world of form is the Great Illusion, he remains free from emotional attachments to those forms, while nonetheless immersing himself in the experience of them in order to use them to serve those who are still deeply entrenched and trapped in attachment to them.

With detachment comes humor. In fact, a deep and childlike sense of humor, which reflects his sense of wonder, is one of the Magician's greatest tools. Laughing in the face of apparent danger that would reduce others to emotional incapacitation, he remains in a state of poise and confident humility. The Magician can afford humor in the face of adversity for he knows that Who We Truly Are can never be harmed regardless of outer appearances to the contrary. Flowing naturally from the wonder and humor is also a spontaneous state of joy in all situations.

- Profound Wisdom

As magicians we also stay consistently in touch with a deep sense of wisdom. That doesn't mean that we know more than others, or even know better. It simply means that we remain patiently open, calmly and fully accepting all that we experience as exactly as it should be, with compassion and understanding towards all whom we encounter.

True wisdom is not so much about intellectual knowledge, as it is about a form of insight that comes from compassionate acceptance and an openness to a moment-to-moment intuitive awareness and responsiveness. Wisdom, the way of the wizard, does not judge, it simply accepts fully with patience and poise and responds accordingly.

If we think of those famous magical characters from mythology and literature: Merlin, Gandalf, Obi-Wan Kenobi, Albus Dumbledore, we notice that in addition to being characters who command the powers of magic, they are also custodians of deep pools of wisdom about life. They teach us of the compassionate use of power and the importance of always avoiding the lure of *the Dark Side*, the temptation to use the powers of magic for purely selfish purposes.

In this sense it represents our own struggle to step out of identification with the ego's incessant chant of "what can I get for me?" Our own inner Magi—the intuitive voice or the Authentic Self—is our magical mentor, guiding us through the trials of temptation and battle with the dark forces (ego identification) which wish to possess us.

As The Magician, we choose to walk the path of life in the physical world surrounded by the experiences of the senses, using the various forms that arise, but without becoming attached to those forms or falling into the temptation of identifying with them.

- Patience

The Magician is patient because all is as it should be, including our desire to improve the world. As magicians we understand and fully accept that all things come in their appropriate moment. The paradox is that we fully accept what is, while calmly and patiently working to fulfill our aspiration to create something better. Passion and inspiration don't imply lack of acceptance or patience. They are by no means mutually exclusive. The Magician understands this.

- Personal Power Used for the Common Good

As magicians we use the manifestation of physical, emotional, and mental forms, and direct and transform them at will, without ever seeking them for their own sake but only as a means to express and fulfill our deeper purpose of intuitively guided service to others, especially those who have not yet awakened to their own magical Identity. Thus we can see ourselves as the architects of our own magical mythology, our own magical work of art, which we share freely as our contribution to the world, meant to inspire others to awaken to the magic within them as well.

This needn't be anything extravagant in scope, and is in fact usually quite simple, since the true Magician understands that all small acts of compassion are infinite in their effects. The true Magician is therefore content to work without any recognition whatsoever, often working behind the scenes disguised as an ordinary person, and keeping his or her magical powers hidden.

- Humility

While wielding great power, the Magician nonetheless remains ever humble. He understands that we all have the same greater sense of True Identity, interconnectedness, and immense creative power, even if most are unaware of it. He therefore never sees himself as better or greater than others. The true Magician remains the humble servant of all those whom he recognizes as extensions of himself, which is everyone.

- Balance

Finally, as the Magician we lead a life of complete balance between the polar opposites of outer appearance and inner

Reality, of patient acceptance and purposeful action, of harmony through conflict. Balance encapsulates many of the other traits of the Magician, and is therefore worthy of examining in a bit more depth.

Chapter Eleven

THE MAGIC OF BALANCE

"Life is like riding a bicycle. To keep your balance, you must keep moving."
—Albert Einstein

A recurring theme throughout much of my work, study, and personal life has been that of balance. It has applied to my interest in physical movement disciplines, to my approach to magic, to my philosophical interests, and on a practical level, to just about everything else I do. Of course, balance in nature and in life are foundational principles in both science and religion. All systems tend to move automatically towards a state of natural equilibrium.

In our modern hectic society we struggle to find balance in our daily lives: a balance between family and career, between work and leisure, between getting things done and maintaining a healthy lifestyle. How do we make sense of it all and order our lives so that everything goes where it belongs and we're not out of balance? The Hopi language has a word that describes much of our modern life: "Koyaanisqatsi", which means "life out of balance".

I've found the subject fascinating for a variety of reasons, not the least of which is that it arises again and again as a key theme and principle in nearly all the world's mythologies and religions, for the simple reason that balance is so fundamental to our existence and advancement as human beings. But aside from a purely philosophical interest, having a thorough understanding for the principle of balance and how it works is also extremely useful and practical in all areas of life. We need balance on a variety of levels in order to be happy, healthy, and fulfilled.

The archetype of the Magician and the use of magic as a metaphorical theme both involve finding balance in a variety of areas. Balance is essential to the understanding and effective use of our process of magic as well as in moving beyond the ego into intuitive awareness and towards self-actualization.

The Masculine and the Feminine

One of the best ways I've found for describing and making sense of the process of attaining balance is to identify specific traits and behaviors as either "masculine" or "feminine". Keep in mind that in this context, we're not talking about whether someone is male or female. These are characteristics common to all human beings, regardless of whether you're a man or a woman. The masculine/feminine description is merely a useful way of classifying and correctly identifying the healthy and most appropriate application of certain behaviors that we all share.

While this might seem a bit abstract and ambiguous, I find that we all seem to have an innate understanding of what I'm talking about with these classifications. Let me give you a quick example. Go through the following list of words, and for each one, determine whether you think it describes something that is masculine or something that is feminine. There is no right or wrong answer for any of them, so don't feel like it's a test that you have to get right. Just take a look and see how you relate to each one.

Accepting	Explode	Logic	Intuition
Abstract	Expressive	Melt	Rigid
Active	Fire	Mental	Science
Aggressive	Flexible	Moon	Soft
Analyze	Flowing	Movement	Specific
Art	Focused	Nighttime	Spiritual
Artistic	General	Nurturing	Spontaneous
Commercial	Give	Objective	Stillness
Compliant	Hard	Passive	Structured
Concrete	Healing	Powerful	Subjective
Conquer	Idealistic	Pragmatic	Sun
Daytime	Inspiring	Providing	Surrender
Determined	Intellect	Receive	Synthesize
Emotional	Dispersed	Receptive	Tension
Emotion	Material	Relaxation	Water

Did you find that you had a definite feeling about each word and where it belonged in our masculine/feminine classification? Most people have a definite sense for this, and I find that, while this is largely subjective, nonetheless most people tend to group the words in the following manner:

Masculine	Feminine	Masculine	Feminine
Active	Passive	Intellect	Intuition
Aggressive	Compliant	Logic	Emotion
Analyze	Synthesize	Material	Spiritual
Commercial	Artistic	Mental	Emotional
Concrete	Abstract	Movement	Stillness
Conquer	Surrender	Powerful	Flowing
Daytime	Nighttime	Pragmatic	Idealistic
Determined	Accepting	Providing	Nurturing
Explode	Melt	Rigid	Flexible
Expressive	Receptive	Science	Art
Fire	Water	Specific	General
Focused	Dispersed	Structured	Spontaneous
Give	Receive	Subjective	Objective
Hard	Soft	Sun	Moon
Inspiring	Healing	Tension	Relaxation

We live in a world of dualities, of good and evil, dark and light, hot and cold, male and female. Even matter itself at its most fundamental level has the dualistic attributes of both wave and particle. Since the masculine/feminine polarity seems to be a universally understood and therefore archetypal concept, it is a very convenient and practical way of understanding our own behavior and guiding ourselves towards a state of balance and healthy equilibrium.

The Essence of Each

Now here's a key insight into how to apply masculine or feminine modes of behavior. Masculine attributes, when appropriately applied, always begin with an *inner directed focus of attention* which then moves outward. And feminine attributes always begin with an *outer focus of attention* that is allowed to move inward.

In general, masculine actions are "expressive", which literally means to "push out". And feminine behaviors are always "receptive", which means to "take in". But the beginning focus is *inner* for masculine, and *outer* for feminine characteristics. Further, you literally can't have one without the other, they are mutually interdependent.

Here's a simple example. In a conversation, expressing yourself, or talking, would be masculine, and receptivity, or listening, would be feminine. When you're expressing yourself, you want your focus within, on your own thoughts and what it is that you want to express.

If instead, you place your attention outside of yourself, for example rather than focussing on your own thoughts you are instead focussed on the other person and trying to figure out what it is you think they want you to say, you won't be effective in communicating your own thoughts and intentions. Conversely, when listening, you want your attention outside of yourself, in this case on the person who is talking to you. If instead you are focussed within, for example you're thinking of what you want to say next, you won't be very effective as a listener. You won't 'get' the other person.

The problem arises when we get these approaches reversed, applying the wrong behavior to the wrong situation. The masculine "active, expressive, directive impulse" belongs focussed within; we direct and control our *own behavior*. Attempting to control other people or outside situations is little more than an experiment in frustration for everyone involved. The appropriate response to anything outside of yourself is receptivity, complete *acceptance* of what is. And of course, we need a balance of the two appropriate approaches, accepting whatever is around us in the outer world, and looking within to direct our own actions.

My Insight Into Balance

I came to my own understanding of this concept in a sudden flash of insight several years ago when living in Los Angeles. I've been a distance runner since I was a teenager, and over the years I've gotten some of my most amazing and profound insights and inspirations when I was out running. I'd been exploring the whole masculine/feminine concept on both philosophical and practical levels for some time and was trying to make sense of it for myself. One day I was on a long run through the part of the San Fernando Valley where we lived, and on this particular day, the sky was crystal clear which was actually relatively unusual since the visibility was often obscured by the LA smog.

As I was running, I was focussed on my running form as was often my habit, trying to relax and smooth it out. One of the difficulties with running long distances is that your body can begin to tense up after a while, and your form becomes more rigid and much less efficient, which can sometimes become a vicious cycle.

So I was concentrating on each part of my body, trying to release any tension I discovered and to get into a relaxed flow. And of course this flow is an attribute that I'd identified as one of the feminine traits. While I was having some degree of success with this, I was finding it challenging to remain aware enough to maintain a decent level of relaxation and avoid becoming too tense.

At one point I ran across a large, open parking lot, and as I did, I happened to look up and saw a beautiful, expansive view of the mountains in the distance. This surprised me for a moment, since on most days the smog was too thick to even be able to see the mountains from there. I experienced a moment of pure awe, of just taking in the beauty of the mountains and noticing how the sun brought out a wide variety of colors in the panoramic view. It "took my breath away", as they say.

I suddenly noticed that, in that instant when I'd been overcome by the beauty of the mountains, my running form had, for just those few moments, become nearly perfect, completely relaxed and smooth and graceful, without any attention to it whatsoever on my part. And then it hit me that all these feminine attributes, such as relaxation and flow and gracefulness, were defined by an *outer focus of attention*. All the tendencies that we can most often identify as feminine are some manifestation of *receptivity*, of putting the attention outside of ourselves and accepting and receiving what is there.

When I'd been focussed on my body and trying to relax, I'd had limited success. As soon as I shifted my attention fully and intensely outside of myself, my body automatically took on a relaxed state. And then, in an example of my own need to think in balanced ways, I also surmised that the masculine modes of expression would be about putting the attention within. The masculine directive, initiating impulse must begin from an inner directed focus of attention.

It's important to not only apply the appropriate focus to the appropriate behavior, but also to have a balance of the two modes of conduct or state of being. If we understand how this applies, it can be a very useful tool for staying on track in just about every area of life.

As I mentioned, we often get these approaches reversed, and apply them where they don't belong. Approval seeking and looking to others to tell us what to do is a misapplication of the masculine "directive" impulse, attempting to begin with a focus on the outer sphere rather than having it focussed within where it belongs. Or you could also say that it's being passive about your own sense of purpose, rather than having a strong inner sense of direction. In other words applying a feminine trait to an appropriately masculine context.

We also try to control things outside ourselves, which is applying the masculine directive impulse to the outer sphere where it also doesn't belong. Particularly in Western society, we tend to try to control all kinds of outside situations. We try to control and manipulate other people, other situations, even nature itself. The only appropriate response to anything outside of ourselves is to accept it exactly as it is. Complete receptivity to the outer world is the appropriate application of the feminine principle.

At this point you might ask, "Does that mean we should never try to change or influence outside situations?" No. What it means is that we simply observe and fully accept the outside situations *exactly as they are*. Then, based on what we observe, we look within to our deepest intuitive sense to know how best to take action, and we act accordingly.

Once we've taken action though, we must then also remain unattached to the *outcome* of those actions, rather than reacting in the normal, fear-based, ego need to control and manipulate them. So we have the balance of going from the feminine receptivity to the masculine creative/directive impulse, back to the feminine acceptance, and so on, in a continuous and harmonious cycle. That is applied balance in life.

Applying the Principle

I discovered one of the most potent and practical applications of this principle a few years ago when I was working on preparations for an educational theatre show for school groups. The show I was putting together was very theatrical, and in addition to writing and preparing new material for my own performance, I was also directing dancers and actors in the show, designing and helping to build large set pieces, designing and creating costume pieces, working with a composer to write original music for the show, and creating lighting design and special effects.

We had a limited amount of time before the show opened, and I was putting in twelve-and-thirteen-hour days seven days a week working on the various preparations for the first performance. A couple weeks before we were set to open the show, I got up one morning and felt certain I was on the brink of coming down with a bad cold. I knew from past experience that if I got sick right then, there was no way I'd be able to have enough energy to get everything done in time.

As I was taking a shower that morning, I could tell that I was right on the borderline of getting sick, and that if I allowed myself to tense up and be 'stressed out' by everything, I was going to push myself into getting a full blown cold. I realized that my only sensible choice was to stay consistently really relaxed so that I could avoid getting ill. And in order to get things done without hurrying and stressing, I'd have to be really focussed on the most important task *right now*. This balance between *focus* and *relaxation*—between an intense, mindful focus on the top priority of the moment and a complete purposeful intention to act on it, combined with a consistent state of mental, emotional, and physical relaxation—is the epitome of balance in practical application.

Perhaps ironically, I find that whenever I apply this process to literally anything I do, I get far more done in less time than when I'm in a 'hurry and rush' mode, and I feel better and enjoy the process much more. In case you were wondering, I did get the show ready on time, and I didn't end up getting sick.

As I said, this approach to balance applies on every level of human life. Let's take a look at a few examples and see how they work out on a variety of levels. Interestingly, as we'll explore a bit later, if you attain a strong experience of balance on one level, you'll automatically and simultaneously be experiencing it on other levels as well.

● Physical Balance

Attaining balance on the physical level can take many different forms. At its simplest and most direct, it applies specifically to how we move and use our bodies for just about every physical activity that we undertake. This is an area in which I've done quite a bit of personal exploration and have developed techniques for learning to be more balanced. My experience with martial arts and other movement disciplines has given me insights into how to do this effectively and efficiently.

One of the strategies I've developed is something that I call *balanced movement technique*. I've taught it to other magicians throughout the country to help them move more gracefully and purposely when performing, and to integrate the techniques of magic with the expression of their personalities. I've also introduced it to participants in my self-improvement seminars as a way of being more fully 'in the body' in a healthy, sound manner. When we use our bodies most effectively and efficiently, we use far less energy to accomplish tasks of all kinds, and we avoid stress and strain on the body's structural and other support systems. Using these techniques, you can learn to generate tremendous amounts of physical power with a minimum degree of physical effort.

Briefly, here's how it works. Simply stated, you begin all movement from a balanced state, in other words, good posture. Then you initiate all movement from the body's center of gravity, and by using applied relaxation, you then allow that initial impulse to flow out to the body's extremities in whatever way is most appropriate.

Good posture may not be what you think at first. It's not about being stiff and straight as a board. It's about a combination or a balance of relaxation and proper alignment. While standing, you can imagine a "central axis", a line that runs straight down through the middle of your body. Then as you stay relaxed, you want to get as much of your body as close to that central axis as possible. As you maintain the centered position around the central axis, you relax further, dropping your shoulders, for example, as though, while staying aligned around the axis, you allow your body to "slide down" the axis. Again, it's aligned but relaxed.

Then any specific movement is initiated first from the body's center of gravity, a point about an inch or two below the navel. For practical purposes, though, this means first moving from your hips. You move the hips first, and then in a whip-like action, you allow that movement to flow out through the rest of your body.

Here's a simple example. Standing erect with proper relaxed alignment and posture, let your arms hang loosely like limp pieces of rope. Then, simply by moving your hips and allowing your arms to swing freely and loosely, see if you can get your arms to swing in specific directions. Can you get your right arm to swing straight up in front of you? Can you do the same with your left arm? Can you get both arms to swing forward at the same time? Remember that you're not using the strength in your arms to do the movement, only the motion of your hips, while letting the arms remain limp.

You may notice that as you make your right arm swing forward, your left arm automatically swings back. So the movement is balanced not only in the sense that you have good balance, but also in the fact that one movement balances out another. For every action, there is an equal and opposite reaction. In Karate, for example, when someone throws a punch they begin the movement from the hips, and as the right fist moves outward to punch, the left fist snaps back to the hip.

Of course swinging your arm in this way is a very simplistic example of how this works. In specific applications the movements are both more complex and more subtle. You redirect and refine the movement as it flows out from the body's center. The main point is that rather than using muscular strength in the arms to move them, to lift an object, or push open a door, for example, you instead generate the movement and the power from the center of gravity, from the hips; and while maintaining proper alignment you let that initial movement move outward, subtly redirecting it here and there where necessary in order to accomplish the task at hand. The momentum generated from the center of gravity actually creates more physical power than if you tried to accomplish the same action with the muscular strength in the arms alone, and yet with far less physical effort.

Of course the various specific applications of this are far more complex than I have the space to go into here. An entire book could easily be dedicated to this technique alone. But anyone who uses their body most effectively and efficiently for any task is automatically using it in this way. Dancers, gymnasts, martial artists, skilled athletes, and literally anyone who has learned to use their bodies with proficiency for literally any type of physical activity, are using this technique. It's just how the body works most effectively.

In case you hadn't noticed, the masculine/feminine rule applies in the sense that the masculine directive impulse begins from the *innermost* point of the body, the center of gravity, and the *outermost* parts of the body, the arms, legs, etc., exhibit the feminine attribute of relaxed flow. This application also has a rather interesting metaphorical context which I'll share with you a bit later.

As we learn to use our bodies in the most efficient, relaxed, proficient ways for moving and accomplishing tasks, we find that we feel better physically and that we use up less energy, don't tire as easily, and that it has direct positive effects on our health. Physical balance also contributes greatly to emotional and psychological balance as well.

Any coordinated form of exercise or physical discipline that requires dexterity or bodily awareness can help you to practice and learn this approach to balanced movement. Tai chi, yoga, and martial arts such as Aikido are all very helpful in this regard. But once you understand the basic principles and have a good sense for balance, relaxation, and moving from your center, you can practice it all the time. I practice it when I'm mowing the lawn, working in the garden, and even in simple activities such as washing dishes and typing at my computer.

So much of the time we get into unhealthy habits of poor posture and inefficient movement patterns. Rather than maintaining a posture consisting of relaxed, well-aligned poise, we hunch our shoulders forward, curving the spine unnaturally. Rather than moving from the center of gravity, we use an over-exertion of muscular strength in isolated areas of the body to accomplish tasks, with little or no integrated connection to the rest of the body.

To go back to the central axis image, when your body is centered around this axis in a relaxed way, as long as you remain balanced, the body's weight is supported by the spine and skeletal system. The more you move parts of your body off the central axis, for example by hunching the shoulders forward, the more the weight of the part of the body that is "off the axis" then has to be supported using muscular strength. This is not only a waste of physical energy, but it also leads to a chronic state of holding unnecessary tension, creating stress.

What we're essentially doing, is unnecessarily resisting the pull of gravity. Habitual tension held in our various muscles pulls them up in opposition to the natural pull of gravity. If we are aligned, our spine supports our weight naturally and we can relax the tension.

You can think of a tall stack of heavy, metal checkers, with thick rubber bands wrapped around the stack from top to bottom. As long as the checkers are aligned in a perfect vertical stack, the rubber bands are unnecessary. If the checkers are misaligned, with some of the upper checkers leaning to one side, you can prevent them from falling over by applying tension to the rubber band on the side opposite from which they are leaning. But this only works so long as you maintain the tension on the rubber band.

The checkers are your spine, and the rubber bands are your muscles. With proper spinal alignment, or posture, there is little or no need to apply tension in the muscles in order to maintain balance and remain erect. And no need to habitually resist gravity.

Similarly, when we move from our center, maintaining proper posture and balance, we can use simple leverage and momentum to accomplish even tasks requiring generous amounts of power, without the need to exert much physical effort at all. So often I see, for example, people who try pushing open a heavy door by hunching forward and pushing mainly with their arms. This pushes them further off balance, which then means they have to use even more effort to get the job done. You can see the strain and exertion they exhibit. This, too, leads to unhealthy habitual tension and stress.   Even though I'm a fairly small person, I can push open the same heavy door by leading with my hips and staying aligned, and with a bare minimum of effort, I can make the door go flying open.

● Breathing

The basic balance technique also applies to habits of healthy breathing. How we breathe actually has a significant effect on our overall health, since proper breathing fully oxygenates our bodies' organs, muscles, and other systems. Often people think of deep breathing as sucking in the air, expanding the chest and raising the shoulders. But what most people don't realize is that the out-breath actually requires the most attention, since if you aren't eliminating the unwanted, waste gases, there isn't room for the oxygen in the lungs. And if you do empty the lungs fully, the in-breath and oxygenation takes care of itself.

By applying the balance technique, we have effective breathing.   You can practice this in the following way. Essentially, you push the air out from the center of the body, the lower abdomen, making sure to push as much air out of the lungs as you can on each out-breath. Then you simply relax from the push and allow air to refill your lungs. You want to relax fully on each in-breath.   As I said, most people get this backwards, putting all the emphasis on the in-breath, and forcefully sucking in air. But the healthy pattern is that the active phase, masculine, is pushing outward, and the relaxed phase, feminine, is receiving, allowing in.

Several years ago I was doing a series of workshops—which among other things included the balanced movement technique —at a weeklong retreat at the Asylomar conference center near Pacific Grove, California on the Monterey Peninsula. One day during break-time a woman approached me and said, "I'd like to thank you for changing my life."

I was a bit taken aback, as you might imagine, and I asked her, "Really? Well, what do you mean?" She explained that she was a professional singer, and that after attending one of my workshops, she began applying the balanced movement technique of initiating movement from her center and allowing it to flow outward, to her singing, her breathing, and her movement. She said that it immediately transformed her vocal abilities, opening new avenues in what for her was a major breakthrough. She felt strongly that by further pursuing it, perhaps by learning Tai Chi or other movement disciplines, that she could see that it would completely transform and enhance everything that she did.

I guess it's another example of the old adage that when the student is ready, the right teacher or information will appear. It certainly seemed to be the right information for her.

- Eyesight

Another example of the "focus/relaxation" balance I mentioned before is in the proper use of our physical vision. Working in the early part of the 20th century, Dr. William H. Bates developed an approach to eyesight improvement which became known as the Bates Method for better eyesight. While somewhat controversial, his techniques have nonetheless been credited by many with having made significant improvements in their vision. I've had consistently good results using the techniques myself.

The main idea behind the system is based on Dr. Bates' discovery that we only see with truly clear and distinct detail at a single point at the exact center of our field of vision. And we only see truly clearly even there for just a brief moment. So in order to use our eyes most effectively, it's necessary to focus on one individual point on an object at a time, and to continuously shift our focus from point to point on the object.

What most people tend to do instead is to try to see all of an object at once, and when that doesn't work well, we stare at the object rather than moving from point to point, and our vision becomes fixed and strained. The more we keep staring at the object, the more it creates even more strain in the muscles surrounding the eyes which, according to Dr. Bates, then changes the shape of the eyeball so that it becomes even more out of focus. Using corrective lenses such as glasses or contacts to correct the problem only reinforces the specific improper usage, so that we then become dependant upon the corrective lenses to be able to see well.

The eyesight improvement exercises that Dr. Bates developed were centered around a combination of learning to relax the muscles surrounding the eyes, to focus only on one small detail at a time, and to fluidly and smoothly shift the focus consistently from one point to another. So again, we have this balance of centered focus of attention, combined with relaxed flow: masculine and feminine.

One of the more famous proponents of Dr. Bates work was the author, Aldous Huxley. He credited the techniques with having significantly improved his failing vision. He wrote a popular book on the Bates Method, titled *The Art of Seeing*. In it he describes the process of proper vision by saying that *"Vision is not won by making an effort to get it: it comes to those who have learned to put their minds and eyes into a state of alert passivity, of dynamic relaxation."* These two phrases, "alert passivity" and "dynamic relaxation", strike me as two rather apt descriptions of our masculine/feminine balance.

- Emotional Balance

On the emotional level, healthy masculine forms of emotional expression would be a focussed desire for a positive outcome, enjoyment, and enthusiasm. Examples of feminine emotional traits would include empathy, compassion, and forgiveness. A note about forgiveness in this regard is necessary, however. In this context we're not talking about forgiveness in the sense that it is usually used, which is to identify a wrong or a violation and then pardon it. This is the ego basis for "forgiveness", which elevates the forgiver above the person being forgiven. True forgiveness is more about a deep and complete acceptance of what is, and a recognition that no true wrong was committed in the first place. In that sense, you could say that it is actually a correction of our misperceptions.

True receptivity is about complete acceptance without judgement of any kind. The destructive emotions of anger, resentment, blame, fear, and guilt all have mainly to do with judgement and unforgiveness. We perceive that a wrong has been committed, which "justifies" our anger. As we've discovered though, our perceptions are never accurate, and particularly inaccurate are those which tend towards justifying negative emotional reactions.

We hear people say things like "He *made* me angry." The fact is that no one else can make us experience a negative emotion. We choose, most often unconsciously, habitually, and often automatically, to react with anger or other negative emotions based on our *perceptions* of someone else's actions and the effect which they have upon us. But those perceptions are themselves a choice, often based on other past mistaken perceptions. When we are perceiving more clearly, we begin to see that anger and fear are never actually appropriate responses to situations *as they truly are*.

This is a position which can be truly difficult for many people to relinquish. We rationalize it by arguing that other people really do harmful and destructive things that hurt us. And of course it is true that people do destructive things and that they do have an effect upon us. But Who we truly are, our Authentic Self, cannot ultimately be harmed by those actions. It is only the ego, our false self, that suffers loss. To the Authentic Self, even suffering is just another experience, neither inherently good nor bad. From this higher perspective, even difficult and painful situations are in truth to be appreciated as bringing us an opportunity to grow and become more.

Of course for most of us this is much easier said than done. Being at peace and experiencing only a forgiving attitude in the face of trying and often painful situations can be one of the most challenging obstacles on our path to self-actualization.

But "wait a minute…!" the ego wants to argue, "Does that mean we should never stand up for ourselves or others and just act as doormats, letting immoral people walk all over us?" No, not at all. It simply means that anger and other negative emotions are not warranted. In fact, anger and fear make us far less effective at dealing with difficult people and situations. When we stand up to others who are acting aggressively or destructively, the most effective way to do so is with a sense of calm detachment.

Here's another seemingly magical paradox to consider:

"In my defenselessness my safety lies."
—*A Course in Miracles.*[12]

When we choose, consciously or unconsciously, to perceive a situation as something that we must defend ourselves against, we are literally using our magical creative abilities to bring about results that "prove" our defensiveness is "justified". It becomes a self-fulfilling prophecy. It's only when we give up completely our need to defend ourselves, and the emotional position that goes along with it, that we are truly safe from "attack".

When others act in attacking and destructive ways, it is inevitably because they, at some level, consciously or otherwise, are themselves in pain and afraid and feeling threatened in some way. When we perceive this clearly, the appropriate response is not further attack on our part—which will only reinforce the other person's perception that their own attack was warranted. The only truly appropriate response is compassion. This compassion can sometimes take the form of simply standing up to the other person. But it is never done with hostility or "justified" resentment.

This is the compassion inherent in the passive resistance of protestors in the face of violent opposition by tyrannical governments. Ghandi and Martin Luther King both understood and advocated this form of compassion.

From our perspective of emotional balance, the appropriate, feminine receptive response to anything outside of ourselves is complete acceptance, compassion, and forgiveness. Anger comes about when we misapply the masculine, more active emotional response to a situation outside of ourselves, and it therefore becomes distorted and out of balance. The active emotions, which when appropriately focussed include ones such as positive desire, determination, and enthusiasm, are meant to move us to action and motivate us, and belong focussed only *within*.

- Mental Balance

On the mental level, as with the emotional, the feminine approach is one of complete acceptance, but in this case, it is a form of non-resistant mental observation and stillness, which is then combined with the masculine side of alertness and mental focus. Basically we "pay attention". This is similar in principle to what Aldous Huxley was calling "alert passivity", but in this case it applies to our mental awareness. The masculine approach has to do with an acute mental focus, or concentration. In fact, the word "concentrate" actually means "to bring to the center". It also expresses itself in what Dr. Wayne Dyer calls the "Power of Intention".

Mental balance would combine an alert, moment-to-moment awareness, interest, and curiosity of what surrounds us, with a similarly 'in-the-moment' mindfulness of purpose, intention, and sharp mental focus. When we allow our minds to wander aimlessly and without focus, we're applying the more feminine "unconcentrated" approach to the inner mental landscape where it ideally doesn't belong. And when we ceaselessly judge, analyze, and over-interpret our outer circumstances and the people around us, we are exhibiting the ego's need to "figure it out so I can control it", by misapplying the masculine, active approach to our outer world where it also doesn't really belong.

True understanding of our outer world more often springs forth not so much from analysis as it does from a combination of open-minded observation and intuitive insight. And so often much of what passes for thought for many of us tends to be little more than a somewhat defensive and narrow-minded rationalizing of our personal prejudices and beliefs. True creative thought is much more rare, and it springs forth from deeper within, from beyond the grasp of the ego mind.

Of course, since for the majority of us our consciousness is most often centered mainly on the emotional level, true mental balance is also relatively rare, because the mind ends up functioning chiefly as a rationalizing device for the emotional desires of the ego. In fact, the ego itself is a false mental construct whose very foundation and existence depends upon us staying out of balance. As we successfully begin to attain any real balance on a variety of levels in our lives, the ego begins to dissolve.

● Superconscious Balance

This is really a redundant phrase. The very essence of experience of the intuitive, superconscious, or spiritual level of the Authentic Self is that of balance. In fact, when we are out of balance we literally can't experience this level. This level is synonymous with balance. At this level, in many ways, the masculine and feminine traits begin to blend together into one.

Just to continue our reasoning though, the examples at this level would combine the feminine detached, open-minded observer and the masculine sense of intuitively (inner) directed purpose. But these distinctions actually become rather blurry at this level, as we'll discuss in a bit more detail later.

● Balance in the Moment

I was tempted to call this "balance in time", but when we are truly balanced, the experience of time actually goes away, and we're simply fully in the present moment. But the applications of the balance principle in this context are *patience* for the feminine trait, and *persistence* for the masculine. I think this is fairly self-explanatory. Patience has to do with total acceptance of whatever is happening right now. Impatience arises when we resist or judge this present moment. And persistence I've sometimes called "patience in action". We simply stay completely focussed on the top priority *in this moment*. In that sense, you could also refer to the masculine trait in this context as "focus".

Finding Our Uniqueness

In my lectures for other magicians, I emphasize the importance of finding their "performing character". It is that unique persona or personality that they will portray in the performance of their magic. Most beginning magicians tend to put all their focus on the magic tricks. I teach them to instead discover their "character" and to make that the main focus, so that the magic becomes an extension of and an expression of their character, rather than the other way around. This is, in my experience, one of the key secrets to being successful as a performer.

One of the challenges for magicians in this context is being able to accomplish the magic technique in a way that seems completely natural and true to their character. This can be difficult for some, since the techniques of performance magic demand that the performer pretend to be doing one thing while actually doing something else. If they can do this successfully, to the degree that they can, it creates the illusion of a magical effect.

The principles that I teach magicians for being more natural also have direct applications to finding our own uniqueness in life. In order to perform magic in a way that appears natural, two things are necessary: *relaxation* and *motivation*, which are of course yet another example of the masculine/feminine balance.

Relaxation is important in magic because without it the performer involuntarily directs the audience's attention where he doesn't want it to be. If a performer holds a lot of tension in the hand where he's secretly hiding an object, the audience will realize something's wrong.

Motivation is an acting term that means having a reason for everything that a character does. When performing magic, in order for the magic technique to blend invisibly into the performance, there must be a reason for doing whatever the magician is doing technically, in terms of what he is expressing openly to the audience.

In the context of discovering our own uniqueness in life, being relaxed means being comfortable with Who we are; to be *at ease* with ourselves. Being able to accept ourselves without harsh criticism is an essential element of transcending the ego and discovering our True Self. This doesn't mean that we deny or overlook our shortcomings, merely that we accept them without making ourselves 'bad' or 'wrong' or making an identity out of them, and instead simply take note of them and act to leave them behind.

Those who are relaxed and at ease with themselves, who are 'comfortable in their own skin', are also moving towards self-actualization. In the sense that relaxation is also about letting go of unnecessary tension, it means letting go of the tension of resisting who we are, which allows us to be ourselves.

Motivation in this context would be whatever 'moves us'. What is it that you are most passionate about; that you value, and that gives you a sense of mission and purpose? When we understand why we do what we do, and begin to see it not just from an ego perspective but in terms of what drives us at the level of *heart and soul*, this is a fundamental element of experiencing and expressing our uniqueness as individuals. It is fundamental to our experience of ourselves as the Authentic Self.

Balance is Balance

Interestingly, whatever we experience on one level—physical, emotional, or mental—we will also experience simultaneously and automatically on the other levels as well. This is why when someone is feeling fearful or angry or happy, it shows up clearly in their facial expressions, body language, and posture. So if we deliberately establish a state of relaxed, well-aligned poise in our physical bodies, to the degree that we can do so effectively, we will automatically experience an equivalent state of emotional and mental balance.

Most all of us carry habitual emotional stresses in our physical bodies. It shows up differently for everyone, but for many it can be chronic tension in the shoulders, lower back, neck, or the abdominal or facial muscles. In our balance context, it is misapplied masculine active energy.

The great thing about this is that we can focus on any one area —physical, emotional, or mental—that's easiest for us to influence, and by creating balance in that sphere, it will also translate into our overall experience. Not only that, but by using the imagination to recreate the state of balance from some past experience that we've had, we can automatically re-experience the balance we previously exhibited.

This principle is the foundation for many of the techniques in Nuero-Lingistic Programming. NLP, as it's most often called, is a method for reprogramming the subconscious mind based on an applied study of how the mind communicates and creates patterns in life. Many of the techniques of NLP rely on mentally, emotionally, or physically creating or recreating a specific state that we wish to become a more consistent habit.

When you have those experiences in which you're feeling most confident and competent, how does your body respond? What are your breathing patterns? How do you hold your shoulders, your spine, your facial expressions? How relaxed are you overall? If you can take careful note of these specifics and then re-experience them by using the imagination to 'put yourself' back into the desired past physical state, you can then also automatically recreate the same emotional/psychological experience in any *new* situation.

Similarly, if you're trying to learn a new physical skill, and can think of some other past experience where you had great physical poise, dexterity, and competence, you can use the imagination to recreate the emotional state from the past, bringing it into the new activity. Your body will automatically respond with a greater level of skill and competence in the new activity.

A Judo Breakthrough

Here's a rather pointed example from my experience in teaching Judo. Judo is sometimes described as a grappling art, similar to western style wrestling, but with the difference that you can grip the heavy costume, called a "gi", of your partner in order to help gain control of their movements. It consists of two main areas, standing techniques, in which the object is to throw your partner onto his or her back on the mat, and "groundwork" or matwork, in which once you've both gone down to the mat, the object is to roll the person onto their back and hold them there in a "pin".

Techniques depend upon balance, leverage, and moving with your partner in such a way as to effectively upset their balance while maintaining your own. Several years ago, I was working on matwork with one of my students, named Chris. Even though I'm fairly small, and Chris was well over six feet tall, outweighed me by at least 80 pounds, and was much younger, stronger, and in better shape than I was at the time, I could nonetheless easily move him around at will on the mat, consistently pushing him off balance and pinning him with relatively little effort.

I was trying to get him to have more stability when working from a defensive position on his knees, in order to avoid being turned over and pinned. I wanted him to relax and not be so stiff, to open his chest bringing his shoulders down and back, to flex his spine more fluidly, and also to drop his elbows and hold his arms and wrists at a particular angle that helped translate power more effectively from the rest of his body. He just wasn't getting it enough to be able to resist me effectively, so at one point I asked him if there was anything else that he knew how to do that he was really good at and really confident with. I said that it could be anything at all, even something simple.

Chris stopped and thought about it for a moment, and suddenly his face lit up, and he said, "Yea, there *is*." As he said this, his face also relaxed into a soft smile, his spine and posture straitened out, and he relaxed and dropped his shoulders.

I asked, "What is it?"

He replied, "Making doughnuts!"

When I asked him what he meant, he explained that a couple of years before, he'd worked in a doughnut shop. He had to go in really early in the morning before the shop was open, and make all the doughnuts for the day, in time for the shop to open at 6 AM. He said when he first started, it took him over two hours to make all the doughnuts, but he decided that he wanted to improve on that. He became determined to get it down to an hour, and so every day, he'd work at getting it all done as quickly and effectively as possible, and eventually he got so good at it that he was indeed able to meet his goal of making all the doughnuts in just an hour.

As he told me the story, I could see the pride and confidence shift his body into a state of relaxed poise. I said, "OK, show me what you do when you're making doughnuts." Chris pantomimed for me the actions of making doughnuts. I could almost see the deep fryer basket and other utensils in his hands. As he did this, his body automatically did all the specific things I'd been trying to get him to do. He moved with a fluid grace, his spine straightened, his chest opened, shoulders relaxed, his elbows dropped naturally, and even his wrists were cocked at just the right angle.

I pointed all this out to him, and then I had him close his eyes and vividly imagine making doughnuts and to really *feel* what it felt like in his *whole body* when he was doing it. After a few moments of this, I told him to maintain that overall feeling as we did matwork. We went back to the mat, and from that moment on, I was never able to budge him from his stable position on the mat. The transformation was immediate, profound, and literally magical.

Of course, Chris' experience with making doughnuts was a perfect example of relaxed but purposeful physical poise and proficiency. On the emotional level, that experience of relaxed, proficient poise can be called *confidence*. When we experience emotional confidence, our bodies automatically relax, become well aligned, and move with fluid grace. And vice versa.

This can also be extended to the mental level if we can identify the mental 'language' or 'self talk' that accompanies the corresponding physical and emotional states. In this context "language" doesn't necessarily refer to words, although that may play some part in it as well. The mind thinks and communicates largely with images, and they form the mental language that we need to recreate. This is also one of the key principles used in NLP. It is the *linguistic* aspect, and it involves identifying the subtle ways in which we communicate, both within our minds as well as with others. This is actually an entire field of study in itself.

As with our process of magic, the key is our imagination. When we find that we are out of balance emotionally in any given situation, feeling anger, fear, or anxiety for instance, we can use our imagination to recreate and re-experience a past experience of emotional balance. Or we can take note of our breathing, our body's areas of tension, and our posture, and correct them by imagining and re-experiencing relaxed physical poise. Or we can change our inner mental dialogue to reflect the state we wish to experience.

As we identify areas of imbalance in our lives, we can address them directly, on the level on which we first notice them. or we can find their equivalent imbalance on another level and address them there. The inner/outer, masculine/feminine model is a very useful tool to help us identify the particular form of the imbalance and understand what needs to be addressed and how. If we're feeling threatened by outer situations, or feeling the need to control them somehow, the solution is simple acceptance. And if we lack poise, confidence, and effectiveness in our own behavior, the solution is to bring a stronger sense of inspired focus and purposeful intent to our inner world.

Mutually Interdependent

Additionally, in case you hadn't yet realized it, we literally can't have a demonstration of any of the masculine traits, in any full and complete way, without an equivalent demonstration of the feminine, and vice versa. We can't have one without the other. In the physical body, if we don't have poise and proper alignment, we can't fully relax, since poor posture uses unnecessary energy and creates tension and stress. Without a relaxed flow in the body's extremities, we can't have coordinated, purposeful movement, since the initial movement is blocked by any stiffness in the various parts of the body.

Without forgiveness and compassion, we can't experience true joy, and vice versa. In relationships and life in general, we can't receive unless we give. And we can't give in any complete way unless we are willing to receive and accept the results that return to us from having given freely.

In each of the areas that we've discussed, and in every other area of life, we can only fully exhibit the masculine traits when we also exhibit the corresponding feminine ones. And the opposite is always true as well. Balance is a universal law, just like the related law of cause and effect, and it always works out, regardless of whether we consciously cooperate with it or unconsciously resist it.

A Few Fascinating and Useful Insights

Interestingly, this model of balance is the same as our process of magic or artistic creativity. The process of having an intuitive inspiration, and moving it outward into mental form, the emotional desire, and the physical manifestation is the same as the masculine expressive formula. We begin with the focus at the innermost point of ourselves, the intuitive level. We then allow the initial inspiration to move outward as an idea, a desire, and then a physical reality.

Once it moves outward, we release it to allow it to be as it is and to become whatever it will. This is the feminine receptive side of the equation. Rather than controlling the outcomes, we simply observe and accept them, and then based on what we observe, we listen within to our intuitive voice once more to see if there is further appropriate action we need to take. As this cycle of inner expressiveness and outer receptivity continues and repeats itself, we have balance in life, the balance of the real "Magician".

I mentioned earlier that the physical balanced movement technique had a rather pointed metaphorical context. You'll remember that well-balanced movement begins by initiating the movement from the body's center of gravity, and then allowing it to flow outward to the body's extremities. In the sense that gravity is the physical attractive force in nature, it is the physical equivalent, or perhaps the physical manifestation, of the spiritual principle of Love, the *meta*physical attractive force in nature. The "center of gravity" could therefore be defined as the Center of Love, which is our innermost intuitive level of experience.

In the creative process of "magic", we initiate movement from the Center of Gravity, the level of our intuitive, inner Authentic Self. It then moves outward into the mental, emotional, and physical realms, the "extremities" of our human expression. As we move increasingly towards self-actualization, and therefore identify more and more consistently with the Authentic Self rather than the ego, we begin to realize that we are not the body, the emotions, or even the mind. They then instead simply become outer vehicles of expression for the inner Self. A deeper experience of balance then begins to manifest.

For example, if we identify with our emotions, and think they are 'who we are', we will try to control them (active, masculine), but by simply stepping back and observing the emotions (receptive, feminine) rather than reacting to them or trying to control them, we detach from identification with the emotions. As we then move our sense of self-identity deeper within, to the intuitive Authentic Self, we no longer see the emotions as 'who we are', but instead as an outer activity or experience. The appropriate response to any tumultuous emotions then becomes to simply observe (receptive, feminine) the emotional activity with detachment.

We can similarly become less and less identified with the ego-based, continuous cacophony of the mind. We step back and simply observe the mental chaos. This act of observation and detachment from the body, emotions, and mind removes our habitual reinforcement of the negative patterns of physical stress, emotional upset, and mental clutter and judgement.

By identifying with the imbalances, we are habitually empowering them, feeding them with our own creative energy. When we simply observe them, we are also removing the energy that has fed them. And we break the pattern of continually empowering them, so that the body, emotions, and mind become more and more at rest—peaceful. Then as we develop the habit of acting from inner inspiration, our outer physical, emotional, and mental personality expressions simply begin more and more to reflect and demonstrate the peace, wisdom, and compassion of the Authentic Self.

As we move more consistently into the realm of identification with the Authentic Self and the boundaries of the "skin encapsulated ego" therefore begin to dissolve—as do to a large degree the distinctions between inner self and outer environment—a whole new level of *balance* comes into play. The differences between the masculine expressiveness and feminine receptivity also become less and less distinct, until they begin to blend together into the same function.

If all points in space are infinitely interconnected and time doesn't exist, then the only place and time that can ever be, is 'here and now'. Our perceptions of inner and outer, self and other, expressive and receptive, active and passive, all begin to blend together somewhat in the magical moment experience of unity. The Great Illusion of our perceptions of the world is transformed into an artistic dance and play of energies, moving in infinite harmony.

To the degree that we experience this unity and harmony, this is what we begin to demonstrate in our daily lives. Our lives begin to embody the reality of our interconnectedness with everyone and everything in an outpouring of harmlessness, compassion, inspiration, and joy. This is balance. This is the Art of Life. This is the role of the true Magician.

PART TWO

The Big Picture

Chapter Twelve

THE WORLD

"The world as we have created it is a process of our thinking. It cannot be changed without changing our thinking."
—Albert Einstein

If you're still with me, perhaps you're wondering at this point what the wider implications are for our various magical principles. I know I am. (Oh, wait, that's right, I'm the one who's writing this. OK. Fine.) A quick word of warning, though. We're about to enter territories that tend to be a bit more controversial and which many if not most people already have firmly entrenched beliefs.

So if the perspectives I'm about to share differ strongly (at least in your perceptions) from those that you currently hold, I understand. And I'm certainly not asking you to blindly go along with any of my ideas if they seem to have no basis in truth. Quite to the contrary, in fact.

You should always look within for your own sense of rightness and truth. I'd simply like to give a gentle reminder of how faulty our perceptions can be, as well as the beliefs which are subsequently based upon those perceptions. And to ask that you merely keep an open mind. I'd simply like to offer these broader ideas for your consideration.

These are ideas that I do currently believe are valid and valuable and appropriate to our present human condition. That doesn't necessarily mean that I'm correct, or that at some point I won't find some further or more all encompassing perspective on them. But I share them in the hope that they will be of some value to you, if not as intriguing new ideas or as ones that resonate with what seems right to you, then perhaps at least as ones that will help you to further clarify your own sense of what is true. With that in mind, let's move onward!

The Social—Political Sphere

Any time there are groups of people living within the same physical locale, all making the effort to live their lives in some sort of personally satisfactory manner, regardless of whether that locale encompasses a few acres, an entire continent, or an entire planet, you will find that perceived conflicts of interest tend to arise. We all need food and shelter and safety from natural dangers in the environment. And we all have different perspectives on how to go about meeting those needs, and how to use the available resources. Often those perspectives can seem to be in conflict with one another.

So if we're going to live together without being in a constant state of conflict and strife, it's necessary for us to come to some kind of agreement as to how to order our shared resources. In the past, that agreement has often been that the Biggest, Strongest, Meanest Dude in the cave gets to say how things are going to be done. And the rest of us, sometimes through painful personal experience, agree that he is in fact the Biggest, Strongest, and Meanest, and that if we don't see things his way, we'll get hurt.

Of course at some point enough of us get together and realize that if we cooperate the Big, Strong, Mean Dude can't overcome all of us at once, and we can agree to work together to take over the reins of power from him. At this point we have to come up with some kind of group decision on how things are going to be done.

Sometimes you have a small group within the greater group that decides to cooperate to *be* the Biggest, Strongest, Meanest, and as a group, takes over the same role that the BSM Dude played previously as an individual. Sooner or later though (even if it sometimes takes centuries), the weaker individuals that make up the greater group get tired of being bossed around. They realize that they have far greater numbers, and therefore decide to cooperate once more to take power and work together to order things according to the needs of the greater group.

The former style of ordering things are the totalitarian forms of government such as dictatorships, fascism, and Soviet-style Communism. The latter style are, ideally at least (though not necessarily in practice), some form of democracy, socialism, or some mixture of social democracy. The totalitarian forms of government are almost entirely ego-based and therefore based on false premises, mainly that might makes right.

However, even from a more idealistic perspective, we still have two polar opposite approaches as to how to order our common resources. The first values liberty and individual freedoms above all else. To relate it to our balance model, this would be the "masculine" side of "freedom of expression". The other approach values the common good. This is the "feminine" side of looking without to see what is most needed. If we lived in an ideal world, free from both individual and collective ego-based motivations, these two would be in a natural state of balance with no conflict between them. Unfortunately, we do not. And so the ideals become distorted when placed into practice.

The paradox that must be addressed is how we can best balance the two poles of personal freedom and common good, inner and outer, *masculine* and *feminine*. As a pure ideal, both communism and democracy are sound *theories* of how to order our shared lives and resources. Each of these are models of how the various individuals within a group can freely cooperate to meet the needs of the group as a whole. Unfortunately, neither *true* communism nor *true* democracy have ever yet been fully demonstrated on our planet, because the instant a sound idea is presented and applied, the individual and collective egos involved begin distorting it for their own selfish aims.

In theory, communism looks to the needs of the entire group, and orders the available resources to best meet the needs of everyone. It focuses on the people and their common resources, looking for the best way to share those resources in ways that are equitable and geared to meet the needs of the people. In practice, those who tried to apply the ideals of communism became so attached to the *ideology* of communism that they refused to trust the people to act as they thought best. They felt they had to control them and force the ideology upon them. So communism as it was actually applied made no allowances for personal freedoms and the respect and sanctity of freedom of choice. It became an extreme form of institutionalized *political* totalitarianism.

In theory, democracy allows each person within the group to have a say over how the common resources will be used and allocated, and as to how they as individuals will choose to order their own lives and contribute to the overall good. It focuses on the individual and his or her personal freedom of choice. In practice, particularly in the West, those who tried to apply the ideals of democracy became so attached to the *ideology* of democracy that they have tended to avoid making allowances for protecting the common resources from those individuals who choose to use their personal freedoms to control and exploit the common resources to their own selfish purposes, and to the detriment of the whole. In that sense, it has become an extreme form of *economic* totalitarianism, which we call "capitalism".

I, for one, do not believe the theory that simply because someone is extremely skilled in the techniques of commerce and finance, that it means they somehow deserve to control and dominate an inordinate majority of the earth's resources upon which we all depend for our survival and happiness, to the detriment of the masses who do not happen to have those same skills.

The BSM Dudes in this context are those who dominate others in a form of 'might makes right' that is based on *economic* power rather than purely physical power. (Although in practice economic power more often than not also tends towards physical power, as with military resources or with simply being able to hire enough BSM Thugs to maintain it.) The ideal of democracy has devolved into an extreme form of capitalism in which those with the most financial resources use that power to stack the deck against the majority of people who do not have unlimited financial resources.

Huge multinational corporations and those relatively few individuals who control them wield enormous power and thereby usurp the overwhelming majority of the earth's various natural and man-made resources for the purpose of gaining even more wealth and power. Even in the United States, which is touted as being the shining example of democratic equality and fairness, the top 10% of the people control well over 90% of the wealth.

In our current state of imbalance, in our so-called "democratic" system, only those who control or who can leverage huge amounts of wealth and power can be elected to high positions in government. This is true regardless of which political party a candidate represents. This being the case, since it is these individuals who set public policy, only those who help maintain the current imbalance of power tend to remain in public office for very long.

Essentially we have government and the market tied together to ensure that the wealthiest individuals can continue to increase their control of the world's resources. The ego perspective says, "There's not enough to go around, so I have to get mine before someone else does." However, this simply isn't true. Although there are some 38 million people literally starving to death each year, and on average one person dies of starvation every second of every day, we actually have a 10% per capita *surplus* of food in the world. Much of this food simply rots in warehouses.

Roughly a billion people are living in utter abject poverty worldwide. But we actually have the natural and man-made resources to provide adequate food, shelter, and life support for them if it were only applied adequately to those needs.

The problem lies in ego-based motivations and rationalizations, both individually and collectively. Since the ego is all about "what can I get for me?", and powerful egos in today's economic world can control levels of wealth, resources, and power unlike any before in history, these imbalances between those few who control far more wealth than they could ever use in 10 lifetimes, and the overwhelming majority who are barely scraping by, are upheld at grotesque levels.

Combine this with the fact that we are now interconnected worldwide by instantaneous communications media that parades this wealth and privilege of the few before the eyes of the many in more blatant terms than ever before, and you have the potential for massive revolution on a grand scale. The question to my mind is not whether the masses will revolt, but when, and how peacefully?

The fact that we are joined together at new levels of interconnectivity by the new technology and communications media means to me that, like it or not, we are on the verge of an enormous shift in human affairs of historic proportions. As we join together into one "Global Brain" of integrated humanity, the only question is, will we function as a healthy, well-integrated organism and thrive in harmony, or will we act as a cancer and destroy ourselves utterly? If we continue to operate exclusively as a collective ego and thereby maintain the current imbalances, our destruction is virtually assured. Luckily, as I hinted earlier, there are definite indications that this is indeed beginning to shift.

Peaceful transitions of power (relatively speaking, at least) have become more and more common over the past twenty years or so, beginning with the fall of the Soviet Union. Those of us who have lived through the end of Soviet Communism, the fall of the Berlin Wall, the end of apartheid in South Africa, and most recently the rising of protests in the Middle East, have seen massive changes that we thought would never be possible in our lifetimes. I believe that we're only at the very beginning of that change.

As with all forms of balance, you literally can't have the *masculine* without the *feminine*. You can't have true personal freedoms without social justice, and vice versa. This becomes unmistakably clear once we step free of being run totally unconsciously by the separative ego mind, even for only a moment. This is as true for a group as it is for an individual. As we wake up, we see the imbalances clearly for what they are, rather than continuing to buy into the illusion as it is represented by the corporate controlled (ego-dominated) mainstream media.

Political—Social Balance

Of course it's one thing to recognize that what we have isn't working, it's another to envision precisely what a healthy, self-actualized society would look like and how it would function. But if we realize that all of the principles that apply to the psychology of an individual apply equally to a group, our understanding of ego dynamics, self-image psychology, and masculine/feminine balance can all serve us to create a vision for a healthy society.

The major false assumption that underlies all of the current distortions is that we are all separate. Even though our interconnectedness and interdependence is becoming much more difficult to deny, competitiveness, greed, and ideological warfare of all kinds are nonetheless based on the continued belief in separateness. And the ego is incredibly clever at rationalizing and justifying behavior that is based upon that belief.

Once we accept that we are not in fact separate, and that what happens to one of us happens to each and all of us, starvation and extreme poverty will become intolerable and we will simply act to eradicate them. Infringements upon the freedoms and rights of others will become similarly intolerable and they will be addressed as well. Destroying our various natural resources and poisoning our environment in the name of profit and greed will also be seen for the insanity that they are, and the demand for change will be answered.

In fact, it is only an ego, whether individual or collective, that could find it even remotely tolerable that millions of people starve while there is a surplus of food available. When we truly understand that we are not separate, sharing and cooperation become the only rational choices. A healthy balance between freedom and justice becomes automatic and flows forth naturally from our intuitive responses to the needs of the moment.

If you understand that there are starving people in the world and those who are living in absolute poverty, and that we actually have more than enough surplus food and resources to meet their needs, the solution becomes rather obvious, does it not? Most of us learned all about this as children. It's called sharing.

Without sharing we can never have true social justice in the world. Without justice, we can have no true democracy or freedom. But perhaps more to the point on a purely practical level, without justice we can have no peace in the world. And without peace, given the level of military technological advancements and the ability to destroy the planet several times over, we will have no *life*.

Even the problem of terrorism is acutely connected to this issue. Terrorist organizations cannot exist without the ability to recruit people to their ranks. Those growing up in atmospheres of chronic hopelessness are easy targets for the hateful ideologies of fundamentalist organizations. If the resources of the world were being shared equitably so that everyone enjoyed an adequate standard of living, trust and accord would be the common experience, and terrorists would be blatantly unable to gain popularity or attract followers.

Unfortunately, rather than insisting that we share the resources of the world with one another equitably, we allow ourselves, in true ego fashion, to get sidetracked and caught up in ideological arguments about *how* we are to allocate those resources. It really isn't rocket science. Although perhaps, from the distorted perspective of the ego, it is! But if we step back with detachment, letting go of the ego attachment to "my way or the highway" for even a moment, clear thinking shows the true simplicity of the issue.

There are in fact some excellent roadmaps for true balance in the social/political arena. In his State of the Union Address in January of 1941, Franklin Roosevelt laid out what came to be know as the "Four Freedoms" that everyone in the world ought to enjoy:

"In the future days, which we seek to make secure, we look forward to a world founded upon four essential human freedoms.

- *"The first is* **freedom of speech and expression**—*everywhere in the world.*
- *"The second is* **freedom of every person to worship** *God in his own way—everywhere in the world.*
- *"The third is* **freedom from want**—*which, translated into world terms, means economic understandings which will secure to every nation a healthy peacetime life for its inhabitants—everywhere in the world.*
- *"The fourth is* **freedom from fear**—*which, translated into world terms, means a world-wide reduction of armaments to such a point and in such a thorough fashion that no nation will be in a position to commit an act of physical aggression against any neighbor—anywhere in the world."*

Interestingly, these Four Freedoms could be seen to relate directly to our four levels of awareness in which we experience life, which we explored earlier:

- *"Freedom from want"* applies to our ***physical level*** needs.
- *"Freedom from fear"* could relate to our ***emotional level*** well being.
- *"Freedom of speech and expression"* could be seen as freedom of thought, relating directly to the ***mental level***.
- *"Freedom to worship"* relates to our relationship to the ***spiritual level***.

These Four Freedoms were also later included in another more comprehensive roadmap for social—political balance, the "Universal Declaration of Human Rights", which was adopted by the UN General Assembly in 1948. Among many other rights that it lays out, it also includes the requirement of adequate food, clothing, housing, medical care, and education as *universal rights* to all people everywhere. While it has yet to be implemented adequately throughout the world, the Declaration does nonetheless give us a very good vision of what is desirable.

The Commons

There is presently a highly practical social movement that is beginning to unify a wide spectrum of social issues into one interconnected whole, bringing together what were once seen as separate issues and interests in a comprehensive manner. It is becoming known as the "Global Commons Movement". Issues as widely diverse as hunger, human rights abuses, environmental issues, genetic engineering, and computer software development and distribution are all seen to be the same types of issues, namely "the commons".

Simply stated, the commons are those resources of any kind that are, or by all rights should be, available for everyone for the common good. In that sense, the commons cannot be privately owned, but can only be shared by all the people of the planet, or in the case of regional or local commons, at the very least by all those people residing in those particular locales (or who are otherwise associated with or considered legitimate stakeholders of a particular resource). "Commons" resources can include natural resources, basic services, cultural traditions, information and knowledge, public spaces, certain technological resources, and just about anything else that can be shared by everyone.

The commons are meant to be held in public trust so that they can be used and enjoyed by everyone. One element of the commons is that they can be used by anyone, so long as that use does not interfere or restrict anyone else from using them. To quote the website, www.otherworldsarepossible.org:

> *"Behind the commons is the fundamental idea that life, information, human relationships, popular culture, and the earth's riches are sacrosanct and not for sale."*[13]

One very obvious example would be the sky and the earth's atmosphere. We all depend upon the atmosphere to protect us from the sun's rays and to provide the sustaining oxygen which we need to live. Therefore global society must work together to protect the atmosphere from any action that could be taken to damage it or reduce its usefulness as a crucial element of life support for the planet. For example, if we discover that certain types of manufacturing or the production of toxic gases damage the atmosphere, it is society's responsibility to restrict those particular activities in order to protect the *commons* that is the sky.

Examples of commons that are already well-established in our society include such things as the public parks systems, and written works and other intellectual property on which the copyrights have expired and that have passed into public domain.

However, the commons can also refer to the *people* who use the various resources and who work together to protect and sustain them. And the Commons can refer to the *process* of protecting those resources. A commons movement, by definition, always rises up organically from grass roots levels whereby the members of a community come together to make decisions about how the commons are to be protected and sustained. Various forms of social activism and public protests can be considered commons movements.

Because the current forms of government and market-based economic systems have failed miserably at meeting the essential common needs of the people, the Commons is envisioned as a useful and necessary means of meeting those needs. Currently we function under two segments of society: the public sector which is government, and the private sector which is the marketplace. These two alone as they currently function are inadequate to meet our common needs because they are prone to ego distortion and to the control of those sectors by the few who hold power within them.

The Commons is seen as a third segment of society, not meant to replace either the public or private sectors but to act as a third segment that will bring balance to our society by constraining the dangerous monopolization of resources that so often occurs within the current "market/state" system. Privatization of a wide variety of resources such as water, health care, human organs, intellectual property, and even genetic information have all begun to endanger our common quality of life.

Because the Commons rises up from grass roots levels and has no hierarchical structure as is the case in the public and private sectors, it is not subject to the same types of monopolization and totalitarianism that have become the norm within the market/state. In point of fact, if some particular individual was somehow able to take over a commons movement in dictatorial fashion, it would then by definition no longer *be* a commons, and another commons movement would inevitably rise up to replace it.

Because the way in which we talk about certain issues literally defines how we think about them, one aspect of the Global Commons Movement is that it is inventing entirely new language to describe and address the issues involved in meeting society's various needs. Many people who are immersed in the structures of the "market/state" are at first unable to comprehend that there may in fact be another way of doing things.

This is why the financial bailouts and other efforts by the government have so far failed to solve the problems of the current economic crisis. They are attempts to solve the problems by addressing them in the same way it has always been done, from within the very same structures and contexts that created them. It's just more of the same. The real problem is that the very structures upon which the system is founded are themselves faulty, since they are based largely upon the ego perspective, and they must therefore be completely overhauled and replaced.

The old ways of thinking about social and political issues and the ways that we talk about them and the very language that we use to describe them, all tend to keep our thinking locked within the very context which is itself the root of the current problems. For example, one of the current distortions that we seem to blindly accept is the fact that a so-called healthy economy is currently measured as a factor of "growth".

It's not enough for income to be steady and sustainable, it has to *increase* each year, or we think something is wrong. This is blatantly insane. In a cell in our body, unchecked growth is abnormal and it is called cancer, and if it continues to grow unchecked it destroys all the other cells around itself. Unchecked economic growth is also unsustainable and destructive.

Another similar distortion is the theory that if we allow the market to run its course unhampered, it will somehow magically meet the needs of all the people. This is based on the idea that there is a level playing field and that everyone has the same opportunities, and therefore the same power to effect things, within the market. Of course, nothing could be further from the truth. The current political and economic system is wildly skewed in favor of those few who already hold the majority of the wealth and power.

We are also trained by media and society to think of ourselves as 'consumers' of goods and services. This very use of language and the largely unconscious implication behind it has led to the disposable, 'throw-away' society which we have developed. Rather than maintaining, preserving, sustaining, and reusing our resources, we *consume* and dispose of them in huge landfills, poisoning the land on which we live. It also subtly implies that we are just *users* and not *participants* in society. Perhaps this is one of the reasons that we passively give over our power to the market and the government.

These and many other similar ego-dominated misconceptions make up the very environment in which the current political economic systems function and the foundation upon which they are based. In order to see the problems clearly and thereby solve them, we have to step outside the current context itself. It's very much like a fish trying to understand the nature of water and the difference between water and air, while it is experiencing it from within the water. It would have no other context in which to understand it. The fish couldn't even understand "water" since it is its only experience and it would have nothing to compare it to.

The commons movement addresses these issues by stepping completely outside the current "that's the way it's always been done", market/state context, to a much broader, "what do we really need as human beings" context. New language is also arising to help shift to the new broader context. For example, "commons" is also sometimes used as a verb. "Commoning" is the act of participating in, and the process of furthering the commons. This could very well lead to a much more well-balanced, healthier, self-actualized form of participatory social democracy that would be far more successful in meeting the needs of people everywhere.

True effective governance to my mind would need to be participatory and local rather than highly centralized as it is currently. In other words, we all need to get involved in making decisions, and the big decisions about how resources will be used *locally* are made at the local level, rather than in some far off national capitol.

Levels of Ego and Authentic Self

In order for our Authentic Self to flow forth and express itself in our lives with inspiration and its natural creative energy, it's necessary to transcend the restrictions and limitations of the ego. True freedom is about freedom from the smallness of the ego. As soon as any aspect of the Authentic Self does show up in our lives, the nature and purpose of its creative expression is always in service and compassion. This is as true at the level of a group as it is for an individual person.

Once we begin to experience, appreciate, and fully grasp the nature of this shift from ego to Authentic Self in our own individual lives, it becomes a simple matter to apply the same principles to our family, our community, our nation, and to the world. All sound principles of psychology and human behavior apply as equally to groups of people as they do to individuals. Moving from insanity to sanity, for an individual or for a society, involves finding the balance of the Authentic Self, the balance between individual freedom and service to others. This is the inner/outer, masculine/feminine balance that demonstrates itself in all healthy systems in nature.

As we move beyond pure ego dynamics, our natural and automatic response to outer need of any kind is that the inner creative impulse flows forth to meet the need. Each person, each community, and each nation will have its own unique perspective on how to address these outer needs, but, to whatever degree we can leave the ego out of the picture, these unique perspectives will always blend together into a cooperative consensus that will inform and guide our actions.

Magical Transformation

Assuming we agree that a healthy *masculine/feminine* equilibrium in society would balance and make allowances for both outer need and personal freedoms, how do we get from here to there? Perhaps our "process of magic" can give some insight into the necessary steps. Essentially, we need to apply the four-step process of intuitive inspiration, mental vision, emotional desire, and physical action and outcomes to the collective level of society.

We already have good examples of the intuitive inspiration in the form of various inspiring visions such as Martin Luther King's "I have a dream", and Roosevelt's "Four Freedoms". These and other similarly powerful and uplifting ideas, including even those as simple as "goodwill and peace on earth", have a deep resonance with almost everyone, and we sense them as profound truths.

The next step is to create the mental blueprint and the image of what it would actually look like if it were accomplished, and to vividly visualize it in the "collective mind". The Universal Declaration on Human Rights is one very good, detailed description of what is desirable. There are many others, including the language and ideas currently being formulated by the Global Commons Movement. What needs to happen is for these types of outcomes to be visualized universally enough that they become accepted as possible, expected as reasonable, and begin to become "real" in our collective imagination. They then become magnetic, attractive "ideas whose time has come", and which therefore nothing can stop.

Currently the majority of the images and ideas being visualized in the collective mind of the mainstream media are mainly along the ego-based lines of "acquiring" and "more", as well as of competitiveness and domination. Images of how attractive we'll be to the opposite sex if we use the right toothpaste, and how happy we'll be if we have a huge LCD television with the latest version of PlayStation, as well as abundant images of glorified violence and other forms of glamorized ego domination bombard us from every direction. If images of a harmonious, just, well-balanced society were presented with the same frequency and urgency, they would no doubt already be well along the way to being realized.

Fortunately, there are other, both high-tech and low-tech, avenues of collective expression that are not directly under the control of the ego-dominated mainstream media. The internet and social media give millions of people the ability to have a voice and to present another image of what could be. With advances in technology making high-quality video production affordable, documentary films and other inspiring video presentations are popping up more and more frequently. Widespread public protests are also bringing another possible vision of the world into our conscious awareness in more definite terms, and allowing people to articulate it more fully.

A different type of self-education is also necessary. The more people who begin exploring ideas like those presented by the Global Commons Movement, and begin to fully 'get their heads around' a completely different, practical, more participatory, well-balanced approach to solving our problems, the more it will begin to become "real" in our collective imaginations.

As these various images become more and more clear and well established in our collective Global Brain, they will also become more magnetically attractive, and will be naturally infused with the enthusiasm that will bring in the necessary emotional energy. The final realization and accomplishment will then come when we set about putting the various plans into action on the physical level. The first step in taking physical action is already beginning to take place, in the form of massive public protest.

If and when the masses of people become fully aware not only of the fact that the overwhelming majority of resources are being monopolized by a tiny group of privileged few, as they are already beginning to do, but also of the various means by which that few maintains its control, and of the real power inherent in a well-mobilized, well-informed public opinion, we will see even more change on a global scale than we can possibly begin to imagine. As I mentioned previously, I firmly believe that in the near future a dynamic, educated, well-mobilized "people power" will become the world's new Superpower, against which nothing can stand.

In the United States, even with the economic downturn and high unemployment and more and more people losing their homes, we still live, for all practical purposes, free from the hardships of the extreme levels of poverty and starvation which billions of people elsewhere face each and every day. Perhaps this is why we have, up until now at least, been relatively complacent in the face of the extreme imbalances and gridlock in our political and economic systems. We get angry about them and complain about them, but how many of us in our society take it upon themselves to take any real concerted action to actually change things? Even voter turnout in the US is among the very lowest of all the world's democracies.

But perhaps this too is beginning to change. As I write the first draft of this chapter in October of 2011, there is a new protest movement arising here in the United States, which initially was not covered at all by the mainstream American media. When it did begin to be covered, it was only in the most flippant, condescending and dismissive of terms; and only in the past couple of weeks have they finally been forced to report on it with any real seriousness. The "Occupy Wall Street" protests have quickly spread to other cities across the country and around the globe. Similar to the protests in the Middle East earlier in 2011, there are no leaders within the movement, participants include people with a wide variety of political orientations and religious beliefs, and they have used the internet and social media to help organize.

Because there are no leaders, because the protests have not formulated any specific, official list of demands, and because many of the early protesters were college age and claimed to be uninterested in politics or the political system itself, those within the current political/economic system, as well as the mainstream media, have dismissed the protests as trivial and irrelevant. However, it's also been suggested that the protests reflect a new 'outside the box' way of thinking about our social problems, and that they express the rising frustration with a political/economic system that is unresponsive and even antagonistic to the true needs of the majority of the people.

There seems to be an intuitive awareness that the entire structure on which our system is based is faulty, that the old ways of thinking about it are distorted and irrelevant, and that we must create a new way of organizing society from the ground up, in acute contradistinction to the top down, ego-based mode in which it currently exists. It remains to be seen as to whether this movement will grow into a new, more self-actualized approach to social self-organization and begin to reflect true group awareness and healthy group mindset, but initially, at least, it appears to hold hope in that regard.

International Cooperation

As we move towards a more self-actualized society, cooperation becomes one of the main foundations upon which our lives are based. The ideals of a participatory democracy give us a fairly sound set of principles as to how this cooperation actually functions. Essentially, this entails a balance between freedom and social responsibility. In a true participatory democratic system, no one would be uninvolved, and all would have both the freedom and the responsibility to take part in the decision making processes.

This would be true locally, regionally and nationally, as well as internationally. Currently the closest thing we have to democratic cooperation at an international level is the United Nations. The main element that is lacking in the current makeup of the UN, however, is the fact that it does not function as a truly democratic system, since the majority of the power rests in the hands of the fifteen nations who make up the members of the UN Security Council and particularly the five permanent Security Council members: the United States, the United Kingdom, China, Russia, and France.

Interestingly, it is only these five nations who are recognized as "nuclear weapon states" under the Nuclear Non-Proliferation Treaty. In true ego 'might makes right' fashion, we still function internationally by placing the BSM Dudes in charge. As we move towards more equitable and cooperative decision making internationally, one step might be to shift this power from the UN Security Council to the actual democratic organ of the UN, the only one in which all member nations have equal representation, the UN General Assembly. As with the as yet distorted ideals of democracy and communism, the true potential of the UN has not yet been allowed to manifest.

A New Vision

The question is, can we, through the means of participatory, peaceful public protest, through an intelligent use of publicly accessible communications media and technology, and through a new kind of participatory dialogue, begin to truly envision, on a collective level, a new, more self-actualized way of living in the world?

What would happen if we simply acted to distribute the surplus food and resources so that people who are currently unable to live at a reasonable level were enabled to do so? It has been argued that these people somehow live in poverty and starvation because they are simply lazy and unambitious. And that if they were given enough to get by it would only reinforce their laziness.

This perspective reveals a shockingly blatant level of ignorance of how people are actually living in many third world countries. Many people toil through longer, harder hours every single day, often walking miles and miles to simply gather water and firewood for their families, than almost anyone would accept here in the developed world. Through no fault of their own, these people are caught in circumstances where resources are simply not available, and they have no means through which to better their own situations, regardless of how badly they may want it or how ambitious they may be.

Can you imagine the creative energy that would be unleashed if these millions upon millions of people no longer had to devote all of their attention, and resourcefulness to merely surviving? The power of this latent creativity has already begun to prove itself with the introduction of "microcredit". Originated by Muhammad Yunus at the Grameen Bank in Bangaladesh, microcredit supplies very small loans to those living in poverty to allow them to begin small entrepreneurial endeavors. The practice has been so enormously successful in allowing people to lift themselves out of poverty that Muhammad Yunus was awarded the Nobel Peace Prize in 2006 for his work with microcredit.

If we were to take definite action to simply guarantee basic levels of food, shelter, and life support resources to all people everywhere as a universal right, an action that is *absolutely possible and even practical* given the simple willingness to do so, can you even begin to imagine the outpouring of unleashed creative energy that would be the result? Can you even begin to imagine the spirit of trust, cooperation, and goodwill it would inspire worldwide?

If healthcare were also guaranteed as a universal right, can you begin to imagine what it might do to transform the current suffering and fear into a climate of security and hope? If education were guaranteed as a universal right, regardless of sex or social status, can you imagine how unleashing this nearly infinite untapped human potential might transform our world?

Can you begin to envision what a more self-actualized, collective human society might achieve? This actually begins as we make this vision more universal by first envisioning it ourselves, and by expressing it in as many forms as possible, by sharing it with as many people as we can, and by making it the common dialogue between us until it becomes absolutely real in our collective imagination.

The ego mind says, "That's just one more Utopian fantasy. It can't happen. People are just greedy and selfish and lazy, and they'll never change. That's just the way it's always been, and that's how it will always be." I would contend that not only is another world possible and practical, but that we have no other reasonable alternative. We are at a definite turning point in history in which the advances of technology and our ever increasing interconnectedness and interdependence are becoming such an irresistible force for universal change, that if we do not consciously and deliberately make these positive changes, we will utterly destroy ourselves by default.

The choice is ours to make.

Some would say that there is no choice, and that we are predestined to an apocalyptic denouement. So, somewhat reluctantly, I suppose it's time for me to address the topic of…

Chapter Thirteen

THE PROBLEM OF RELIGION

"Silence is the language of God, all else is poor translation."
—Rumi

Thus far in our exploration of the various aspects of this magical realm that we call life, I've attempted whenever possible to avoid terminology and language that could be construed as having religious connotations. This is not only because religion can be a very controversial, contentious, and hot-button topic, but also because religious terminology has over time become extremely distorted, stereotypical, and also monopolized by groups that to my mind are deeply rooted in ego-based distortions and prejudices.

When we use words like "God", "salvation", or "sin", most people have strong preconceived feelings and ideas about what they mean, and they tend to induce strong emotional reactions in one direction or another. Rarely are these terms seen as neutral.

Regardless of whether a person considers him or herself to be strongly religious, completely uninvolved and uninterested in religion, agnostic, or atheist, religion is almost never a neutral topic. Throughout human history religion has been used to justify the entire gamut of the ego dynamic of distorted belief and behavior, from hatred to war to outright genocide.

While most organized religions claim to honor the sanctity of free will, in practice they often do nothing whatsoever to encourage it, and in point of fact do everything in their power to exterminate free thought. Guilt and fear are wielded as the weapons of choice, used to control, manipulate, and dominate the wills and behavior of religious adherents. Religion could even be considered the third form of institutionalized totalitarianism, after the political and economic forms which we've already discussed.

In many if not most cases, religion is dominated by the

separative ego dynamic to an extreme that far surpasses almost all other areas of human society and culture. Why is it that the one area of human life which should by all rights join us in common experience in practice is the one that is the most contentious and separative?

I believe that this is because true spiritual experience poses the greatest threat to the existence of the ego, both individually and collectively, and therefore the ego must distort, manipulate, control, and dominate this sphere of influence more strenuously than any other. As soon as a profound spiritual Truth is stated and recognized, the ego immediately jumps on it and begins reinterpreting (*mis*interpreting!) it to its own ends.

For these and many other reasons, many people have become so entirely alienated by the very idea of religion that they avoid it at all costs. They would claim to have no religion and that all religions are simply a means of controlling people. Baby and bathwater springs to mind.

And yet in spite of the extreme distortions, millions of other people are inexorably drawn to religion. Why should this be? What is so attractive about systems of thought that seem to be so controlling and ego-based. Let's take a look at each of these perspectives. First, it occurs to me that those who are strenuously opposed to religion and claim to have no religion, while that viewpoint is definitely understandable, are nonetheless to some degree missing the point.

It's estimated that by the end this month (when I'm writing this chapter—October of 2011), and therefore by the time you're reading this, the population of the earth will have surpassed 7 billion people. I would contend that if there are 7 billion people living on the planet, that means there are 7 billion unique and distinctly different religions, and *necessarily so*. To my mind, a "religion" is a set of beliefs about the nature of life, reality, how things work, and how we can make sense of anything and everything.

One of the dictionary definitions of religion that I found is: *"a set of beliefs concerning the cause, nature, and purpose of the universe."* In that sense, everyone has such a set of beliefs, regardless of whether they've taken the time to consciously identify them or not. Because each person is an infinitely-unique-in-all-of-time individual, they will naturally and necessarily have a completely unique perspective on the world. As Alan Watts put it:

"The individual is an aperture through which the whole energy of the universe is aware of itself."

Therefore I would argue that each of us has our own unique 'religion', and that this is a necessary aspect of being human. This is true regardless of whether or not it involves concepts such as God or anything else even remotely spiritual, or whether it is an entirely materialistic perspective on the universe.

We each ultimately have to find our own way in life and discover our own perspective on how to make sense (or not) of it all. And each one will be uniquely different. You might then ask whether there is an actual ultimate Reality, an ultimate Truth that is beyond our individual beliefs *about* that Truth? Is there an actual nature of Reality and the Universe? Of course, that's the big question, isn't it?

In this sense, both science and religion are exploring the same territory, namely the nature of what is. Both science and religion seek to discover what is true, though they tend in most cases to go about it by very different means. Unfortunately, beginning in the west, there formed a distinct and definite split between science and religion. Up until the 16th and 17th centuries, there was no such strong schism between science and religion or science and philosophy.

Around the time of Galileo, however, a split which was largely instituted by the Catholic Church firmly established the material realms as acceptable to scientific investigation, but the non-material realms, and anything to do with what we might call "consciousness" as *only* to be addressed by the Church. Since that time, science has as a result become much more materialistic in its approach, and anything remotely spiritual has come to be regarded as unscientific and therefore without merit from that perspective; whereas religion has become less and less inclined towards the processes of rational thought and the "proof through experience" approach which is the foundation of science.

In my view both science and religion have suffered greatly and become distinctly out of balance as a result. In yet another example of ego separativeness, left brain/right brain, or masculine/feminine ways of thinking and approaching life have been split apart and seen as in opposition to one another, instead of as mutually interdependent and complementary as they truly are.

Secondly, there are a variety of reasons why so many are attracted to organized religions in spite of the seemingly obvious distortions within them. One is simply that people naturally need a sense of belonging and community. Even when we are immersed and polarized in the largely unconscious, emotionally ego-based, "what can I get for me" sense of separateness, we can never completely cut ourselves off from the need to experience our interconnectedness since it is the essential nature of Who we truly are. Organized religions fill this role for many.

We also all have an innate need to make sense of the "mysteries of life". Even at the purely ego level of control, there is a need to find meaning and purpose in life, to sort through the more confusing trials and tribulations and make sense of them. Even the ego has its limits beyond which it can no longer sustain extremes of pain, fear, and confusion.

In fact, if the pain becomes too acute we will eventually surrender, at which point there is the possibility to leave behind the continual resistance of the ego and to transcend it entirely. Most organized religions supply a ready-made perspective on how to organize our beliefs to at least attempt to deal with the confusion and pain in a way the ego can accept.

On a somewhat more superficial level, it's my experience that many people choose specific religions because the ego-distortions within them most closely reflect and agree with their own personal forms of ego-distortions. Those with strong personal prejudices, for example, tend to gravitate towards religions with similar beliefs in exclusivity and separatism. "We are the chosen ones. We, and only we, will be saved. Everyone else is wrong and doomed to damnation," or at the very basest, most childish level, "My god can beat up your god." This to my mind is the real ego intent behind the familiar refrain of many religions of "My god is the one and only true god."

However, at a much deeper level, there is a much more significant and potent reason why people are attracted to religions, and that is simply that they are all founded on profound truths that resonate with us at our deepest levels. At levels far beyond ego-distortion, we all sense that Love is real. We all understand the wisdom of "Do unto others..." And to the degree that we've had magical moments, peak experiences, true intuitive inspirations, and other deeply profound spiritual experiences, we sense the utter reality of them and aspire to re-experience them and to share them with others. These inspired, "in-spirit" experiences are often revelatory and bring deep insights into life.

It's my sense that most all religions originally sprung forth from one or more persons who had one or more of these experiences, and did their best to explain and share them with others. In many cases, these individuals may have even transcended the ego entirely and became Great Teachers and shared their insights with others so that they could benefit from them as well. Of course there are limitations to our ability to communicate these experiences. We can *experience* the spiritual realm—the spiritual Reality—but it cannot be conceptualized or understood through the medium of the finite human mind.

Unfortunately, since the ego wants desperately to control any experience that is remotely spiritual in nature—because those experiences are by definition beyond the realm of the ego entirely and therefore threatening to its very existence—it does so by analyzing, conceptualizing, and attempting to reduce to concrete ideas and symbols that which cannot be so reduced.

It then clings just as desperately to these artificially-contrived mental constructs *about* the spiritual experience as if they *were* the experience. As soon as a spiritual Truth is recognized and communicated, the ego mind immediately recognizes the inherent threat to its existence that the Truth poses, and it systematically goes about distorting it to its own purposes. This is the very reason that various religions, theologies, and other similar belief systems *seem* to be in conflict with one another.

Ultimate Truth

It does seem logical to assume that there is an "ultimate Reality", an ultimate nature of *how things are*. It also seems likely that whatever it is, it is also by its very nature far beyond the ability of the human mind to comprehend. How can the finite human mind begin to grasp infinity?

To my mind the Bible, as well as many if not most of the world's other spiritual scriptures, through the centuries has been and continues to be distorted and misinterpreted. The tendency, especially amongst fundamentalist Christians and fundamentalist sects of other religions, is to try to interpret the scriptures in purely literal terms. This strikes me as a total contradiction and misuse of the essential purpose of the spiritual writings of the world.

The fact, so often stated in many different ways throughout the Bible and other scriptures, is that "Truth", meaning "the Truth of God" or absolute truth, sometimes called the "Word of God", is infinite and beyond human knowledge or understanding and therefore is not expressible in finite terms or forms such as human spoken or written language. It cannot be stated, but only experienced.

The scriptures are consequently approximations of the Truth at best, and extremely imperfect ones at that because of the limitations of language. To take the scriptures only literally strikes me as a complete and total misunderstanding of their usefulness and importance. The Truth in the scriptures lies hidden *behind* the words for the individual reader to discover for him or herself. They are merely signposts pointing the way to a personal *experience*, which is the only way that any real understanding of the Truth can be gained.

I would argue that the tendency of the world's religions to take them only literally is to mistake the forms for the content. The symbols used, the stories told, the histories expounded in the scriptures are simply the metaphors that represent some *aspect* of the Truth. If one assumes that the symbols *are* the Truth, that individual is assiduously avoiding the very experience that the scriptures were meant to help bring about. As has been stated so clearly:

> *"There can be no universal theology, only a universal experience."*
> —*A Course in Miracles.*[14]

It's also important for us to understand that since spiritual writings are *approximations* of the Truth, there are many different ways in which those approximations can be expressed; even some forms which, within the limitations of language, seem to be in contradiction with other forms. It is only the "forms" which seem contradictory, not the "content" to which the forms were meant to point.

Since these approximations of the Truth can be expressed in so many different ways, we might also want to keep in mind that each of the scriptures, including the various books of the Bible, was written at a specific time in history for a specific group of people with specific cultural backgrounds and levels of understandings. This is not to say that the ideas expressed are not universal ones that are still as true and as useful as when they were written, but they are expressed in terms which relate specifically to the people for whom and the time in which they were written.

Often, as is the case with the Bible—Christ even says so specifically—the people of the time were not advanced enough spiritually to understand many of the ideas that the Teacher or writer of the scriptures wished to convey, and so the ideas were hidden in metaphorical language or in "parables". In this way the teachings were protected from the misuse and distortions of those not ready for them, but could be found by those who were spiritually awake enough to understand them.

If we truly want to transcend the ego, both on an individual as well as a collective level, we inevitably need to relinquish our need to be right and to make others wrong, and the most firmly entrenched need to be right often tends to lie in our religious beliefs. If we do indeed have 7 billion unique perspectives on the world, I believe it's paramount that we treasure this "unity in diversity". It is in our uniqueness that we are drawn together. Once we begin to even faintly grasp the true significance behind spiritual experience, we can learn to have true respect even for those perspectives which on the surface seem to interpret those experiences differently.

I often like to use the analogy of a huge wagon wheel. The hub at the center of the wheel is Ultimate Truth, or God, or Absolute Reality, or whatever else you may wish to call it. Each of us is on our own unique spoke of the wheel, moving back towards the center. This is our own personal path to Truth or God or Enlightenment or whatever you wish to call that Nameless Source from which we sprang, in other words, our personal "religion" if you will. We all seek truth in our own unique way. The farther out on any given spoke a person happens to be, the farther away the other spokes will *appear* to be. And the closer to the center we move, the closer all the other spokes are to our own.

We could also say that the more firmly enmeshed in ego-dynamics any particular person is, the more he or she will perceive others to be separate and different and threatening. And the closer we move towards self-actualization, the more we recognize our oneness and cease to perceive the illusion of separateness.

My Religious Upbringing

My own early religious background was, I suppose, relatively typical for someone raised in the midwestern United States. I grew up in a highly fundamentalist Christian church that had a strict literalistic interpretation of the Bible and placed a great deal of emphasis on sin, fear, guilt, and damnation. They regularly made a point of taking issue and finding fault with any and every other denomination of Christianity, picking apart their various theologies and identifying what was wrong with them. Only those Christians who believed as we did were "saved", and all others were destined to spend eternal damnation in hell. Of course non-Christian religions were beneath consideration, and more often than not simply considered evil, the work of the devil.

While I always fully accepted the idea of salvation through faith, I nonetheless at a relatively early age began rebelling against the more manipulative, fear-based, dogmatic, and intolerant aspects of our church's theology. Though I certainly couldn't have consciously identified it at the time, so much about their approach felt deeply wrong, coercive, hypocritical, and inappropriately self-righteous.

As I got a bit older and was exposed to Eastern philosophies through my involvement in the martial arts, I came to feel that there was something very right about many other religious approaches. I had a deep sense for example that the Tibetan Buddhist monks that I learned about on television were truly spiritual people, and that condemning them as evil because their beliefs were different struck me as so incredibly misguided as to be virtually blasphemous in its own right.

When I began studying the various self-help and peak performance literature in my mid-teens, I was also intrigued to find that I was already familiar with many of the ideas, although in a very different form. The principles were those found in the Bible, except that our church's strict interpretation was that they were "holy laws". It began to occur to me that most of the "laws" in the Bible were not in fact strict rules that you had to "obey" or suffer punishment and damnation, but were in fact impersonal laws of nature, laws of the universe. In the sense that if you follow the "law", you'll get the best results from life. If you try to break the law of gravity, for example, you'll fall down and skin your knee. But if you work in harmony with it, you can dance and run and learn to do backflips.

Another insight came when I began learning more about self-image psychology, and I realized that everything that made any sense to me and that felt sound and true down deep said that we do best when we have high levels of self-esteem. When we feel good about who we are, we treat others with respect and compassion, and we get the best results from everything we do. This was the complete opposite of what I'd been taught in church: that we are by our very nature worthless sinners, doomed to damnation unless we repent.

In short, I came to believe that the fundamentalist approach in which I'd been raised had deliberately, if unconsciously, distorted spirituality into the epitome of the ego dynamic, and was the complete antithesis of everything that actually felt truly spiritual to me. This realization was also quite liberating, however, because it allowed me to leave behind the confusion and contradictions with which I'd been indoctrinated as a child and freed me to explore the experience of spirituality in a much broader and more inclusive context.

Moving Beyond Religion to Spirituality

While there are profound truths to be found even in traditional Christianity, I've found that it's only by exploring them in much broader contexts that they can be applied in more universal and all-encompassing ways. Truth is Truth, no matter where it's found. When we find two or more expressions of Truth that seem to be contradictory and mutually exclusive, it's almost always because we're misinterpreting one or more of them. Many if not most of the confusions and contradictions to be found in organized religion come from interpreting universal concepts that are literally beyond the realm of the ego from the strictly limited perspective of the ego itself. To clarify, let's take a look at just a few of these as examples.

God

It's my contention that we "create God in our own image", and since most people are immersed in identification with the ego, we personify God as having the same ego-based characteristics. Since the prime filter through which we perceive the world, as well as everything else, is our self-concept, and we project that concept onto literally everything, why would our perception of God be any different? The ego personifies God as a vengeful, controlling father figure who relentlessly punishes disobedience. In other words, as an omnipotent super Ego!

"Man was created in the image and likeness of God" is often interpreted to mean that God has a body, a personality, and human thoughts and emotions. Perhaps it actually means that *we don't*. That Who We Truly Are is not merely our body, feelings, and thoughts; not merely the limited, separate self of the ego. Perhaps it also means that like the Creator, we too are essentially creative Beings.

A friend who identifies himself as an atheist recently asked me, "Do you believe in God or don't you?"

I said, "Yes. And no."

Whereupon he became exasperated, and exclaimed, "It can't be both, either you do or you don't!"

Finally I said that, "I believe in a spiritual Reality that is far beyond anything that can be limited to the finite *idea* which is generally associated with the word, 'God'."

I tend to avoid using the word "God" when talking about spiritual ideas, since it has become so identified with a personification. If we understand, however, that when we talk of a greater spiritual Reality, one which cannot be limited to the personal pronoun "He" (or "She" or "It", for that matter), one which cannot even be conceptualized or expressed in human terms or language whatsoever, and if we then choose for the sake of convenience in conversation to refer to this infinite, unknowable, incomprehensible Reality as "God", I'm OK with that.

Sin

The idea of sin is one that to my mind has become extremely distorted, and goes to the heart of the attempt to keep people trapped in the prison of guilt and self-contempt. The original root of the word "sin" came from archery, and meant "to miss the mark". It implies an error or a "missed attempt", and not an immoral transgression as it has come to be interpreted. The appropriate response to an error, seen from any perspective other than purely ego-based, is correction, not punishment.

One reason sin and punishment have become associated with one another is that most destructive errors, because of the law of Cause and Effect, bring about painful results. The ego interprets this as punishment. It is not punishment, it is merely feedback about how things work. If you act destructively, you get destructive and painful results. The destructive actions aren't wrong or bad or evil, they're simply mistakes. Seen clearly, this often painful feedback brings our attention to the nature of the error so that we can learn to avoid repeating it.

The guilt-based interpretation of sin also plays into the ego's need to avoid the present moment and to live instead in the past. Guilt and blame are about the ego's illusion of past. Since the present moment is all there ever actually is, this is where we address the error. Holding onto guilt or blame only reinforces the error and makes it more likely it will be repeated. By responding appropriately to the present moment, we leave behind the past errors and can move towards actions that are consistently more sound, harmless, and beneficial.

Evil

In much the same way that many religions personify a Supreme Being, they also anthropomorphize evil by interpreting stories of the devil in exclusively literal terms. While there is little doubt that some individuals and even groups of people often behave in deeply destructive and selfish ways, and that it is certainly understandable that we would want to resist their selfish actions, branding them as embodiments of evil can ultimately be a problem in its own right, since it plays into the ego's need to justify hatred and retribution.

The belief in a "Great Evil" which is completely unredeemable is one of the ego's ultimate tools for upholding and justifying its continued belief in separativeness and blame. Throughout western history, this has been the justification for the brutal slaughter of untold numbers of so-called witches, heretics, and infidels, not to mention the basis of many "holy wars".

If we accept the principle that "sin" is actually error, or actions based on false premises, and that the appropriate response to error is correction rather than vengeance, then evil must also be reinterpreted. Even those who have committed great atrocities and crimes against humanity, such as Hitler in Germany, Pol Pot in Cambodia, and Slobodan Milošević and others in Serbia, can be seen in a somewhat different light. While the actions of such groups and individuals absolutely demand that we do whatever is necessary to put an end to their reign of destruction, they nonetheless also play a crucial role in our collective advancement.

In a very real sense, these destructive personalities serve mankind by exhibiting in no uncertain terms the ultimate consequences of the ego belief in separatism and mass aggression. They place clearly before us the choice of whether to act as a collective ego and follow the path to destruction, or to cooperate for our mutual benefit. In this way, we can see clearly and distinctly the horrendous results that ultimately can result from institutionalized forms of prejudice, bigotry, intolerance, brutality, and other types of ego dominance.

Salvation

In our church the common refrain was often, "Are you saved? Have you accepted Jesus Christ as your personal Savior?" The idea goes something like this: that, in total ego identification with error, we didn't just make mistakes, *we* **were** *sinners*. The sin was us, and we were the sin. Since sin was seen as a completely intolerable transgression which demanded endless punishment from a vengeful God, *somebody* had to be punished.

Since we were not only worthless sinners, but also completely incapable by our very nature of rising above the sin in any way, and since sin *must* be punished mercilessly, the only way to be saved from the eternal damnation which we inherently deserved, was for someone else to be punished in our place. That's where Jesus came in. Sounds like a classic ego scenario to me. Make error unforgivable, then shift the retribution onto someone else who doesn't deserve it so the unforgivable could be "forgiven".

What?

No kidding.

If however we accept that the ultimate nature of Reality is that of infinite wholeness, infinite interconnectedness, omnipresence, and infinite possibility (which is what both science and religion state that it is), and that the ego is a false mental construct based on the erroneous belief in imperfection, separateness, individuality, and limitation, wouldn't "salvation" be *correction* of those false perceptions, and therefore the release from the prison of the ego's limited perspective? Wouldn't the move towards self-actualization be salvation from the suffering of the ego?

From this perspective, the interpretation of the Gospel story is quite different. It's not a story of punishment, crucifixion, and death, but one of transcending them. Metaphorically speaking, it isn't the crucifixion which saved us, but the resurrection.

Suffering

One point of great confusion where religion is concerned for many people and one which is often used as an argument against religion itself is the question of how a loving God could create a world filled with war, cruelty, starvation, and extremes of human suffering. Or even how could a loving God allow such things? Of course the answer is that God doesn't make suffering, we do. All suffering comes about through actions we take, based on the ego's belief in separateness.

It is, once again, simply the law of Cause and Effect in action. If a Greater Spiritual Power (you can think "God" here if you want) were to interfere with this process it would be not only an infringement of our free will, it would also prevent us from getting the feedback that we need in order to learn to correct our mistakes.

From a spiritual perspective, freedom of choice, or free will, is sacrosanct since it is essential for the effective working out of cause and effect, which in turn brings about the lessons which are required for our spiritual growth.

If the spiritual Reality called God is involved in our personal human affairs at all (which does seem at least possible if not likely) and if God is in fact infinite Love, the most loving thing to do for us would be to allow the errors of our actions to work out in the valuable, painful lessons which are the natural results of those actions. Though completely impersonal, I believe the law of Cause and Effect nonetheless ultimately reflects a loving perspective, since it consistently moves us towards correction of error, and therefore towards self-actualization.

Freewill Versus the Will of God

Another similar point of confusion that often arises with regard to religion is, "If the Will of God is omnipotent and has therefore predetermined our ultimate destiny, how can we in fact have any free will whatsoever?"

I think this question in a certain sense goes to the heart of the nature of life itself. Albert Einstein was said to have made the observation that the most important decision we can make is whether we believe the universe is friendly or hostile, and that that decision would determine how we live our entire lives.

If we believe the universe is hostile, then life ultimately becomes an unending struggle and an exercise in futility. We'll see enemies everywhere, and we'll be in a constant state of resisting and fighting against the flow of life. If we believe the universe is friendly, then trust, faith, and goodwill become warranted. We'll look for the best around us, and see opportunity and possibility rather than limitation and imminent doom.

If there is in fact a greater purpose to life and to the universe itself, and if that purpose is benevolent, do we then have the freedom to choose to either follow that purpose or to work against it? And if we do, what effect do our more destructive actions have upon its ultimate outcome? How can any particular outcome be predetermined if we can mess it up?

Again, I believe the answer is cause and effect. If there is a greater purpose to the universe, and to the life of humanity itself, it seems to me that it would be built into the very fabric of the natural order and that the laws of nature would reflect that purpose perfectly. Perhaps we are safe from self-destruction, relatively speaking, because Cause and Effect places a natural limitation on how destructive we can ultimately be.

We can continue to choose destructive actions only until the painful results of those actions become so intolerable that we are eventually forced to change our ways. Perhaps it's only the timing which we get to choose: whether to cooperate with our ultimate destiny now, or to struggle against it until our resistance becomes too painful to continue.

How Do We Know What is True?

It seems to me that the blind adherence of many people to organized religions that have so many seemingly obvious contradictions and distortions within them is based upon a specific type of faulty logic which is quite common to the ego. Those who have accepted as true a particular theology or religion had at some point to make the decision for themselves that they believed that it is in fact true. How and why did they do this?

Sometimes this occurs because an individual is exposed to a particular religion as a young child and is told over and over that this particular interpretation of spiritual life is not an interpretation at all, but is the inviolate "Word of God". Because children are completely dependant upon their parents and the other adults guiding them, and because they are also completely trusting and open by nature, they simply accept what they've been told and take it to heart as the "truth". Some never question this even after they become old enough to think for themselves, and it becomes a lifelong, deeply entrenched belief system which they never bother to open to further dispute, in spite of the often uncomfortable contradictions.

But many people who do in fact learn to think for themselves also choose dogmatic religions, and I suspect that this is because at some point, after being exposed to a particular religion, they either have one or more deeply profound spiritual experiences which they associate with the religion, or they connect deeply with some particular truth expressed within the context of the religion. They sense deep within themselves that these experiences are absolutely *true* for them.

Unfortunately what often happens next is that they forget that this profound experience of the truth came from *looking within themselves at a heart level* to discern the inherent truth of the experience itself. And because they may have never had such a profound experience before, and because it occurred within the context of the particular religion, rather than continuing to measure the truth by their own inner experience, they instead "logically" assume that since the experience was absolutely true, and the experience "came" from the religion, the religion as a whole must also be true.

They choose, often unconsciously, to blindly accept all of the various theological doctrines of the religion, regardless of how true they may feel at a deeper level, including even those ideas that may not resonate at all with what feels true, and in many cases may even be in sharp conflict with it.

The ego simply comes up with rationalized justifications for any specific beliefs within the religion that feel erroneous at deep levels, sometimes in quite convoluted ways. The person then abdicates responsibility for discerning the truth to the "higher authority" of the particular dogma of the religion. To question any of the more disturbing aspects of the religion would then be seen as heresy, and is often even seen as grounds for expulsion from the religious group itself.

Such people conveniently forget that the very reason they accepted the religion in the first place was because they felt deep within that something was true about it, and from then on out, they give up using this approach as their means of evaluating various aspects of the religion for fear they will lose their connection with it.

Having "faith" is then interpreted as the blind acceptance of all the various precepts of the religion, regardless of how false they may feel deep down at the level where *true faith* actually resides. True faith has more to do with "listening with the heart", with trusting the voice of the Authentic Self, that place within where we *know* that something is true or not. Not merely at an intellectual level of rationalization and logic, but at a heart level.

Early sects of Christianity known as Gnostic Christians, as well as many eastern religions, believed that the highest source of authority and truth always came from within oneself. The highest truths were those that sprung up from within our own consciousness, our own "inner knowing", and that these always superceded any written or other "outer" teaching.

Of course, the ego doesn't trust this, since ultimately it doesn't even trust itself. And ego-based institutions such as organized religions could never trust others to think for themselves in this way since it would be impossible to control them. So these early Christian groups were quickly stamped out by the mainstream Christian Church.

Institutionalized Egotism

Since both the individual and collective egos within dogmatic organized religions are highly fearful of the actions of those who think for themselves, they systematically built institutionalized forms of control into those religions in an attempt to prevent free-thinking. Fear of punishment, not only in temporal terms but in the form of eternal damnation and torment, became the weapon of choice against any who would dare to question any of the religion's doctrines.

And since those who held opposing beliefs were deemed deceivers, agents of the devil, and inherently evil, it was seen as completely justified and even mandatory that they be annihilated. Thousands of people were tortured and put to death during the Inquisition in the name of religion. But even today, particularly in the western world, many within fundamentalist branches of Christianity and other religions brand anyone with differing belief systems, as well as the religious practices they employ, as absolutely evil. Hatred and aggression towards these "evil others" is seen as completely justified and the "Will of God".

What began as a message of love, peace, and goodwill has somehow been distorted into a justification for hateful divisiveness. This particularly pervasive form of ego-distortion can be especially difficult to overcome since its adherents build their entire worldview around it. They convince themselves that only they are right, and only they are favored in the eyes of God. It's difficult to imagine how such an arrogant and obviously egotistical perspective could continue to be upheld even by educated, relatively intelligent people, but sadly, it is.

Predestined Destruction

Finally, another form of particularly destructive ego-distortion that plays a major role in many religions is the belief in the predestined apocalyptic destruction of humanity. This is a highly convenient belief from the ego's perspective, since it justifies an outlook of hopelessness and complacency. "Believers" are seen as God's chosen, and therefore exempt from the destruction to come. And since the apocalypse is absolutely preordained as the Will of

God, there's simply no point in working towards humanity's advancement, since it's doomed to failure anyway.

This justifies the ego's refusal to take any real responsibility for the various social and political problems in the world. If, however, we accept that we create our own experience by choosing our perceptions of the world, and if we do in fact choose to believe that the universe is friendly, it seems to me that to any degree that we give relevance to scriptural prophecies, it would seem wiser to interpret them as warnings, rather than as predetermined fact. In other words, rather than seeing their more destructive predictions as meaning "this is absolutely how it will be," they are instead simply meant to indicate, "this is what would happen if you refuse to stop acting destructively."

This means that the wise choice would be to envision a positive future, rather than focussing our attention on a destructive end. After all,

"You become what you think about all day long."
—Earl Nightingale.

Or in the words of the Bible,

"As a man thinks in his heart, so is he,"
—Proverbs 23:7

And this is as true for humanity as it is for an individual.

If we become what we think about, and if there is even the slightest chance that we can advance beyond the limitations of the current world situation, then both logic and intuition dictate that it is our absolute responsibility to believe in a positive future and to envision it as often and as vividly as possible. Regardless of whether we ultimately succeed or fail in reaching our highest ideals, if we want life to change at all—for ourselves, for others, and for humanity as a whole—we must choose both our beliefs and the perceptions on which we base them from those that reflect the future we want, rather than what we don't want.

Neither our perceptions of the world nor our beliefs about the world are ever completely accurate. Therefore it's wisest to choose beliefs based on how well they serve us. By believing in a positive future, we move towards it. If we believe that all of humanity is inherently bad by nature, and only the small segment of people who believe as we do can be saved from utter damnation and destruction, how is that belief serving us except purely in ego terms? If we believe that humanity deserves to be destroyed and that its destruction is unavoidable, how does that belief help us?

The nature of spirituality is wholeness and compassion. Spiritual and religious beliefs are meant to join us, to bring us together, and to save us from our more destructive actions. If our beliefs are divisive and destructive, how can they be truly spiritual? And what do they say about who we are? Are we merely an ego who cares only about itself? Or are we something more? These are to my mind, at the very least, questions worthy of consideration.

Chapter Fourteen

THE CHILDREN

"Children see magic because they look for it."
—Christopher Moore

S ome of the most magical creatures on our planet are giggling gleefully somewhere right this very moment. If you truly want to learn about the wonder of magical moments, about living in the present, and about being in touch with a genuinely inspired, creative perspective on life, go spend an afternoon with a three year old. Children are both our greatest teachers and our greatest responsibility.

It should be no mystery to anyone who spends any time around young children why Jesus said that you must be as a little child to enter the Kingdom of Heaven. Children understand intuitively that the essence of the Universe, of Reality itself, is that it is truly awe-inspiring. And the experience of awe, of wonder, is the experience of ultimate reality; it is the wellspring of all joy, inspiration, and all forms of creativity.

And yet it is amazing how soon we begin to forget this simple truth. We grow up and get side-tracked with all the fears and anxieties and menial expectations of the world we live in and the society around us. It's so easy to forget.

Often three year olds are my favorite people. In my experience, when you get to know someone when they're three, you get to see who they truly are as a unique individual. At three, in most cases at least, we haven't yet been conditioned out of the innocence and wonder of our True Self, but we're just old enough to be able to begin actually communicating with others. It's the most magical of ages, because Who We Are comes shining through clearly.

All too soon, the "adult" egos around children who feel seriously threatened by their joy, enthusiasm, and free thinking, do their utmost to control those exuberant little bundles of energy into subservient egos which they can dominate and manipulate into "safe" areas of expression. But if we want to 'live on the skinny branches' and actually begin to transcend our own attachment to ego identification, we need to pay attention to really young children and *model our behavior* on them!

Egos are childish, but the Authentic Self is child*like*. Egos are immature in that they are selfish and completely egocentric. But our Authentic Self has the childlike perspective of pure joy and a completely in-the-moment outlook which is completely free from the illusion of past and future.

Children *know* that life is wonder. Children *know* that life is joy. Children *know* how to live in the present moment. And when suffering does arise, they *know* how to accept it completely without getting stuck in it. Little children can be singing one moment, crying pitifully the next, and giggling gleefully the moment after that.

Several years ago after my wife, Kathi, and I had recently moved back to Illinois after having lived in California for many years, we were walking out the door of our local YMCA one day at the beginning of the winter season, only to discover that it had started snowing while we'd been inside. It had just snowed enough for there to be a few thin spots of accumulation on the ground. As soon as we saw it, we looked at each other, groaning, and almost in unison said, *"Ugh! Snow!"* with utter grumbling aggravation in our voices.

A bare moment later, there was a little boy about three years old who'd just gotten out of the car with his parents, and as he rushed to one of the small, thin pockets of snow on the ground and bent over to try to scoop some up in his hands, he gleefully exclaimed, "Yay! Yay! YAY! **SNOW!!!**", with the absolute, unbridled enthusiasm that only a three year old can convey.

Kathi and I looked at each other and laughed out loud. Now, quite often when one of us is tempted to get aggravated about something, the other will just go, "Yay! Yay! YAY! **SNOW!!!**", as a reminder to not take things so seriously.

Once several years ago we were visiting Kathi's family and got to babysit our nephew and niece, Jimmy and Alicia, while their mom, Kathi's oldest sister, went out for the evening. They were about three and four years old at the time, and we decided to take them to a movie, which they'd never done before. They were used to watching old movies on VHS video that they regularly borrowed from the library, but we weren't completely sure they'd be able to sit still in a movie theater for an extended period. We needn't have worried.

We decided to see the live action version of Disney's *The Jungle Book*, with Jason Scott Lee. We arrived at the theater a few minutes late, and when we came in, the previews had already started. As soon as we walked in and began to find our seats, Jimmy and Alicia's eyes were immediately glued to the screen. Even as we sat down and helped them take off their coats, their attention never wavered for an instant from the projected images.

For well over an hour and a half, Jimmy and Alicia sat transfixed, in a complete state of awe and wonder. I'd never seen either of them sit so still or be so quiet for such an extended period before. Occasionally we'd whisper to them, commenting on something that was happening in the film, and they'd respond with a brief comment or nod, without ever once looking away from the screen.

Afterwards they were both talking incessantly about what an amazing thing it was. When their mother got home and asked Jimmy how the movie was, he was still filled with wonder and enthusiasm. He exclaimed, "Mom, you wouldn't believe it! It was the *biggest video tape you've ever seen!!!*"

When my sister's son, Joe, was about five or six years old, he was helping my parents and the rest of our family get ready to have a yard sale. Kathi and I arrived a bit later to help with the sale, and when we got there, Joe had been busy carrying things outside. As soon as he saw me, he ran up to me and began enthusiastically shouting, "Uncle Mitch, Uncle Mitch, I've been working really hard!"

I said, "I can see that."

He then immediately held his hands out to me and said, "Feel my hands!" I smiled at him and wondered where this was going, but decided to play along, so I grabbed hold of his hands and felt them. Whereupon, he blurted out with enthusiastic sincerity, "Do my hands feel tired?"

The Perfect Students

Children are also naturally curious little learning machines. Literally everything in their world is a field of discovery and exploration. In the first several years of life, children assimilate a mind-numbing amount of information about the world around them, from their language to how to move and walk and tie their shoes. If they're exposed to several languages regularly at a young age, they can as easily learn all of them as only one. If you want to learn how to learn, spend time with children. If you want to discover how to be open-minded and naturally inquisitive and filled with the joy of learning new things, spend time with children.

What if we all retained this joy of discovery and learning throughout our lives? What if we continued to have an accelerated learning curve all our lives? Isn't learning and growing what life is about? Isn't the very nature of becoming trapped in the limitation of ego identification the fact that we want to think we already know, that we have nothing more to learn? Of course, that path leads only to stagnation and death.

Children are like sponges that soak up everything around them, both the positive and the negative. Whatever happens, whatever they see or hear or experience, they take it in, without judgement, and it becomes integrated into their perspective. And because of their innocence and initial lack of bias, they often have amazing insights into that experience.

Children as Teachers

Ego perspective tells us that children should be "seen and not heard", that their interests and preferences are trivial and irrelevant to real life. The "adult" viewpoint says that things like play, adventure, and fantasy are a pointless waste of time, with no real purpose or significance in the "real world".

But young children are disarmingly honest. They're completely genuine. With kids, what you see is what you get. Initially at least, there are no complex ego games going on geared to manipulate and control others, although that does begin to change rather quickly once children are forced to attempt getting their needs met amongst the other egos in their environment.

This childlike honesty and authenticity is terrifying to the ego mind. And all too soon the innocence and sincerity of childhood gets conditioned out of children by the emotional competitiveness and neediness of even many of the most well-meaning of adults in their lives.

Of course, we rationalize much of this restrictive conditioning as being "for their own good". It's not safe to be so open and honest and innocent. Children "don't know what's best" for them, and so we have to impose it upon them. And if children are allowed to live with fantasy, they'll never "grow up" and be able to live in the "real world".

It's true that there are physical and other dangers that we must protect children from, but I think it's a mistake to assume that children don't know what's best. Often they know much better than we do. Often they have a wisdom and intuitive knowing that far surpasses anything the adult rational mind can grasp. Thanks in part to their innate simplicity and innocence, with even just a little guidance in the right directions, children can often go to the heart of any problem and address it with compassion and insight.

On another occasion visiting her family, Kathi and her mother, Jimmy and Alicia's grandmother, were left watching the kids one day while their mom was at work. At some point Jimmy, who was still only three at the time, for some reason didn't get to the bathroom in time, and "made a mess in his pants", which was unusual but shouldn't have been a huge deal.

Unfortunately, he went to his grandmother for help, and she became absolutely furious with him, and as she manhandled him into the bathroom, she berated him with an unending torrent of nearly hysterical screaming about how horrible he was for making a mess that way. Kathi's mom had a lot of great qualities, but like all of us, she had her issues, and for some reason, this was one that would really set her off, bringing out the absolute worst of her control and anger issues.

Meanwhile Kathi was in the bedroom across the hall, shocked by what she heard going on, which brought up old memories of her and her younger siblings being terrorized by their mother in potty-training incidents. Kathi knew she couldn't allow this to happen and had to intervene to protect Jimmy from being traumatized, but she was afraid that if she wasn't careful how she did so, that it would just escalate the situation and make things even worse.

At that moment Alicia, looking visibly upset by what was going on, walked shyly into the bedroom and said, "Jimmy's *bad!*"

Kathi looked at her and said, "No, sweetie, Jimmy's not bad. He just had an accident. Anyone can have an accident."

Knowing that she couldn't wait any longer to do something,

Kathi went out into the hallway and stood outside the open bathroom door, and Alicia followed her. Still struggling with what to say or do, Kathi was just about to speak when Alicia said with complete innocence and sincerity, "It's OK, Jimmy, you just had an accident. Anyone can have an accident."

Kathi's mother immediately stopped her tirade, and looked up at them with an expression of utter shock on her face. Kathi later said it was like she'd suddenly "awoken from the madness" and realized what she was doing. Alicia's simple, compassionate approach completely diffused the situation, and Kathi's mother continued helping Jimmy get cleaned up, but she was quiet and gentle with him, where before she'd been aggressive and hostile.

Kathi described it as one of the most amazing instantaneous transformations of a volatile situation that she'd ever seen. She'd felt fairly certain that if she'd said anything herself, that her mother would have become even more entrenched in her position, and the situation would have become even more out of control. Whereas, four-year-old Alicia had simply taken what she'd been told, accepted it as completely true, and repeated it with complete innocence and conviction, and the results were nothing short of miraculous.

Rather than feeling we need to control children or get them to stop being so inquisitive or imaginative or rambunctious, we could instead pay attention to them and emulate their openness, honesty, and enthusiasm. Instead of talking down to children, assuming we know better, we could step into their world and treat them as equals, allowing them to guide us into unexpected avenues of inspiration and joy and compassion.

When my nephew, Joe, was little we would often have these amazing extended conversations about all kinds of things. Even as a child, Joe has always been naturally curious and a real "thinker". Whether the topic was time and how it works, responsibility, nature, or relationships, I could always count on him to have something interesting to contribute.

Often our conversations would consist of me simply asking a series of pointed questions and drawing him out on whatever we were discussing. He'd often come up with the most amazing, insightful answers. While he couldn't always get there on his own, by asking him the right questions and giving him the space to think through an issue, more often than not, he'd be able to find his way to the heart of the matter, and express it with simple clarity.

I remember in one conversation when he was about ten or eleven, Joe brought up the topics of "sin", "wrongdoing", and "evil", as he'd had some confusion about them from what he'd been told in church. We started talking about behavior and what was right and wrong. Rather than just telling him what I thought, I'd ask him questions and tried to get him thinking about it for himself.

I'd ask him, "Well, what do you think sin is?" At first he just repeated some dogmatic phrase he'd been told in church. So I'd suggest that he apply the idea to different situations to see how he really felt about it, and what he thought was true.

I'd ask things like, "So if you do something other people think is bad, but you don't know there's anything wrong with it, did you 'sin'?" And we'd explore that for a while. He decided that a lot of what we think of as "bad" are really just mistakes, and eventually he said that the only thing you could do that is really "wrong" would be to deliberately do something on purpose that would be hurtful to someone else.

I told him that made a lot of sense to me.

Teaching Discipline

Raising and guiding children is one of the most important responsibilities that we have as adults in society. And this is true regardless of whether or not we have children of our own. We *all* need to take responsibility for the welfare and nurturing of our most valuable resource, the children around us. Of course this can often be a challenging undertaking, both for parents as well as for anyone else who touches the life of a child in any way, which ultimately is each and every one of us.

There is often a fine line between healthy essentials, such as keeping children safe, setting appropriate boundaries, and creating consequences for destructive behavior on the one hand, and what is essentially spirit-crushing ego dominance such as the need to control, emotional manipulation, and physical and other forms of "punishment" used as retribution, on the other.

Children do need to be taught that selfish behavior brings about painful or undesirable results. And while it is indeed our responsibility as adults to teach this lesson, *how* we do so is an enormous responsibility with far-reaching consequences that can often impact a child for the rest of his or her life.

As with everything else, it always comes down to whether we are acting from the ego perspective or from one of honesty, sincerity, and detachment. Unfortunately, our ego mind is often ingenious at rationalizing its perspective as "compassionate" when in reality it is nothing of the sort. It's all too easy to fall into the trap of justifying abusive behavior as being "for their own good".

Children do need discipline. We do need to step in when they're about to stick a fork into an electrical outlet, or stick their finger into a sister's eye. And it's also essential to address selfish, mean-spirited, or disrespectful behavior. But it's crucial to be as fully present as we possibly can be in these moments, and to be utterly honest with ourselves about how and what we are actually communicating on all levels.

We often tend to think of "discipline" as forcing children to do what we think is best. But discipline isn't something you can force, it is something that we learn—or not. Ultimately it needs to be seen as something desirable, so that children will choose it for themselves. When we talk about discipline, we're really talking about our *own* ability to direct and organize our *own* actions and conduct. Discipline is a powerful and highly valuable tool for ordering our lives and improving the results we get from our efforts.

If we don't learn discipline as children and make it a habit, it becomes much more difficult as adults to achieve the things we want to achieve and to lead the lives we want to lead. Discipline is one of the key enabling factors in aspiration. And we teach discipline to children by demonstrating it ourselves. If we are emotionally undisciplined and fly easily into fits of anger, that's what children will see, internalize, and imitate.

When we're in a position to discipline children, if we're acting from a need to control, if we're attempting to manipulate behavior with emotions by "guilt throwing", if we're acting from a position of anger, outrage, or self-righteousness, if we're attempting to label the child as "bad" and identify *them* with their inappropriate *behavior*, or if we're acting purely from a need to impose our own will on the child, then we're coming from the ego, and our actions will be abusive and harmful to some greater or lesser degree. True compassion comes from a place of detached involvement.

It is in fact possible to impose discipline on children without anger or attachments to specific outcomes. It requires complete acceptance of what is, which includes unconditional acceptance of the child, as well as fully accepting whatever behavior we are addressing. By "accepting the behavior" I don't mean to imply that outrageous or hurtful behavior should be allowed to stand unchallenged. It can and must be addressed, immediately and unequivocally.

But it's also important to simultaneously communicate that the child is completely acceptable and loveable, and that they do in fact have the freedom to behave in whatever manner they choose. However, if they choose to behave destructively or selfishly, they won't like the results. We can still impose decisive consequences for destructive behavior without making the child wrong or bad or making the behavior an "identity" for the child.

Of course, this isn't always easy to accomplish in any given moment. Our own unmet emotional needs and ego-based manipulative tendencies are often most strongly triggered by children acting outrageously around us. If you've ever found yourself yelling at a five-year-old, and later thinking, "he makes me insane!", you may not be too far from the truth. Of course, the five-year-old didn't "make" you anything. But insanity is a very good description of our unconscious ego traits that are often activated in such situations.

The important distinction here is that the child is not their behavior. Some would feel threatened by the idea of communicating to a child that they can behave however they want. But this is simply the honest truth. Children *can and will* behave however they want. We teach most effectively, not by labeling the child as "bad" or by trying to control their behavior, but by simply making it clear, as dispassionately and kindly as possible, that if they do "A", then the outcome will be "B". If they hit their sister, they get sent to their room. If they apologize sincerely, they can come out.

It doesn't have to be an emotionally charged issue at all. It can be done with complete dispassion and complete detachment, which ultimately, perhaps paradoxically, is the most *compassionate* approach. In fact the more detached we are, the more effective the discipline becomes as a teaching device, so long as we are also fully involved, engaged and present. Detachment doesn't imply lack of involvement or concern, it simply means we're not emotionally attached to having things our own way. And we can still convey kindness, firmness, and conviction along with detachment. If we discipline with anger, we're teaching anger. And we're making the behavior a big deal, treating it as an insurmountable obstacle. We're essentially communicating that the behavior is going to be tremendously difficult to change.

If we communicate that inappropriate behavior is no big deal, but that it simply creates consequences the child won't like, they are much less likely to become attached to the behavior itself. If we make it a fight, we're teaching them to fight, and they're more likely to develop an attachment to the very behavior we're trying to guide them away from. Further, if we *identify* the child with their behavior, they're likely to begin doing the same thing at an unconscious level and see the behavior as *who they are*, so that the negative behavior actually becomes a part of their unconscious self-image and therefore something they must defend as a part of "themselves".

On the other hand, if we do find that we're reacting with anger to a situation, it's also important to not simply repress it or try to pretend that we're not angry, since this only creates confusion for children. We can admit to being angry and take responsibility for it ourselves without making it the child's fault for making us angry. We can simply say something like "I'm really angry right now. I don't like what you did. So you need to go to your room, and we'll talk about this when we've both calmed down a bit."

We've all seen adults who yell and scream at children, and try to make them feel guilty, and threaten them over and over, and yet never seem to impose any actual *consequences* for their inappropriate behavior. This is simply insane. It is also extremely ineffective. And ultimately it is confusing and emotionally abusive for the children.

We teach respect not by demanding it, but by demonstrating it. We can impose discipline and still be completely respectful, kind, and compassionate. First and foremost, children need to be given unconditional love, respect, and acceptance. This is the foundation upon which all guidance and discipline will stand—or not. From a purely practical perspective, if we treat children with disrespect they will have no respect for us in turn, and any discipline we do impose will be seen as unjust and unwarranted. Then, even if we do succeed in imposing our will on them, they won't learn discipline but only that aggression and manipulation are the way to get what we want.

On yet another occasion several years ago, Kathi and I were visiting her family and were left in charge of Alicia and Jimmy. At some point, Alicia, who I think was about five or six at the time, became upset over something that she wanted that we wouldn't allow her to have. She began throwing an absolutely hysterical crying and screaming fit.

Kathi simply took Alicia back to her room and told her something like, "I know you're upset, and that's OK, but you need to stay in here until you feel better. You can cry and scream as much as you want, but while you do, you have to stay in here by yourself. Whenever you're done and are feeling better and calmed down, you can come out." And she left her there.

After a little while, Alicia quietly came out and joined us again, and was calm and apparently feeling fine. By respecting Alicia's feelings and giving her permission to express them, but also making it clear that it wasn't acceptable to impose her tantrum on everyone else, Kathi empowered her to discipline herself emotionally. She established clear boundaries without needing to try to control or manipulate Alicia emotionally.

And yes, I do understand that it's much easier to have this type of detachment with someone else's children than it is with your own, and I realize that not all situations are as easy to address as this one. But the point is detachment, respect, and compassion should always be our objective, the ideal for which we are striving. In any given situation it's unlikely that we'll express it perfectly, and we will inevitably slide back into our own ego tendencies from time to time. But to the degree that we can be fully present as well as honest, sincere, and have detached involvement with our children, to that exact degree will we be effective at teaching them both discipline and compassion.

As I mentioned, we teach respect best not by demanding it, but by giving it. We teach compassion by being compassionate. We teach fairness by being fair. And we teach discipline by disciplining our own behavior, leaving behind ego-based motivations in favor of a more balanced approach. As we strive to more fully demonstrate these qualities in our own lives, we teach by being the examples for the children around us, and therefore create a foundation for their lives as well.

Paying Attention

One of the most crucial needs that children have, and sadly one of the most often lacking, is to simply receive real, open, focussed, accepting attention from the adults around them. In fact, one of the most profound needs that we all have as human beings is to simply feel accepted and valued as individuals. We want to feel "gotten" by others.

By paying real attention to children, we communicate that they are relevant, that they are valuable as individuals, that their thoughts and feelings are important to us, and worthy of our time, energy, and attention. Ideally when we have this experience as children, it serves as a foundation for our entire lives, and allows us to experience ourselves as relevant. Simply taking a truly receptive attitude with children can often have a profound impact on them.

Unfortunately, as children, most of us did not have these needs for attention from the adults in our lives met to a sufficient degree. Since most adults are still experiencing life through the ego framework of not having their own needs for attention completely met, they are unable to give the kind of intense and dedicated attention to their children that they truly need. But luckily, sometimes even short spans of intensely focussed, unconditional, undivided attention given to children at key moments can make a huge difference in their young lives.

When Kathi and I moved back to the midwest after having lived in Los Angeles for several years, it had been some time since I'd been able to visit my family here. So my nephew, Joe, was already four years old when I met him for the first time. He was a bit of a handful, to say the least. Exuberant, unruly, with boundless energy, Joe was not accustomed to being disciplined in any truly focussed way, and he had no real understanding of personal boundaries.

One evening, we were playing together, and he kept jumping up into my lap, and repeatedly insisted on putting his hands into my face really forcefully and aggressively. It wasn't that he was being deliberately mean-spirited as much as he just wanted to connect and had no idea how to do so appropriately. I told him that he needed to keep his hands out of my face, and when he continued doing it, I told him that if he kept it up, I'd have to make him stop. I took a serious tone so that it was clear that I wasn't just playing, without being angry at all. Of course, he kept right on doing it, so I finally wrapped his arms around him, and hugged him so that he couldn't move.

Joe said, "Let me go!"

But I simply said, "No. I told you to stop, and you didn't, so now you have to stay here for a while."

Joe kept trying to get me to let him go, and when I didn't, he got really angry, and finally said, "I don't like you! I hate you!"

Refusing to take the bait, I just responded in a completely accepting tone with, "That's OK. You don't have to like me. You just have to keep your hands out of my face."

Since this was one of the first close, personal interactions that Joe and I had had with one another, and because he wasn't used to being disciplined in such a definite manner, it set the tone for Joe's feelings about me at first, and while he knew he couldn't get away with anything with me, he also didn't like me very much and, particularly when I was in a position to discipline him, he would often exclaim, "I don't *like* you!!!"

This completely turned itself around however one evening when Joe was staying at my parents' house and I happened to be there visiting. We were sitting alone together in the living room, and he was telling me about something, animatedly chattering away in his normal, energetic way. I decided that I was just going to give him my complete and undivided attention, to really *listen* and try to just *"get"* him fully.

I listened closely to the story he was telling me, about something he'd done that day or something he was imagining doing. Every so often I'd ask a question about what he was telling me or I'd respond with an encouraging nod or smile. But mostly I just paid attention, with complete openness and intensity of focus, like he was the most important thing to notice at that moment, which to me, he was.

After spending several minutes like this, at some point, Joe just stopped and looked at me with this look of curiosity and wonder, which in itself was noteworthy since he normally seldom stopped talking for long. After a moment, he exclaimed enthusiastically, "I really *like* you!"

"Well I really like you too!", I replied with a smile. And from that moment on, it seemed as though I was Joe's favorite person. We developed a great relationship, and even in situations where there was conflict and I'd need to discipline him over something, we'd always see it through to a point of resolution, so that he was able to take responsibility for his actions and how he felt about them, and feel empowered rather than merely feeling reprimanded.

This one moment of really giving Joe my full attention seemed to set the groundwork for an atmosphere of true trust and respect between us. It seemed to communicate that, while I might find his *behavior* unacceptable at times, no matter what he did, *he* was OK with me. I saw him as valuable and acceptable for who he was, and somehow Joe seemed to get that.

Though it's unusual for one instance of focussed attention to have this kind of impact, it can happen, and I've had many other similar experiences with children in this regard. The important point is that children need to be given pure, undivided, unconditional attention. It's necessary for the development of a healthy self-image. And given how rare it can often be in the lives of so many children, sometimes a little unconditional attention can go a long way.

Unfortunately, it's all too easy to fill up family time with activity and places we need to be and things we need to do. In our ego-driven striving for "more", it's a common problem in our society that we don't just stop and pay attention. This is important enough in our own lives, but in the lives of our children it's paramount.

Education

A similar problem pervades our educational systems. We're not paying attention to the real needs, inclinations, and capacities of individual children. And we often take a cookie cutter approach to schooling.

One of the main problems with how we approach educating children is that we assume that they need to be "taught", and we interpret this as needing to tightly control the direction of their thinking and practically force-feed them information. Children learn naturally and even joyfully when allowed to do so, but when we interfere with this process by trying to control it, we take away the joy and turn it into drudgery and introduce extreme imbalances and limitations into the process.

Of course we do have an essential part to play in educating children, but it actually has as much to do with getting out of their way as it does with setting the curriculum. Rather than force feeding them pre-ordained bundles of information, we need to direct children to inspired and creative avenues of discovery, and then we need to allow them the freedom to explore them. We need to capitalize on their natural creativity and joy of learning and help to enhance them, rather than killing them off in highly regimented and narrowly controlled "education factories".

I met recently with the directors of the community outreach department of a local community college to see if I could offer to develop some workshops on creative thinking and problem solving. One of the needs that we discussed was that in their role of working with employers and prospective workers in the community, one of the main issues that comes up again and again is that students are leaving school with no creative problem-solving skills or abilities in critical thinking that are in fact so essential to functioning effectively in the work force.

It turns out that one of the detrimental effects of the emphasis on standardized testing in public schools is that, since it forces teachers to focus almost exclusively on getting students to get the correct answers on tests, there is little or no attention given to creative thinking of any kind. Students are simply taught to absorb and regurgitate predetermined bodies of information. Their creative abilities are discouraged and allowed to atrophy until they can no longer think for themselves and are unable to come up with solutions to even simple, everyday work-related problems.

Employers are finding that these students who are graduating from high school and entering the work force are woefully unprepared for meeting even the simplest of creative demands that arise naturally in the workplace. Of course, this imbalance is unnecessary and is being artificially imposed on students. It needn't be.

In fact, Richard Barrett, author of the book, *Liberating the Corporate Soul*[15], points out that research indicates that we all have profound creative abilities that are quickly driven underground by the social conditioning of parents, school, and work. A group of children who were tested for creative abilities showed that 98% of them had genius level abilities at ages 3 to 5 years. Five years later when these same children were tested again, only 32% still scored in this genius category for creativity. Five years after that, it was only 10%. When the same test was given to 200,000 adults over age 25, it showed that only 2% of them had creative abilities in this genius category.

Memorizing facts is only one aspect of true education. Without the abstract thinking skills to reorganize, manipulate, and make sense of the information, it has no meaning. The problem is that if we're coming from an ego perspective, allowing children the freedom to explore and discover for themselves rather than interpreting everything for them, is unacceptable. In fact, generally speaking, creativity itself is threatening to the ego since it can't be controlled. So the fear-based ego approach is to artificially impose what is actually an extreme imbalance, with no *feminine*, right brain, abstract thinking allowed.

What children do need is a balance of focussed, purposeful but accepting attention, pointed, well-directed guidance, and the encouragement and freedom to explore new territory for themselves. Learning is fun by nature, and when we remove the fun, we remove both the joy and the effectiveness of learning.

I encountered one of the best descriptions of healthy balance in education several years ago when I was teaching at a weeklong summer magic camp in California. The camp was held on the grounds of a science camp in the mountains near Idyllwild, California. The name of the organization that managed the camp was *"Guided Discoveries"*. To me this is one of the simplest, clearest definitions of what education should be.

Children do in fact need guidance. They need to be pointed in the right directions, and they need help in focussing their attention, otherwise their activities become chaotic as most of us have experienced with children at one time or another. But then they also need the freedom to discover things for themselves within that focussed framework. When we discover something for ourselves, those are the lessons that we take to heart and make our own.

A Lesson in Influence

At this same camp, I had what for me was a profound teaching experience and a huge lesson in the power that just a little guidance at the right time can have. The first year of the camp at the very first group session, when we were meeting the kids for the first time, there was one boy who dominated everyone's attention from our first moments together. His real name was Brad, but he went by the nickname "BJ". He was about 9 or 10 years old.

BJ was extremely outgoing, charismatic, and funny, and he also loved giving everyone a hard time in a friendly, but 'in your face' kind of way. He was also really clever, obviously intelligent and a fast thinker like a miniature Don Rickles, continuously jabbing people with his verbal sparring but never in a mean spirited way, really just having fun. Before long, all the other kids were giving it right back to him.

One day towards the end of the camp, I happened to walk up to BJ and one of the counselors and saw that BJ was in tears and really upset about something. I asked what was wrong, and the counselor told me that BJ thought that none of the other kids liked him. I asked him why he thought that, and he said it was because they were always giving him a hard time.

I said, "Everybody likes you, I think they all like you a lot. And they think you're funny and fun to be around, they just give you a hard time because that's how you are with them, and they figure you can take it from them too." There was a group of science kids at the camp at the same time, and I pointed out that, "If any of the science kids were to start a fight with you, all of our kids would be there in a heartbeat to defend you."

I got him to see that the other kids thought that he was funny and likeable, and they were just giving back what he was putting out, but he was still upset. So I asked him if he liked being how he was, and he said, "No."

So I told him, "Well, if you don't like how you are now, that's OK, because you can change if you want to. All you have to do is really want to be different." We talked for a bit longer and he felt better, and I didn't really give it another thought.

The following summer I went back to teach at the camp again and BJ was back again too, but he was no longer "BJ". Now he wanted to be called Brad. And he'd undergone an amazing transformation over the ensuing year. He was still outgoing and charismatic, but he was also extremely respectful and considerate, and where before he'd been a real 'live wire' and needing to be the center of attention, now he was simply calm and confident. He was truly like a completely different person.

I was really impressed with the difference, and one morning

when he came along on a hike that I was taking with a few of the kids, I told him so. I said, "You know, Brad, you've really grown up a lot in the last year."

He said, "Yea, I know."

"And I don't mean just physically," I added.

He said, "Yea, I know. That talk we had last year really made an impact on me."

At the time we'd had the conversation, I really just wanted him to feel OK about himself, so I was totally blown away to discover that he'd not only taken it to heart, but had literally transformed his personality in a profound way as a result. It's so easy to forget how impressionable children are, and how they take in everything around them. With children we teach as much just by being who we are as we do by trying to teach them. Which is yet one more reason for us to leave behind our own ego tendencies as often as possible.

In Brad's case, as "BJ", while he was definitely fun, smart, and likeable, he also needed to be the constant center of attention. Somehow what I had to say to him at just the right moment, along with the fact that he looked up to me and respected me, allowed him to take the idea to heart: "You're OK, you don't need to try so hard". And he took the ball and ran with it. The story is to my mind the perfect example of leaving behind the neediness of the ego, and simply becoming Who We Truly Are. Brad taught me a valuable lesson I'll never forget.

Balanced Education

There actually are some great examples of truly balanced approaches to educating children that combine both analytical and creative thinking skills and that inherently utilize creativity, fun, and "guided discovery" as key elements of everything they do. One of these is Waldorf Education. Here's a brief introductory description:

> *"Developed by Rudolf Steiner in 1919, Waldorf Education is based on a profound understanding of human development that addresses the needs of the growing child. Waldorf teachers strive to transform education into an art that educates the whole child: the heart and the hands, as well as the head.*
>
> *"Teachers in Waldorf schools are dedicated to generating an inner*

enthusiasm for learning within every child. They achieve this in a variety of ways. Even seemingly dry and academic subjects are presented in a pictorial and dynamic manner. This eliminates the need for competitive testing, academic placement, and behavioristic rewards to motivate learning. It allows motivation to arise from within and helps engender the capacity for joyful lifelong learning."
—David Mitchell[16]

In Waldorf schools, drawing, music, drama, and other cultural activities are not only an essential and regular aspect of the curriculum, they are also included and integrated into other subjects such as mathematics, science, language, and history. When students dramatically portray the life of Julius Caesar, or create colorful drawings of various plants or insects, or recite poetry that reflects important grammatical rules, they come to understand and integrate the knowledge of each subject in a way that makes it truly their own.

Waldorf schools are also structured around three seven-year developmental phases in a child's life. It's a well known fact in biology that it takes about seven years for every cell in our bodies to be transformed; every seven years we literally have a completely new body. And in childhood, seven-year cycles reflect specific phases of development which also relate to the first three "levels of awareness": physical, emotional, and mental, as we discussed in Chapter 7.

From infancy to about age seven, children tend to learn through imitation. They model the physical behavior around them, and thus learn to walk and talk and interact with others.

The phase between the ages of seven and fourteen is defined largely through imagination and feeling. Children's emotions and creative capacities become more finely developed and are the prime vehicles for exploration and learning.

Then at around age fourteen, the search for truth becomes one of the key motivators, and in adolescence, young people begin to truly develop the capacity for rational thought, and learn to actually think for themselves.

Waldorf schools address these phases not only by making the educational content relevant to each developing phase, but also by assigning children to the same Class Teacher in grades one through eight, for example. While not their only teacher by any means, this teacher accompanies the students as they advance from one grade to the next until they reach the next major phase and enter the high school ages.

A More Effective Approach

Studies have shown that Waldorf students who go on to university significantly outperform their peers from mainstream education. Waldorf students also scored notably higher on tests geared to measure moral reasoning than students from either public schools or even religiously oriented schools.

In studies in Germany comparing success on college entrance exams it was found that Waldorf students passed the exams at double to triple the rate of students from the state education system. Further, students who had attended Waldorf for their entire education passed at much higher rates than those who had only attended Waldorf schools for part of their education.[17]

I know a woman who sent her children to a Waldorf school when they were young. She told me that whenever they were too sick to go to school, they'd plead to be allowed to go anyway, because they were so afraid they'd miss something really great that day. They were highly motivated to "get better" so they could return to school. The content at Waldorf schools is constantly varied and creative and fun-filled, and it brings out the natural joy of learning. Contrast this with the way that most children feel about going to school, and you'll have some insight into how effective this approach can be.

Waldorf is just one example of a truly balanced approach to education. There are others who also successfully combine both "right brain" and "left brain" styles of learning. The collective ego-based approach to educating, which is the common strategy currently imposed on most public school systems, stresses the need to control children's progress through an overly structured, exclusive focus on a left brain, highly rigid curriculum.

Waldorf and many other more balanced approaches to education are available and could be more widely implemented and even integrated into public education, but they are completely unacceptable from the perspective of ego, since they can't be controlled, and they encourage and help facilitate creativity and free thinking.

The purpose of education should by all rights be to help each individual child to explore and discover his or her own unique talents, predilections, and personal passions; and to find his or her own area of genius. It should be about helping each individual to discover Who they truly are, and what their unique mission and contribution in life might be. Instead we use the standardized, 'square peg in a round hole' approach of force fitting all students into becoming good little consumers, working in concert with society and the media to deaden their thinking and get them to fit into the status quo. This need not be.

Chapter Fifteen

THE MAGIC OF ART

"It is through art, and through art only, that we can realize our perfection."
—Oscar Wilde

From April 5, 1992 to February 29, 1996 the "longest siege of a capital city in the history of modern warfare"[18] took place when shortly after Bosnia and Herzegovina had declared independence from Yugoslavia, Serb forces surrounded the city of Sarajevo and bombarded it with all manner of modern weapons. It's been reported that as the city was cut off and devastated through incessant bombing, and the siege progressed, there were certain people who were not allowed to leave under any circumstances. Among these were the artists and those in the creative class.

The Serb forces apparently realized that the artists, musicians, and creative types were also those who, if they had access to the outside world, could most clearly and passionately communicate and inform the rest of the world of the atrocities taking place within the city. Meanwhile, within Sarajevo, while even medical complexes and cultural properties were specifically targeted and destroyed by the bombardment, musicians, actors, and artists helped to keep the spirit of the people alive.

Vedran Smailović, a cellist with the Sarajevo Philharmonic Orchestra, and principal cellist for the Sarajevo Opera Company, regularly visited the sites of bombed out buildings and played his cello there. A photo of him playing in the ruins of the partially destroyed National Library[19] has become famous, and his story captured the imagination of people around the world.

The first *Sarajevo Film festival* was also held during the siege, in many cases using VHS videos which belonged to the organizers, and over 15,000 people attended the viewings over the 12 nights of the festivals with each night sold out. It has since continued, becoming the most influential film festival in southeastern Europe.

Art exhibitions were held, and some artists even created sculpture from the twisted debris left by the bombings. Plays were produced and held, as well as theatre festivals. In acts of peaceful defiance that proclaimed "you can bomb our buildings and even kill many of us, but you cannot kill our spirit or our culture", artists of all types helped to keep the heart and soul of the people of Sarajevo flourishing.

Throughout history, art has played a defining role in shaping our society, our culture, and the direction of our collective progress as human beings. Art in all its various forms proclaims more loudly and clearly than perhaps anything else who we are, both as individuals as well as in terms of our common humanity. Art also enriches our lives and is the means by which we share our deepest inspirations with one another.

"There is no pulse so sure of the state of a nation as its characteristic art product which has nothing to do with its material life."
—Gertrude Stein.[20]

As we saw in the previous chapter, art in education has a profound effect on the development of the growing child. In fact, long-term studies at UCLA show that, all other factors being equal, students who attended "arts rich" schools did significantly better in all areas of academic achievement, they were far more likely to attend college, and achieved higher grades in college. Further, the "arts engaged" students, those who had art and music as a regular part of their curriculum, had significant advantages in terms of the types of jobs they got after school and their levels of volunteerism and political participation.[21]

In studies done at the University of Pennsylvania it was also found that community-based arts programs "increase civic engagement and participation, improve child welfare", and even help combat poverty. Further, economist and social scientist, Richard Florida has shown that it is the "creative class" who are the driving force in economic development. He sites research that shows that those cities, and countries, that are able to attract and retain creative residents, especially those in creative professions, will prosper economically, and those that don't will not.

In the United States, the non-profit arts-and-culture-related industries support approximately 5.7 million full time jobs. Compare this to the US automobile industry with only 3 million jobs. These arts-related industries also generate $166.2 billion (yes, that's *billion*) every year, and $29.6 billion dollars in revenue to local, state, and federal governments. These three levels of government together spend less than $4 billion dollars annually to support arts and culture, which means they are getting a 7:1 return on the investment, an amount that would thrill even the most jaded Wall Street investor.[22]

Artistic expression and creative innovation are driving factors in education, social success, and economic development. Given all the overwhelming evidence of the essential nature that artistic and cultural expression play in our society, I find it shocking how often we tend to dismiss their significance. Arts programs are generally the first to be cut from a school's curriculum when budgets are tight. Even though the arts are a strong economic driver, the same is true for funding public arts programs.

Unfortunately, the arts are often seen as frivolous. Nothing could be further from the truth, and yet many are blissfully unaware of this fact. Recently when asked why he wasn't supporting funding for the development of a new museum, a member of the city council in a nearby city said that he'd never gone to a museum, he'd never taken his children to a museum, and he wouldn't attend the new museum if it were built. This in spite of the fact that it had been shown that the museum would be a major attractor of tourism dollars for the city.

On a more personal level, art inspires us in ways that effect all areas of our lives, from our effectiveness at work, to our relationships, to our spiritual well being. When we surround ourselves with stimulating architecture, design, music, and other forms of art, and allow ourselves to be inspired by them, our lives are changed in profound ways on all levels. Having our own outlets for artistic, creative expression can also be liberating, therapeutic, fulfilling, inspiring, healing, and absolutely essential to our mental, emotional, and physical well being. And literally any aspect of our lives can be a potential avenue for artistic, creative expression.

On her television show, Oprah Winfrey once told a story of having traveled to Africa and visited a small village. While there she spent some time going from hut to hut taking note of the poverty and struggle that the inhabitants lived with, until she came to the hut of an 18-year-old girl who was raising four younger siblings by herself. Although they were living in utter squalor, they'd somehow managed to create a small kitchenette and living quarters in the hut.

Everything was ragged and even smelled bad, but then Oprah suddenly noticed a small piece of fabric hanging in the corner above the girl's pillow. The girl had hung it there because she wanted something small and bright and beautiful and "nice to look at". It gave her a sense of hope. It seems we all have an innate need for beauty in our lives.

Art and creativity are an essential aspect of Who we are, and this is as true on the collective level as it is on the individual level. Our society needs art and aesthetic expression as a natural and necessary quality of human life. Both the individual and the collective ego mind resists creative expression, except in cases where it can be turned to purely narcissistic or egocentric self-aggrandizement. This is because true art, which comes from a place of inspiration, an expression of the Authentic Self, has the ability to take us out of the realm of ego and into the realm of wonder, harmony, presence, and true magic.

Anything that we can do as individuals to support artistic expression in our society as a whole will assist in moving our society towards equilibrium and health. A few nights ago, we turned on the television to watch a DVD movie. When the TV came on, it happened to be tuned to our local PBS station, and there was a "Great Performances" presentation of the San Francisco Ballet's production of *The Little Mermaid*. We sat in awe, transfixed by the truly amazing choreography, sets, lighting, acting, and direction. We ended up watching it all the way to the end, and we were completely inspired.

Having access to such wonderful, inspiring performances is of true value to our society as a whole, one which we can and must support through our financial contributions, our political process, and by choosing to take advantage of the offerings that are presented. A huge percentage of the content on television and other media is filled with glorified violence, materialism, and obscenity. But we have the freedom to make another choice. We can change the channel, we can attend an opera, we can visit an art museum.

Which brings me to...

Chapter Sixteen

THE MEDIA AND TECHNOLOGY

"Any sufficiently advanced technology is indistinguishable from magic."
—Arthur C. Clarke

(I hope you'll pardon me while I step up onto my soapbox for a bit...)

The collective ego mind feels threatened when any one of us chooses to step outside the influence of its domain. So it does whatever it can to prevent us from doing so. As we discussed in Chapters 9 and 12 on the "Global Brain" and "The World", a great deal of our mass-communications media reflects this collective ego separativeness in rather blatant terms.

Since the airwaves, internet, and other media are in essence our collective thoughts made manifest, they potentially reflect both the collective dysfunction as well as "the highest and best to which men have risen". Unfortunately, the majority of the mass media content has been and for the most part continues to be directed and controlled by a relatively small number of people who "hold all the power" in the form of the financial and technological resources.

We are seeing the very beginnings of a trend away from this, as we'll discuss shortly, but for the most part, this is still very much true of the major media outlets, such as network television, major news organizations, and other media conglomerates. In fact, there has been a move towards the further monopolization of even greater levels of media power in fewer and fewer hands over the past several years.

Currently, just five huge corporations: Time Warner, Disney, Rupert Murdoch's News Corporation, Bertelsmann of Germany, and Viacom (formerly CBS) own the majority of all newspapers, TV and radio stations, magazines, books, and movie studios in the United

States. Notably, two of these five conglomerates, Murdoch's News Corporation and Bertelsmann, are foreign owned.

Since maintaining this monopoly depends upon keeping the masses of people from demanding change, the media giants tend for the most part to promote content that influences commercialism, consumerism, polarized and divisive political perspectives, and other separative, ego-based behavior. Each and every day our senses are literally bombarded with messages of materialistic salvation in the form of "more".

We're told over and over, both blatantly and covertly, that what we *really* need to be truly happy and fulfilled is... and here you can fill in the blank with whatever product is the current lure for our attention. If you just drove the right car, wore the right clothes, took the right vacation, ate the right foods, watched the right movie or TV show, listened to the right music, or drank the right soft drink, *then* you'd be *truly* happy. You'd be loved and admired by everyone you know.

Here we see perhaps more clearly than anywhere else, the ego's continual refrain of "more is never enough." A vivid picture of "work—spend—consume, work—spend—consume" gets blasted into our conscious and subconscious minds from all corners, supporting one of the ego's most insistent mottos of "seek but do not find".

We're also taught to worship the idols of celebrity, fame, riches, and a highly artificial and overly sexualized physical perfection. They entice us with implied messages of "look what you could be if you only worked a little harder, spent a little more, became a bit more glamorous." This artificial, unrealistic, and unnatural ideal of physical attractiveness, fame, and endless material prosperity becomes yet another unreachable "more" that we then feel inadequate to realize. Of course, seen through the eyes of sanity, none of this is real, and none of it will bring true happiness or fulfillment.

But it would be a mistake to assume that none of this has any power. As we've seen, our subconscious minds take in whatever messages we give them, and they go to work to create the world that we've seen in our imagination. So by allowing ourselves to be continually inundated with these messages, we come to believe that they are true and that we are inadequate unless we are striving for "more" in all its myriad, seductive forms.

Another incessant media message that passes for "entertainment" is that of "me against you" and "might makes right". So many of our movies, television shows, song lyrics, and video games glamorize conflict and aggression in its many forms. Whether it's portrayed as the cutthroat, merciless, take-no-prisoners conquests in the corporate boardroom; the sarcastic, mean spirited, highly disrespectful banter of sitcoms that passes for comedy; or the highly stylized, glorified, and overly "justified" graphic violence and mayhem, the message is clear: winning in life means annihilating your opponent.

Similarly, the majority of the news media slant their perspective to focus almost exclusively on dire, negative, and ultra-controversial topics. There are in fact some very significant, far-reaching, positive, progressive, *inspiring* events and trends taking place each and every day, in locations throughout the world, but you'd never know that from reading the newspaper headlines or watching the network news on television.

The news media tend to focus on the most negative and divisive of events, and they tend to slant coverage of all events in ways that keep us in fear, frustration, and hopelessness. Even with important issues that actually need to be addressed, key details are frequently neglected in favor of sensationalism and what often amounts to little more than fear mongering. Those who depend upon major news sources to stay informed are most often left feeling powerless, frustrated, and according to recent studies, *woefully misinformed of the actual facts*.

One result is that political candidates are almost never elected based solely on their positions on issues. Campaigns have become glamorized, media-driven popularity contests, usually with little or no real, meaningful content taking part in the process whatsoever. One "blind taste test" survey taken during the 2008 Presidential primaries, indicated that if candidates were chosen based solely on their stand on issues rather than on how "electable" they were portrayed as being in the media, the nominees to the two parties would have been Dennis Kucinich on the Democratic side and Ron Paul on the Republican.

According to the study, these two candidates most closely reflected the actual interests and concerns of the electorate. They also happened to be the two candidates who were most strongly marginalized, ignored, and often even ridiculed by the media as being hopelessly "unelectable". The implication would seem to be that the mainstream media isn't really interested in the political concerns of the public at large.

As long as we continue to base our beliefs and our choices upon the sensationalized misinformation of these huge, corporate media conglomerates, these trends will continue. However, we now have many more choices than ever before in this regard, and as I mentioned, there are indications that this situation is beginning to shift, perhaps slowly, but with ever-increasing momentum.

The Movement of Technological Empowerment

Advances in technology are making a variety of resources, which in the past were the exclusive domain of large media companies, available to ordinary people. Independent music artists can now affordably produce their own music. Independent filmmakers can now affordably produce their own movies. Writers can upload manuscripts digitally to self-publishing services and can affordably publish their own books.

With the rise of social media sites such as Facebook and YouTube, as well as online ordering services such as Amazon, these same artists can now often affordably promote and distribute their own work, in many cases completely avoiding dependence on huge record companies, movie studios, publishing companies, and other media conglomerates.

Similarly, the widespread availability of handheld mobile devices with both video and internet capabilities, combined with blogging and social media, has led to a rise of what is being called "citizen journalism", "grassroots media", or "participatory journalism". Ordinary people are taking part in the dissemination of news and information by using technology to create, augment, and fact-check media, either on their own, or in cooperation with others. The "Arab Spring" and "Occupy" protests are two recent examples of how public coverage of events have strongly affected the wider public perception of those events.

It's becoming more and more common for "breaking news events" to be first covered by someone who happened to be there with a video phone, capturing footage of the event, and then posting it online on YouTube or other similar sites. The flow of news and information which formerly moved in only one direction, from the media to the public, is now flowing both ways.

On a more personal and practical level, access to cell phones, smartphones, and other similar devices can have a significant effect on quality of life for many who previously had severely limited choices. Author and economist, Jeffrey Sachs, has said that "the cell phone is the single most transformative technology for development" in poverty stricken areas of the world, noting that the availability of cell phones in rural villages in third world countries is allowing access to a wide range of services, markets, information, and a connection to the outside world that was simply not possible before. All of these are having a profound effect on people's ability to lift themselves out of poverty.

Our Technological Responsibility

Of course, with greater individual, public empowerment comes the necessity for greater individual and public responsibility. *How* we use technology and media becomes more important because of our extended individual reach and empowerment. One criticism of "citizen journalism", for example, is that it can often lack objectivity, quality, and accuracy. Traditional journalists argue that only those who are trained in their field can understand the precision and ethics involved in reporting news events.[23]

We've all been shocked by stories of young people driven to suicide because of public humiliation on social media sites. Common, everyday cruelties of youth become exponentially amplified when blasted publicly across the internet. Mobile communication devices, internet access, and social media are powerful, and in some cases potentially dangerous, tools which we have a responsibility to use mindfully, wisely, and harmlessly.

It seems to me that the conversation on the ethical and moral implications of the new media technology is currently being largely ignored. For example, we don't allow children to drive automobiles because it's too dangerous, and they're not mature enough to do so safely. But we often give them unhampered, unsupervised, unguided access to the internet, cell phones, video games, and other media which can be potentially dangerous in their own right.

Exposure to extreme images of graphic violence, pornography, and hate speech, not to mention the seductive lure of overly addictive and antisocial behavior surrounding the use of such devices, are often overlooked or rationalized as being somehow not all that significant. These are all issues which in other contexts would *never* be allowed or seen as even remotely acceptable. Of course, children and young people are not by far the only ones who use such resources irresponsibly.

On a simple personal level, I'm amazed at how frequently I see adults using cell phones in ways that are blatantly rude, antisocial, and thoughtless. Rather than using these devices as a means for making a true connection with others, people so often seem to use them to avoid and ignore the present situation in which they find themselves. Time and time again, I'll see a couple in an otherwise intimate setting in a restaurant, and one of them spends nearly their entire time together chattering away on a cell phone or totally engrossed in sending and receiving text messages, meanwhile completely ignoring the person they're with.

Recently during our family Thanksgiving dinner, one of the only times in the year that our entire extended family is together, numerous times one or another of the "adults" interrupted their meal and the conversation to retrieve a text message that they'd just received.

Actually, in these and many other cases, I'm not so shocked by the behavior itself. We all slip into ego-based, antisocial behavior in one way or another from time to time. I'm certainly no exception. What I do find shocking is how we seem to have come to find the behavior completely acceptable, reasonable, and normal simply because it involves handheld mobile devices. I'm sure many would say I'm just 'behind the times' in my attitudes. But I wonder how acceptable similar behavior would be seen in other contexts.

If I sat reading a paperback novel during a holiday meal or in a restaurant with my wife, would that be reasonable? Would we allow children to talk to their neighborhood friends on toy walkie-talkies during a family meal? Perhaps. But my point is not whether any of this behavior is right or wrong, or good or bad, but simply that we may want to take a look at it and pay attention to what we're really doing and what the implications may be.

Like most people today I do have a cell phone, but I rarely carry it with me unless I know that I'll be needing it for something specific. Generally I leave it in my car. I honestly don't want to be that accessible and prone to constant interruptions of my day. I'm not suggesting that this approach is right for everyone, or for anyone else for that matter. Cell phones and other mobile devices can be incredibly useful and valuable tools for accomplishing a variety of tasks more effectively. But they can also be seductively addictive time wasters, sapping our valuable energy and "now moments" with trivialities.

In a recent lecture given to the plebe class at West Point Military Academy, writer, literary critic, and English professor, William Deresiewicz[24] argues that true leadership comes not from jumping through the hoops and achieving the goals that society sets for us, but from learning to think for ourselves. And that the only way to learn to do so is to spend time in solitude with one's own thoughts.

He points out, for example, that recent research has proven that so called "multitaskers" are actually not very good at multitasking. People who multitask a lot, who for example, spend time on social media while texting, while trying to hold a conversation with several other people, actually aren't very good at the very skills which allow one to multitask effectively. These include the ability to think clearly, to distinguish between important and useless information (and to be able to ignore the latter!), and the ability to switch effectively from one activity to another.

This also prevents the development of the main skill inherent in truly good leaders: the ability to think clearly and distinctly for oneself. Deresiewicz contends that effective leaders are those who spend time regularly in solitude with their own thoughts and in concentration on one thing at a time.

He points out that our constant habitual immersion in the trivial, non-essential distractions inherent in not only social media, but also television and other media, is seriously interfering with our ability to be effective at literally anything. We need to take time for contemplation and solitude, even the solitude of a long, in-depth, heart-to-heart, one-on-one conversation with *one* other friend. We need to go deeper than the surface level of continual distractedness.

Similarly, the *type* of content which we allow ourselves to be immersed in is our choice as well. Our televisions, radios, and web-browsing devices have these wonderful mechanisms that allow us to change the channel, surf to a different website, or simply turn them off and do something more productive. We can limit our exposure to mindlessly violent images, hopeless and divisive news content, and a wide range of other negative influences. We can choose instead to watch inspiring performances, listen to uplifting music, and seek out and pay attention to sources of news and information that reflect a positive perspective on national and global events.

As with everything else in life, it once again comes down to whether we are following the superficial and divisive dictates of ego-mindedness, which consistently avoids being fully present—or of a higher, more altruistic, benevolent, and socially awakened perspective which is focussed on "living in the now". In and of themselves, technological resources are neutral. They are neither inherently good nor bad. They are simply tools, in this case very powerful tools, which like anything else can be used in mind-numbing, isolating, divisive, and destructive ways, or in ways that are creative, cooperative, unifying, and beneficial.

The choice is ours to make. We can do so unconsciously and mindlessly, which will inevitably tend to devolve into ego-based behavior of one kind or another. Or we can do so consciously, deliberately, and with an awareness of the responsibilities and implications inherent in our actions, in which case our choices will tend to reflect a more sound perspective that will move us forward into those magical realms of true accomplishment and self-actualization.

Chapter Seventeen

PRACTICES

"Seek freedom and become captive of your desires,
seek discipline and find your liberty."
—Frank Herbert

Let's talk about some examples of practical ways that we can actually apply the various ideas we've been discussing, and begin to lead a magical life filled with inspiration, fulfillment, and joy. Some of these are techniques we've already discussed, but they're all activities that have the ability to bring us more into alignment with the moment to moment immersion in the experience of our intuitive Authentic Self.

The fact of the matter is, in my experience the only thing that prevents us from living the life of magic is our resistance to it. So most of the tools, techniques, and strategies that I've discovered for applying these principles in our everyday experience have to do with uncovering and releasing the various levels of resistance.

It's only the resistance that keeps us from living fully immersed in the experience of each present moment, which is where the magical moment exists and where the ego cannot follow. That present moment awareness is not only the realm of the magical moment, it's also the place of openness to inspiration, the connection with the Authentic Self, the birthplace of the Process of Magic, the source of artistic inspiration and of all true discovery, the light of truer perception, the experience of true balance in life, and the ground for the transformation of the false self-image of the ego into the wholeness of self-actualization, both individually and collectively. In short, it's the foundation for everything else we've been exploring here.

We habitually, and for the most part unconsciously, judge and resist nearly the entire range of the circumstances, events, and experiences in our lives. And yet it is the resistance itself that creates suffering and the "need" for resistance. It's also what prevents us from fully experiencing each present moment.

Recently I allowed myself to get really stressed out over a difficult situation I'd been dealing with, and as I've discovered can often be true when I let that happen, my immune system suffered as a result, and I came down with a cold. A few nights ago I was lying awake in the middle of the night, unable to get back to sleep. I had some rather significant sinus pressure, a headache, and that scratchy feeling in my chest that felt like I might go into a coughing fit at any moment.

Sometimes when in similar situations, I let myself sink into the misery, grumbling my way through the illness. Of course there is a certain sense of satisfaction that we derive from being miserable. We get attention and sympathy from others, and we can sometimes use it as an excuse to avoid dealing with the pressures of daily life for a short time.

On this occasion, though, I decided that rather than judging the experience as "bad" and fighting the cold and feeling miserable and upset that I couldn't sleep and get the rest I needed, I would instead simply pay attention to the experience itself, without judging it as either good or bad. My objective was simply to be fully present in the experience of the moment, rather than resisting it or feeling like "this shouldn't be".

I brought my attention to each physical discomfort, deciding to simply notice it and experience it as a sensation in my body, neither good nor bad, just a neutral sensation, and to merely take note of the feeling of whatever it was without judgement or resistance.

As I began to actually become more fully aware of the sensations in my sinuses, rather than unconsciously fighting them, and instead began feeling what was really going on, I started to notice that I'd been clenching the muscles in my face without realizing it. As I became aware that I was doing this, I was able to relax the tension, and as I did, it relieved most of my headache, and also released the constriction in my sinuses enough that I could breathe freely in spite of the congestion.

As I began paying attention to the constricted, scratchy feeling in my chest, I realized that I was tensing up my shoulders and abdominal muscles in reaction to it, and when I released this tension, my breathing opened up and the need to cough went away completely. I began to realize that my unconscious reactions and resistance to the initial sensations in my body were actually causing a great deal, if not the majority, of the discomfort that I experienced. And when I became aware of the resistance and released it, I was able to relax and feel at ease.

But then as my attention wandered, I found that I'd go right back to holding tension and resistance again. So in order to remain fully aware and to pay attention to my body's various sensations, I found that if I made a conscious choice to breathe in a smooth, relaxed way, in the way I would if I weren't sick at all and were completely at ease, I was able to maintain awareness of my body and stay relaxed and comfortable.

This conscious choice to alter my breathing by focussing on how I would breathe if I were feeling completely comfortable was the necessary "masculine" active role that actually allowed me to maintain my present moment attention, preventing my mind from wandering, and it also allowed for the "feminine" acceptance and non-resistance.

Recently as I've given this more of my attention on a regular basis, I've been amazed to discover how many of the minute aspects of my everyday life that I habitually judge and resist without even seeming to realize it. I catch myself grumbling internally about this or that, instead of saying, *"Yay! Yay! YAY! SNOW!!!"*

By choosing instead to simply notice what's going on at any given moment, we not only free ourselves from the resistance, but we are also making the choice to *fully accept* what is, rather than judging it as intolerable, bad, or something to be fought and resisted as somehow wrong. This choice of awareness and acceptance is really a choice to say "Yes!" to life, rather than continuing the unconscious "No!" of our judgement and resistance.

Really noticing something for what it is, is impossible without accepting it fully. And, of course, acceptance is impossible to experience while we resist what is. So if we are judging or resisting a situation, it means we aren't seeing it clearly; and yet, we are basing our resistance on this false perception. It becomes a vicious cycle. Paradoxically, if a situation requires action or change, it is only through complete acceptance of it that we can know what action is truly required and act most effectively to change it.

Some would argue that if we don't judge a situation as undesirable or "bad", that we're doomed to stay in it; that resistance is required in order to address it. But is this really true?

If we spill a glass of milk, there are a variety of ways we can react or respond to the situation. We can beat ourselves up over it: "I'm so clumsy. I can't believe how I'm always messing things up. I'll never amount to anything!" Or we can get angry: "You idiot! You bumped into me and *made* me spill my milk! *You* have to clean that up!" Or at the extreme, we can avoid dealing with the situation at all: "I'm not cleaning that up. It's not my problem. It's just milk." Of course these are all forms of resisting and not fully accepting the situation as it is. They each lead to more suffering.

Or, when we spill the milk we can simply accept it fully, without wasting energy on anger, guilt, or resistance, in which case we simply respond appropriately to the situation. We clean it up and get some more milk without any need to make an issue out of it. It is what it is, and once we accept that, appropriate action becomes obvious.

In fact, if we really pay attention, we may discover there are hidden treasures: "Hmm? I just realized that I spilled my milk because I was upset and distracted by that problem at work instead of simply being here in the moment. And now that I think about it, the problem at work came up because I was distracted there! I guess if I'm really paying attention, I'll avoid those problems in the first place, both here *and* at work. I'm sure glad I realized that." With acceptance of "what is" may even come gratitude. When gratitude becomes our habit, magical things begin to take place.

Anything that brings us fully into the present moment is a means to practice and experience the magical state of balance and self-actualization. This is the prime purpose of meditation, for example.

Meditation

Meditation is essentially the process of quieting the mind, relaxing into a state of alert, restful receptivity. If we were all to practice a daily discipline of spending a period of quiet, reflective time, it would dramatically transform our lives, both individually and collectively. Making it a priority to turn off our involvement in the incessant mind chatter even for a short period each day loosens the grip of the ego on our consciousness.

Studies have shown conclusively that meditation has measurable positive effects on a wide range of health issues, including blood pressure, stress reduction, immune system function, circulatory issues, chronic pain, brain chemistry, memory, learning abilities, attention deficit hyperactivity disorder (ADHD), and many, many more. Regular meditators have also been shown to have dramatic improvements in their ability to concentrate and to deal with stressful situations in effective and healthy ways.

There are many different types of meditation, but they all include some form of focussed, mindful, directed concentration. It can be a very simple process, more or less scientific, depending upon the form of the meditation. It isn't necessary to stop the normal thoughts completely, just to have a different relationship to them.

Many meditation techniques rely on focussing the attention on some specific object, idea, affirmation, or sensation. Simply mindfully focussing attention on your breathing is one approach. Another is to mentally step back and notice whatever thoughts pass through your mind, much as you might sit and watch clouds moving across the sky.

Anything that brings us into a state of relaxed, alert, one-pointed focus of attention for a more or less extended period can suffice to quiet the mind, emotions, and body and have significant positive effects. This can be as simple as sitting and closely observing the flame of a candle, or it can be more involved, as in the deep relaxation and visualization used in techniques such as autogenic conditioning, which I described in Chapter 8 on the process of magic.

If you've never experienced some form of meditation before, you can experiment by simply sitting and focussing your attention on your breathing, calmly noticing the rise and fall of your breath. Many first time meditators complain that they are unable to stop the constant clamor of the thoughts racing through their minds. But this actually isn't necessary.

All that's required is to allow the thoughts to continue, and perhaps notice them as they do, but to maintain the attention on your breathing, or whatever other focus you choose to use. Whenever you notice that your attention has wandered and gotten distracted by extraneous thoughts, simply bring your attention gently back to your breathing or other focus. You may find that your thoughts naturally begin to become more still, but even if they don't, just maintaining a single focus is enough.

It's usually best not to lie down, since it's too easy to fall asleep. Sitting in a relaxed, well-aligned position is generally more conducive to remaining alert and mindful. For most people, it's good to begin and end the day with some quiet time, since doing so can set the tone for the day, and it puts us at ease before going to sleep.

How long you meditate and the form that you use really just depends on your own preferences. Many people begin with just a few minutes at a time. Others find that an hour or even more is often desirable.

Keep in mind that regardless of the form of the meditation, the point is to bring your attention fully into the experience of the present moment, whether that is the sensation of your breathing, of noticing the flow of your thoughts, or simply being fully present in your body. You simply focus on whatever the experience of your focus of attention may be.

Meditation is also a potent means of tapping into the intuition. For example, you can pose a question, and then sit and wait for an answer to arise. It may or may not do so during the meditation itself, but just the practice of "listening" helps to develop the intuitive receptivity. Many find that creative solutions to problems can often pop up, either during or following meditation. And this practice of quiet, open, receptivity is a good focus in its own regard.

Service

One of the main distinctions between ego-mindedness and alignment with the Authentic Self is that the very nature of the Self tends towards service to others. Making the choice to be of service to someone in some way every single day is not only a worthy habit to develop but it is also a discipline that will bring rich rewards on our path of escaping the stranglehold of the ego. Any act of selfless service is an act to go beyond ego and to see another's needs as not at all separate from our own.

Further, as we serve others, the Law of Cause and Effect ensures that we will also receive as we have given. As we inspire others, we will be inspired. As we offer love and compassion and respect, we will receive them. As we help others to lead more secure, fulfilling lives, we too will experience security and fulfillment.

One rather potent form of meditation is to sit quietly and ask inwardly, "How may I serve?", and then "listen" for an impression. Just the simple act of shifting our focus from the individual, separate self of ego identification to the needs of those around us is a powerful transformative process in its own regard. Just as an experiment, try being of service in some way every day, and see where it takes you.

Movement Disciplines

Practices such as yoga and tai chi can be another healthy, practical way of practicing present moment awareness and attaining more balance in our daily lives. Disciplines that require a mindful, balanced use of the body are excellent approaches to both physical fitness and mind-body awareness.

Yoga actually refers to a wide variety of spiritual disciplines that originated in ancient India. When used in the West, it has become a somewhat generic term for hatha yoga, a specific discipline which utilizes a combination of holding postures that stretch and relax the muscles along with deep breathing and relaxation. Many of the common stretching exercises we're all familiar with were first derived from hatha yoga.

This type of yoga has become vastly popular as a form of fitness exercise and is an excellent method of stress relief and physical conditioning for toning and flexibility. Most health clubs offer yoga classes, and there are many instructional videos available as well.

T'ai chi ch'uan is a Chinese martial art form which most people in the west know simply as tai chi. The tai chi practice that has become popular in this country utilizes "forms" which involve a sequence of slow motion movements emphasizing well-aligned posture, relaxed breathing, and a natural range of motion.

Sometimes referred to as "moving meditation", the regular practice of tai chi has been shown to have a wide range of health benefits, including balance control, strength, flexibility, and cardiovascular health. Tai chi has been shown to burn more calories than surfing, or playing football, and almost as many as downhill skiing. Preliminary studies also indicate that it has positive effects on anxiety and depression, chronic pain, lowering blood pressure, sleep quality, increased energy and agility, and an overall feeling of well being. And a recent study at the Oregon Research Institute[25] has shown that tai chi is highly effective for patients with Parkinson's disease at preserving balance, improving walking, and preventing falls

While there are tai chi instructional videos available, the complexity of the techniques makes it somewhat difficult to learn from video alone. Finding a competent instructor is advisable, since a "hands-on" approach is most effective. Tai chi classes can be found in most cities.

Unfortunately, because of its popularity, many diluted forms of tai chi have popped up which are much less effective than the traditional forms. My personal recommendation would be to seek out an instructor who teaches a traditional style with at least some emphasis on the martial applications of the forms. In my experience, having an understanding of the purpose of each movement is extremely helpful in learning the proper balance and emphasis.

Along the same lines as tai chi is a practice called chi gung (or qigung). Chi gung also involves slow, gentle movement along with focussed breathing. The main difference is that chi gung is almost entirely focussed on health and vitality, with none of the martial arts applications of tai chi. Tai chi is in fact sometimes classified as a form of chi gung. Chi gung classes are a bit harder to find, but it is available in most larger cities.

Most any martial art form can be a relatively good approach to learning and practicing balanced movement, since nearly all of them rely on coordination and balance as key foundations. I personally have come to have little or no interest in the "harder" martial art styles such as boxing, taekwondo, and the hard styles of karate, since they tend more toward a violent approach which can lean towards the "me versus you" tendency of ego tactics.

Along with tai chi, one of the most balanced and harmonious martial art forms is aikido. Rather than forcefully opposing an attack, aikido techniques rely on blending movement with the movement of one's partner and then redirecting it. Using balance, leverage, and harmonized movement, students learn to avoid and deflect attacks with a minimum of physical force. Judo, which I personally have the most experience in, is similar in principle, although it is much more of a "full contact" sport. It is extremely dependant upon balance and agility, however, and is therefore a very effective approach for some people.

I'd certainly recommend nearly any type of dance training, since they are all excellent at teaching harmonious, well-balanced movement. For the more athletically inclined, gymnastics and tumbling are also outstanding in this regard, since they demand a high degree of coordination, fluidity, and balance.

For the more adventurous, surfing, ice skating, snowboarding, skiing, skateboarding, rock climbing, and other similar activities demand a high degree of "in-the-moment" concentration and mind-body awareness. In short, any physical activity which requires our complete, focussed attention, and that requires coordination and discipline, can serve as a means to practice this moment-to-moment awareness and lead to a more well-balanced approach to life.

And of course we all know that getting the body moving in some form of exercise has a plethora of health benefits, not the least of which is the release of endorphins into our system, which can also aid in maintaining a mindful, present-moment awareness. Even walking, if done with full awareness, can be a wonderful way to explore the present moment experience of physical movement, balance, and our relationship to the pull of the earth's gravity.

At the purely *receptive* end of the scale of physical disciplines are various forms of massage, body work, and stress relief. These contribute to our overall balance, poise, and equilibrium by helping to release habitual tension held in various parts of the body. Two related disciplines which also work towards improved alignment through awareness and release of tension are Alexander Technique and the Feldenkrais Method. Practitioners of each can be found in most mid-to-large-sized cities.

Any or all of these movement disciplines can be useful in increasing our present-moment awareness and developing balance and higher levels of mind-body coordination. But even simply getting into the habit of being more aware of how we hold, move, and use our bodies in our everyday activities can often be just as valuable, and it is in any case one of the main goals of these other disciplines.

Writing

There are several types of daily writing disciplines that can contribute to our advancement towards self-actualization. In her book on leading a creatively-based life, *The Artist's Way*, Julia

Cameron recommends what she calls "morning pages". The practice is to begin each morning by writing at least three pages, by hand, in a journal or notebook. It makes no difference whatsoever *what* you write, just put down whatever comes to mind.

In fact, if you can't think of anything, you can simply begin by writing something like, "I just can't think of anything to write. I wonder why that is?" And just keep writing. When I've done this as a daily discipline I've been truly amazed not only at what would often come through the writing itself, but also how it opened up previously untapped avenues of creativity in my daily life. Frequently I'd struggle coming up with the first couple of pages, but more often than not, by the time I reached the third page, I'd be into such a strong flow that I'd end up writing another page or two.

I've been thoroughly amazed time after time at the gems that would come out of these morning pages. Perhaps even more importantly though, one of the main benefits of the process is that it clears away the clutter that is keeping the creative channels blocked. By getting whatever extraneous thoughts we may have out of our head and down onto paper, we eliminate much of the constant, usually ego-based, mind chatter that interferes with true creative thinking. Along with daily meditation, morning pages are one of the most vital and potent ways to begin the day and align our thinking in creative directions.

Another useful tool is to have written, imaginary dialogues with distinct aspects of ourselves. One approach is to have a dialogue with our Authentic Self. Imagine that aspect of yourself that is whole and complete and not at all separate from anyone or anything else: your True Self. You can pose questions to this "Higher Self", and see what you write in response, imagining the answers that your Self would give. If you prefer, you could instead do this as an imaginary dialogue with an older, wiser version of yourself.

Particularly if you first get yourself into a relaxed, meditative state, you may be amazed at the truly profound answers to personal issues and dilemmas that may arise. I find that at the very least, this process always forces me to be completely honest with myself, and it's a very effective tool for getting to the heart of any problem.

Here's an example of a "Higher Self" dialogue that I wrote several years ago, in November of 2003, and that I've re-edited slightly for inclusion here. It actually illustrates well many of the principles we've been discussing:

Me: Why am I having such a problem with focus lately? And with getting things done? What am I missing? Or more likely avoiding? What is it I don't want to face? What is the right question to ask? Are you there?

Higher Self: I Am always here. But this you know already. You hesitate in uncertainty. But that's just an excuse, isn't it? Uncertainty is not the issue. Trust is. With trust, uncertainty matters not. You are in fact learning this. But your rational mind still wants to cling to the belief that it is in control. And thus you over-rationalize everything and minimize your accomplishments and your effectiveness.

It's simply because you've not yet learned to trust beyond what you can see. Yes, you did begin to write "to see beyond what you can trust", which is, of course, also true. And thus you've stumbled upon another important paradox. You can't see because you don't trust what *might* be there to be seen.

Trust My uncertainty. The paradox is that if you give up your *attachment* to seeing everything—which in this case simply means needing to control it—you'll then be able to *truly* see it clearly. Remember that perceptions are selective, and therefore an attempt to control or define that which you see—in such a way that you only perceive that which your rational mind believes will be safe.

This is, of course, impossible, and only leads to a vicious cycle of fear, control, and refusal to trust. Identify the pattern. Recognize it first. Yes, you're beginning to see your resistance to seeing clearly. Just note it. Begin with that. Just stop to note your experience in the moment. Yes, you're also realizing that, although you have some intellectual understanding of this, it is not the same as *experiencing* it.

So simply begin with observation. Let that be your first step in practicing trust. And keep in mind that a first step, sincerely taken, always leads to a second. That's what trust is really about—taking that first step. And of course, that's where you've been stopping yourself. Just do it. Whatever "it" may be in the moment. And then allow yourself to experience that first step.

Another approach is to have this type of written dialogue with your "lower self", or with the part of yourself that is formed by unconsciously held fears and other emotional resistance. I've used this in the past to move beyond self-limiting habits. By asking our "fear self" what it wants, what it's afraid of, and why it's resisting us, we can give voice to those fears and emotional blocks of which we may not be completely aware, and thus *become* aware of them and begin transforming and moving beyond them.

The Creative Process

As we discussed previously, there really is no choice as to whether or not we will be creative and whether we will use our natural creative abilities. Because creativity is an innate and fundamental aspect of who we are as human beings, it happens naturally and automatically, just like breathing, regardless of whether we choose to be creative or not. The only real choice is whether we will use our creative abilities consciously and deliberately in healthy, forward-moving ways, or instead use them by default in unconscious, fear-based, self-limiting ways.

That is perhaps the one truly significant choice which we face each and every day. This is really a matter of becoming ever more aware of the directions of our thoughts. Are we allowing our thinking to be scattered helter skelter by whatever haphazard, emotional tumult the ego throws our way from one minute to the next? Or are we choosing to instead focus our attention more consistently in progressive directions: on the person we want to be, and the life we want to live?

Getting into the habit of applying our artistic "process of magic" to even the seemingly insignificant, menial tasks and problems that arise throughout the day is a truly worthwhile endeavor. Whenever a troublesome situation presents itself, rather than resisting it or trying to force our way through it, we can instead choose in that moment to ask whether there might not be some creative solution that will turn the perceived problem into a creative opportunity.

If we find ourselves resisting or judging a situation as a "problem", we can fairly safely assume that we're not seeing it clearly. As soon as we realize this, we can choose to ask for an answer or a solution, and pause a moment to see if some intuitive impression may present itself. Sometimes a completely new perspective on the situation may present itself, and we may find that we can then act immediately to transform the situation easily and completely. Other times patience may be more appropriate, and we can simply trust that if we're willing to wait for it, the most appropriate line of action will become obvious when the time is right.

Often just getting into the habit of asking for the most appropriate creative response will attract unexpected opportunities that seem magically synchronistic and serendipitous. My close friend and skilled sleight-of-hand magician, Andrew Dakota, told me that when he was preparing to go to work at one of his jobs performing magic, he would often say a little prayer, asking to be allowed to touch those people he was meant to touch in whatever way he was meant to do so, and to be able to keep his own ego out of the picture.

One night Andrew was performing for a group of people with some kids and a handful of adults at a restaurant he was working, and everyone at the table was having an absolute blast—except for this one woman. She was sitting with her arms crossed, a rather sour expression on her face, and every time Andrew tried to get her involved she refused to even smile. She seemed bound and determined to not have fun or to even be in the least bit impressed or entertained by Andrew's magic.

Andrew said he tried to have some fun with her, but when it became obvious that there was little he could do, he just let it go and finally finished up at the table with everyone else there truly thrilled by his performance. After leaving the table, Andrew saw another table of people that he wanted to work for, and since there were also some kids there, he decided he'd do something special for them.

Andrew has a really wonderful magic routine where he blows soap bubbles, and when he gets one that's just the right size, he reaches out and grabs it, and changes it into a solid crystal ball. He then does some magic with the crystal ball, and it eventually vanishes. This particular routine takes some special setup right before he can perform it, so he went into the back where he could prepare in private, and got ready to perform this routine for the next table.

In order to get to the table he intended to work next, he had to walk right past the table where he'd just been, with the woman with the sour expression. As he walked past, he suddenly realized that the kids at the table he just performed for had brought bottles of soap bubbles into the restaurant with them, and they were now blowing soap bubbles. Just as Andrew walked past their table, a bubble that was exactly the right size floated right up in front of him. He looked at the people at the table, and pointing to the bubble, said, "May I?"

When they nodded, he grabbed the bubble, turning it into the small crystal ball, tossed it up and down into the air a couple of times, and then pretended to throw it at the woman who'd been so resistant, and as he did, he made it disappear. Andrew said this woman went absolutely nuts. She screamed and began laughing, and he said that every time he saw her for the rest of the evening, she was raving on and on about how Andrew was the best magician she'd ever seen, and that he was absolutely wonderful.

Of course, the point is not whether the woman thought Andrew was great, it was the fact that by asking for opportunities and being open to them when they arose, he was able to help facilitate a transformation in this woman's openness to the experience of joy and wonder, and presumably to be of significant service to her and her friends.

Making Art

While the artistic, creative process can be applied to any area of life, making art for its own sake is another extremely valuable personal pursuit that can bring us into the present moment, teach us more about the creative process itself, and help us to further discover "Who" we are. As with morning pages, finding an outlet for our creativity that we are passionate about can be one of the most potent avenues for exploring self-expression.

Whether we find ourselves drawn to painting, sketching, creating music, performing, dance, sculpture, woodworking, gourmet cooking, or literally any other artistic endeavor, spending time immersed in purely creative pursuits has a power all its own. It can transform our attitudes, open up new ways of thinking, and allow our spirit to shine into the world in ways we might not have imagined.

After several years of not having played my guitar, I've recently unpacked it and now leave it sitting out on a stand in my office near my computer. When I'm feeling stuck, I'll often pick it up and play for a few minutes, just letting myself go wherever the music takes me. More often than not, it helps me to clear my head and get back on track with whatever I'd been doing.

Artistic expression, in any area of life, also helps us to experience the uniqueness of Who we really are as distinct individuals. It is an act of Self-expression. Through it, we discover both our individual uniqueness and our unique contribution to the world. Once when Agnes De Mille was having a crisis of severe doubt in her ability to access the value of her own work, Martha Graham told her the following:

> *"There is a vitality, a life force, an energy, a quickening that is translated through you into action, and because there is only one of you in all of time, this expression is unique. And if you block it, it will never exist through any other medium and it will be lost. The world will not have it. It is not your business to determine how good it is nor how valuable nor how it compares with other expressions. It is your business to keep it yours clearly and directly, to keep the channel open. You do not even have to believe in yourself or your work. You have to keep yourself open and aware to the urges that motivate you. Keep the channel open. ... No artist is pleased. [There is] no satisfaction whatever at any time. There is only a queer divine dissatisfaction, a blessed unrest that keeps us marching and makes us more alive than the others."*
> —Martha Graham[26]

Taking time out of our busy lives for artistic expression (or ideally, devoting our lives fully to that expression) is a wonderfully empowering and rejuvenating discipline, and who knows, we might just inspire someone else with the results of our creative efforts.

Recognizing Beauty

Stop. Look. Listen. Feel. It's in nature. It's in great works of art. It's in everyday moments. It can *take our breath away* and *make time stand still*. The ability to recognize and appreciate beauty is one of the main characteristics that makes us distinctly human. To "recognize" means to "know again". This implies that what we "recognize" as beautiful resonates with what we have within already.

As it is said that "beauty is in the eye of the beholder", it is our responsibility to recognize and appreciate beauty. For if we don't, who else will? Getting into the habit of regularly noticing and appreciating the beauty around us allows us to truly realize that, as Dan Millman said, *"There are no ordinary moments."*

Inspiration

Are you inspired by life? Do you share that inspiration with others? Do you appreciate and acknowledge the inspiration that does come into your life? As we seek out and allow this inspiration to be a regular part of our experience, we move out of the realm of the ego and into the realm of inspired living.

Many years ago when we were still living in Los Angeles, I was going through a frustrating period with my career. I was becoming well-known and respected as a performer in the professional entertainment circles in which I worked, but I felt that I should be making more progress than I was, and that I wasn't moving forward fast enough towards achieving my goals. I felt stuck and discouraged, like I was spinning my wheels.

Around this time, I was hired to appear as one of the headline performers at a magic convention in Phoenix, Arizona. Magicians have these types of trade conventions periodically throughout the year, and they often hire the top magicians to perform and conduct teaching workshops, called lectures. I was invited to perform on the evening gala show and to present my lecture which was on approaching magic as an actual art form.

Frequently the majority of magicians are much more interested in lectures on how to do the tricks, the technical aspects of magic. But my lecture was on how to *perform* magic better, to make it more artistic and expressive and to have more emotional impact. Though I'd been really down on myself before attending the convention, I was astonished and inspired by the responses of my fellow magicians to both my stage performance and my lecture.

I received a standing ovation on the evening performance, and I was touched and heartened by the overwhelming positive comments on my show afterwards. Similarly, the other magicians responded to my lecture with utter enthusiasm and a seemingly endless stream of appreciation and thanks. Many said it was the best magic lecture they'd ever seen, and that it had radically transformed how they saw their magic and their approach to it. One young man in his late teens or early twenties who approached me following my lecture was nearly in tears, he was so inspired and grateful that he'd finally been given practical ideas on how to more effectively approach his own magic in the artistic way to which he aspired.

I was inspired and humbled by the various responses that I received, and I realized clearly for perhaps the first time that my greatest mission in life is to *inspire*; to be inspired myself and to share inspiration with others. For me, that is the essence and the purpose of all art and of artful living.

It doesn't matter what we do in life. It only matters that we allow ourselves to be open to inspiration. Inspiration can come in any form, in any area of our lives. We can be inspired by an uplifting musical performance. Or we can be inspired by finding a creative new way to fix that squeaky door on the kitchen cabinet. The only matter of true importance is whether we allow, accept, and appreciate the inspiration that we receive.

By allowing myself to become frustrated and judgmental about my progress with my career, I temporarily shut myself off from the experience of my own inspiration. When I let myself see the effect I was having on others, I was humbled to realize the powerful channel for inspiration that I could be, and deeply grateful for the experience of it. And I rediscovered my own inspiration as a result.

Incidentally, I found it somewhat interesting that this experience of renewal occurred in Phoenix, since in mythological terms the Phoenix represents rebirth. The Phoenix was the mythical sacred firebird that every 1000 years would burn to ashes, from which a new Phoenix would arise. And my inspired experience in Phoenix was most certainly one of psychological rebirth for me.

It's important that we pause on a regular basis to check and make sure we haven't cut ourselves off from the experience of inspiration. And if we have, that we re-connect with it. The wonder of inspiration leads to the joyful pull of aspiration, leading us ever onward and upward.

Practicing Humor

I once heard a story, supposedly true, of an Eastern spiritual guru who was giving a talk before a large western audience. At one point in his talk he became very serious and told them that he was about to reveal a sacred mantra that held the secret to self-realization. He asked the audience to chant each part of the mantra with him.

First he chanted "Zen!", and the audience responded with "Zennnnn!" Next came "Zaaahhh!" Followed by "Yuuuu!", and finally "Maaahhh!" Then he had them put it all together: "Zennn, Zaaahhh, Yuuu, Maaahhh!" And then a little more quickly, "ZEN, zah,YOO, mah!" Gradually, as they began to 'get it', the audience burst out into laughter.

It's incredibly valuable to have a great "zenza humah" (sense of humor, in case you hadn't 'gotten it' yet). As I mentioned previously, we know we're making headway in letting go of the ego when someone pokes one of our 'sore spots', or 'pushes one of our buttons', one of those issues that would have once set us off in anger or agitation, and instead our immediate response is to laugh about it.

A healthy sense of humor is about detachment, about letting go of attachments to those issues that the ego clings to so strenuously. Our practice of honesty, sincerity, and detachment is embodied in the healthy experience of laughter and humor. Are you able to laugh at yourself and your shortcomings and take them lightly?

Of course, it should go without saying that we're not talking about the more caustic forms of humor such as sarcasm and put-downs. These are little more than the ego's thinly disguised attempt to justify attack and aggression as just "being funny". That can often be a form of (not so passive) passive aggression.

Stop for a moment to think of all the various situations and issues that really get you stressed out and upset. Is it being stuck in traffic after that long day at work? Is it that overbearing numbskull of a boss at work? Is it when your spouse acts thoughtlessly towards you? Now, can you imagine yourself laughing about it and taking it lightly, even laughing at your own need to get upset? Laughter can be an incredible release for those pent-up emotions that normally eat away at us.

My wife Kathi's mother, Maxine Brown, was an absolute force of nature. On the one hand, she was enormously selfish in certain areas, a completely fanatical dictator with her children, and totally insane when it came to getting her way. By all accounts, growing up with her was in many ways a horrendous experience for Kathi and her eight siblings.

However, Maxine also had a terrific sense of humor, she was tremendously generous in many ways, and she could be forgiving and compassionate beyond all expectations. And she was absolutely masterful at creating wonderful, large family events, filled with an atmosphere of hospitality, love, laughter, and abundance. She consistently made all visitors feel welcome and included.

When she passed away, the family was devastated. It was truly difficult to accept that she was gone, especially for Kathi and her brothers and sisters. Maxine had been this ever-present, unstoppable, all-encompassing *Power* in their lives, in both positive and not so positive ways. And after overcoming and constantly living with a seemingly endless stream of severe health problems for years on end, it seemed inconceivable that her bigger-than-life presence could ever be gone from our lives.

The days surrounding Maxine's funeral spent with Kathi's family were an astonishing, cathartic experience. The most amazing aspect of it to me, though it also seemed completely natural, was that along with the intense grief and tears and anguish, there were just as many moments that were equally rich with hilarity, laughter, and exuberant good humor.

I can't begin to count the number of times we were all doubled over with gut-wrenching laughter at a story someone told of how extreme and stubborn and absolutely outrageous their mother could be. Through the laughter, they all expressed and celebrated their absolute acceptance and love for their mother, in spite of her many excessive and even extravagant faults. There was no question of forgiveness, as it was an already accepted, clear but unspoken, accomplished fact for virtually everyone.

Kathi's mother loved to laugh, and she shared that incredibly valuable gift with her family as one of her undying legacies.

Humor can be healing, uplifting, and a source of both detachment and of true joy. Make sure that you find something to laugh about today.

Play

Along the same lines as humor, it's also really important to schedule time for pure fun and enjoyment; to just play and have fun. Children learn through play, but we can too. More to the point, play brings us directly into the present moment, opens the channels for creativity, and allows us to relax and recharge.

Recreation is not just an optional pastime, it's how we renew and refresh ourselves and release the stresses and tensions inherent in our normally ego-dominated lives. Re-creation literally means to "re-create", to create anew.

Some of my best, most memorable experiences with family have been when playing with our little nieces and nephews, or playing interactive party games, or simply playing frisbee in the park. In my experience, engaging in activities where the only purpose is to have fun is a crucial element of emotional and mental health.

Large corporations are finding that staff training sessions get exponentially better, quantifiable results when fun activities such as team-building games are used as training tools. Introducing relevant but fun activities into any kind of learning event makes it more memorable, and participants take in new information more effortlessly and retain it much longer.

So many people in our modern society have come to believe that daily work is by nature boring, difficult drudgery. Why? Why can't it be fun? The ego objects to this on the basis that fun is frivolous and a time waster. But making work fun and enjoyable can more often than not make it more productive. Fun is its own motivator. People who have jobs that are fun don't dread getting up to go to work, they love it and can hardly wait to get there.

Play can and should be a fundamental element of our everyday lives. It's a great way to be creative, connect with others, and reinvigorate our lives in a variety of ways. But if left to the ego, the only kind of "fun" we'll be likely to pursue are mind-numbing escapist activities, such as addictive, violent video games, or highly competitive, cut-throat 'trounce your opponent' types of sporting activities. We can do better.

Like humor, taking a fun, playful approach to life gives us more detachment and a much healthier perspective on daily events. Why not make life an adventure?

In the Moment

As I mentioned, being fully in the moment is the main point of the entire range of principles we've been discussing. So why not simply go there directly? Using the practice of simply choosing to mindfully, and consciously pay attention to the entire range of experience in any given moment *as a discipline in its own right* is surely fertile ground for our process of self-actualization. This is where the real magic ultimately lies.

Our resistance doesn't always take an obvious form. More often it's subtle. Mild impatience in the form of wanting to be on to the next thing while we're still in the midst of something else makes us miss the experience of each of them. A good model for being fully in the experience of a moment is the act of walking a tightrope. When doing so, it's essential to be fully and intensely aware of each step we take. Otherwise, we fall off the rope. Our life is that rope. Are we practicing awareness on each step? Or falling off?

We can in fact practice this intense, present moment awareness in any and every activity that we undertake. And we can also practice it in non-activities, such as simply sitting for a moment to take a break from our constant busy-ness. Often when we choose to do so, even ordinary moments can become extraordinary.

As I mentioned earlier, in his book, *The Way of the Peaceful Warrior*, as well as in the movie based upon the book, *Peaceful Warrior*, Dan Millman is told by his teacher, Socrates, to go sit on a rock until he has an important thought. After several unsuccessful attempts, the one meaningful thought he has is, "There are no ordinary moments."

When we make it our habit to be acutely aware of our present experience, every moment has the potential to become a magical moment, a peak experience. What are you experiencing right this moment? Are you fully aware of it? Do you notice your breathing? The sensations in your body? The sounds in the room? The textures brought out by the light falling upon the page you're reading? What can you notice that you didn't notice a moment before?

This type of complete attention to the experience of Now brings with it a highly effective responsiveness to situations. We respond immediately, naturally, and with ease to the needs of a situation, often without any need for analytical thought of any kind. The choices are made *consciously*, but in the moment, we simply know what to do, and we do it, without really even thinking about it. We simply respond appropriately to the needs of the moment.

In these moments there is commonly an artful perfection to our actions. This can sometimes happen in the clear-minded intensity of a crisis situation. I've had a handful of experiences over the years of being behind the wheel of a car when some pressing danger has suddenly arisen, only to find myself responding immediately with complete detachment and adeptness. An oncoming car is suddenly and unexpectedly in my lane almost upon me, and I simply swerve smoothly completely off the road, around the car, and back into my lane, without the slightest hesitation or even a clinched muscle.

Later I was amazed at my own adroit responsiveness, but in the moment, I simply acted. The same kind of in-the-moment, dexterous responsiveness can sometimes occur when we are immersed in meaningful work. We become completely focussed on the task at hand, and an hour goes by in what seems like a moment. And we find not only that we've been highly effective and even masterful at our work, but that also, rather than being the least bit fatigued, we end up feeling energized and invigorated.

One of the reasons we are so effective when in this in-the-moment awareness and flow is that in these moments, we are completely open and receptive to intuitive direction without the need to analyze. We simply know the appropriate course of action, and we take it, without judgement or second guessing of any kind.

The key is choosing to pay attention. We make the definite choice to pay attention, vividly and directly, to whatever the experience of this present moment holds. And by so doing, we leave behind, at least for that moment, the judgement and turmoil of our habitual 'mind chatter'. From this experience of intense present-moment-awareness comes not only clarity of thought, but also clarity of action. By seeing things clearly in the present moment, we have a much clearer perception of the needs of the moment, and can take action to meet them if appropriate.

A Profoundly Inspired Message

While it's a core principle in this book, this idea was first brought home to me in a rather definite way during what was for me an extraordinarily profound experience that I had one day in April of 1992. The neighborhood where we lived in the Los Angeles area was in the San Fernando Valley about two miles away from a small community college. The college had a quarter-mile track that was open to the public, and I would often run over to the track, do a few laps, and then run back home.

Often when running, as I mentioned earlier, I would concentrate on my running form. On this particular day though, I wasn't paying much attention to my form, but was instead practicing some of the Bates eyesight improvement exercises that I discussed in Chapter 11. I'd focus on objects in the distance, shifting from one to another and from near to far, also relaxing the muscles in my face and opening my eyes a bit wider.

I was about a mile and a half into my run, not quite to the track, when I suddenly realized that my running form was nearly perfect, perhaps the best it had ever been. My first reaction was to worry that I wouldn't be able to maintain this harmonious, balanced flow, but then I simply accepted that it didn't matter. The important thing was that I'd experienced it, and if I could do it once, I could do it again, and eventually learn to become more consistent at it.

Having let go of the worry, I then made the rather interesting realization that the reason I'd been able to attain such a level of proficiency was that in the context of doing the eyesight exercises, I'd been *looking honestly* at what was right in front of me, and sensing what seemed like the most appropriate response to what I *saw* in each moment, and then simply allowing myself, and in this case my body, to respond accordingly. As a result, I'd gotten into a highly dexterous, agile, and gracefully balanced *flow*.

It then occurred to me that this was a profoundly simple, highly practical principle that had far-reaching implications for literally any situation I could think of. When dealing with other people for example, if in the moment we make our only objective to simply *see them clearly*, to just pay attention and 'get' them for who they are in that moment, something truly magical takes place.

We can choose to do this at any moment, in any situation. And as soon as we do, in the act of choosing to simply 'see', for that moment at least we leave behind our normal judgements, fears, irritations, and blame, and we simply choose to see what there is to be seen without prejudgment of any kind. Of course, in this context

I'm using the term "seeing" to mean not only physical sight and other five-sensory perception, but also a mental alertness, interest, and perceptive acuity, as well as an emotional openness, receptiveness and curiosity.

As we make the definite choice to *see* the other person clearly, while those aspects of their personality that we previously perceived as threatening or distasteful or irritating may still be present in our awareness, they no longer hold any negative emotional association whatsoever. We see those issues simply as *needs* that the other person has. As soon as we see this clearly, we'll also know immediately whether there is anything we can do to help meet those needs.

Of course, I'm not talking about trying to figure out what's going on with another person or what they need. That's just more mental gyrations based on the ego's need to control things. What I really mean is simply *paying attention*, with an intensely focussed openness, interest, and curiosity, to whatever the experience of the present moment brings. In that state, the mind actually becomes still. And then from that place of open alertness, we then allow ourselves to respond naturally to whatever we 'see'.

For example if someone is angry and acting with hostility, it's usually because they feel the need to be accepted or 'gotten' or supported. If, rather than feeling threatened by their anger, we instead choose to just see them clearly in the moment and see their true needs (which may or may not be what they think they are), we can respond accordingly.

Sometimes just 'getting' them will be enough. Other times we may need to take action to help fill their needs in some way. And in other situations, doing nothing in that moment may be appropriate. But if we make 'seeing' our only objective, to the degree that we can do so successfully, we'll know what is appropriate without having to think about it or try to figure it out. This is the essence of true compassion; simply accepting and seeing someone for who they are, and being willing to act accordingly to address any needs that we may see.

As I ran onto the track and began running some laps, my mind was racing a mile a minute with hundreds of examples of how this simple principle applied to anything and everything. I literally couldn't think of a situation that it didn't address thoroughly. By simply approaching any situation with an attitude of complete open-minded but intensely focussed interest, curiosity, and the intention to *see what's there*, along with the willingness to act accordingly in light of what we see, we can respond capably and compassionately to whatever life brings us.

I began expanding the concept to even wider applications and realized that this is also how we, as individuals and as collective society, will solve the various crises, problems, and the myriad dire situations in the world. It's when we can simply look clearly at the conditions of the world around us, without personal bias or prejudice or ideological preconception or emotional attachment of any kind, that we will know exactly what must be done to address every single problem that confronts us. We open our eyes to current needs, see them clearly for what they are, and take action to resolve them, and thus we solve the problems of the world.

I was thoroughly and completely blown away by this simple yet tremendously potent insight, perhaps the most profound I'd ever had. This was for me, at the point where I was in my life, a literally life-changing epiphany that had flashed into my mind complete and whole in the blink of an eye.

As I continued running laps on the track, I was finally just getting to the point where I was stepping back mentally to catch my breath and to try to begin making sense of all the various ramifications of my new understanding, and at that exact moment I happened to pass another runner on the track. As I did, I glanced up at the back of his t-shirt, and on it I read the words, *"Open Your Eyes, and Save the Earth!"* I felt a shock jolt through me as I saw the very essence of my newfound epiphany spelled out perfectly and succinctly in those simple words.

At this particular time in my life, I'd become quite accustomed to the experience of seemingly bizarre, almost magical, serendipitous 'coincidences'. But this was a bit much even for me. I'm not sure that I could have been more thunderstruck if the sky had opened up and a booming Voice spoken to me by name. The message seemed so pointed and personal and directed specifically to my thoughts.

As it was, I knew clearly and distinctly that I'd certainly 'gotten the message', so to speak, and there was no question of the power of the experience and the implications it had for me personally. Since these inspired gifts normally don't come through so blatantly, I felt blessed by the experience, and it occurred to me that I also owed a debt of acknowledgement to the guy wearing the t-shirt. I needed to thank him for the part he played.

But that made me really uncomfortable, since I was afraid he'd no doubt think I was some kind of nutcase, especially given the way I was likely to communicate in the idealistically enthusiastic state of mind I was in at the moment. After struggling with this for several minutes, I finally decided that if I was meant to make some kind of contact with him, I'd be presented with an opportunity to do so. And I let it go.

A few short moments later, I was about to lap the guy and pass him again, when he turned, passing right in front of me and went out the gate to leave. So I followed him. As I slowed and walked up behind him, I said a friendly, "Hi there!"

He turned around and said, "Hi." He was a small man in his mid-twenties, with dark complexion, a friendly face, and a Middle-Eastern accent.

I said, "Hey, I just wanted you to know that the message on the back of your t-shirt was particularly inspiring for me today."

He glanced down at his shirt and said, "Oh yeah, the Earth Day." (I could see then that it was a t-shirt promoting Earth Day on April 24.)

"Well it was especially pointed for me in terms of what I'd been thinking about today," I told him. (Understatement.)

"Yea, that's funny," he said, "I'm not pro or con on it, but I was just reading an article about it this morning, and I was thinking about it because it's the day after my birthday. Actually I hadn't really even thought about this shirt, though. My brother had it and didn't want it, so he gave it to me. I just happened to put it on today. It's the first time I've worn it in over six months."

I told him that was really interesting, and said that I just wanted to thank him for the inspiring message, and we parted with a warm smile. I couldn't help thinking the whole thing had come together for some inexplicable reason. Talk about magically inspired wonder!

While not entirely new to me in principle, the message that I got that day in such specific and blatant terms has become one of the main guiding fundamentals for how I aspire to live my life. Ever since, I've set about working to apply and integrate this experience into my life in practical ways on a daily basis, and I'm certain that I'll continue learning how to do so more consistently, no doubt for the rest of my life. In that sense, it is for me a true Life Lesson.

Chapter Eighteen

A CALL TO MAGIC

"That's the thing about magic; you've got to know it's still here, all around us, or it just stays invisible for you."
—Charles de Lint

Our problem is not that life is not magical. It is that we forget or in some cases even refuse to *experience* it as magical. A quotation that is often attributed to Einstein sums it up:

"There are only two ways to live your life. One is as though nothing is a miracle. The other is as though everything is."[27]

If we expect magic, we'll get it. If we expect monotony and hopelessness, we'll get that. I have complete conviction in the belief that we all have miraculous, untapped potential, just waiting to be released. I believe that we can all accomplish miraculous, seemingly impossible achievements.

I don't believe that human beings act in destructive and evil ways because they are inherently evil. To the contrary, I believe they do so because they are disconnected from Who they are at their deepest levels as human beings. The ego would have us believe that we mustn't look within, because we will find only evil there. This belief only reinforces the disconnection from our True Self and justifies a sense of fatalistic hopelessness. I reject this belief as untrue.

I believe that it is this "disconnect" that is the source of all pain and suffering in the world. However, I also believe that our eventual destiny is to move beyond it to a deeper, truer experience of the magic inherent within our lives. I believe that a better world is not only possible, but inevitable. And I believe that we all, each and every one of us, have a role to play in its manifestation.

We do have a choice. We can choose to destroy ourselves and

our planet. Given the current trajectory of competitiveness, greed, violence, and complacency, that is certainly a possibility. But I believe that this dire outcome is not the way things will go.

Many would argue that there will always be war and greed and suffering and disharmony between human beings because that's the way it's always been, that's just how people are, and they're never going to change. But I believe that this is utter nonsense. We *have* changed, and we *are* changing. Change is in fact the only constant, for the universe and for humanity. Change is a given. We *will* change, the only question is how?

I believe that ultimately this change is always progressive in nature. Even destructive change eventually serves to move us forward, since it teaches us the painful lessons of the importance of harmlessness and compassion. In my lifetime, we've seen positive, progressive, beneficial changes that most people thought could never happen.

In our house we have a small piece of broken concrete that we keep on display in a closed container. One side is smooth, with paint on it. With it is a photograph of our two friends who sent it to us. The picture shows them chipping pieces out of the Berlin Wall when it came down in 1989.

Yes, there are problems in the world. Yes, there are war and hunger and pollution. But there is also progress. There is compassion. There are outstanding human achievements in all areas of life.

On 9/11/2001, after the airplanes struck the World Trade Center and the Pentagon, the rest of the world joined together to send us a seemingly unending abundance of empathy, respect, and support. When the 7.0 magnitude earthquake hit Haiti in 2010, there was an outpouring of compassion, financial contributions, and aid. When the earthquake and resulting tsunami hit Japan in 2011, the world responded immediately with compassion and assistance. When tragedy strikes people in our own communities, we all are moved to offer support and compassion.

Although the headlines sensationalize the hatred and violence and political divisiveness in the world, the overwhelming majority of human interactions are actually cooperative and constructive. Our societies are literally founded upon and completely dependant upon our continual cooperation with one another. Without cooperation and trust, nothing would happen.

Without a measure of cooperation and trust, no financial transaction could take place, no laws could be passed, and even society itself could not exist. I would contend that cooperation is a much more potent and ever-present quality inherent in all of our human interactions than any of our more destructive behaviors.

The problem is not that we don't have cooperation and trust, it's that we take them for granted, overlook them, and even deny that they are the foundation for everything we do as social creatures. Instead we focus the majority of our attention on the examples of hostility, intolerance, divisiveness, and animosity.

But where we focus our attention is not without effect. Do we want to reinforce destructive behavior and situations, or do we want to reinforce something more positive and progressive? Given that, *"As a man thinks in his heart, so is he,"* do we want to envision a future of doom and gloom, or one of inspiration and fulfillment?

The Choice

Humans have a monumental choice before us at this, most momentous moment in history. It is a choice that becomes ever more blatantly clear with each day that passes. Will we choose to continue in the ways of the past, with a focus on competitiveness, greed, conflict, and the "every man for himself" perspective of the ego? Or will we choose sharing and cooperation and the realization that we're all in this together, and move forward into the future as one humanity?

One choice undoubtedly leads inevitably to destruction and devastation for mankind. The other leads to a world *"where no one lacks, where no two days are alike, where the Joy of Brotherhood manifests through all."*[28] Each of us individually is making this choice each day. Do we order our lives in creative, progressive, compassionate ways, or in the mind-numbing, backward, separative ways of the ego?

What About You?

On a more personal level, what are you choosing? Are you part of the problem or part of the solution? This will be determined by the choices you make, the beliefs you adopt, the thoughts you habitually hold in your mind, and consequently by the actions you take in life.

Are you content to live as a separate ego, completely caught up and lost in the conflicts and stresses and turmoil of our so-called modern lives? Or do you aspire to more? Will you act to transform the smallness and pettiness of ego thinking to the inspired inclusiveness of the Authentic Self?

The fact that you have chosen to accompany me on this journey of the exploration of the magic of life tells me that you do in fact aspire to more. By connecting your thoughts with mine during this time we have shared, by taking my ideas into consideration, and by stepping momentarily out of time into the realm of thought and contemplation and *magic*, you have demonstrated the reality of our interconnectedness. For that, you have my gratitude and respect. I hope you have found value here, and if so, that you will make it your own, and share it with others in your own unique way.

As individuals, we have an enormous responsibility for the health and salvation of humanity. You might be thinking, "What can I possibly do to help change the world?" The answer: Begin with changing yourself. As we each move towards self-actualization, we contribute to the "group actualization" of the human race as a whole.

You can choose to live your life with joy and compassion and inspiration. You can choose to share that joy and compassion and inspiration with others. You can choose to answer the call to magic and choose a life of magic, first for yourself, and consequently, inevitably, for the world. The choice is yours.

ABOUT THE AUTHOR

Mitch Williams is an international award winning magician and sleight of hand artist, an inspirational speaker, and an authority on creativity, personal transformation, and peak performance. For over thirty-five years, he has been an avid student of cutting edge information on human development, transformational psychology, future studies, and psycho-spirituality. A true modern Reinnassance man, he is an accomplished artist, musician, poet, author, athlete, gardener, gourmet cook, woodworker, and a martial artist with a fourth degree black belt in Judo. Mitch currently lives in Canton, Illinois with his wife Kathi, his spiritual and creative partner.

NOTES:

[1] (A little tribute to Eckhart Tolle.)

[2] *Psycho-Cybernetics*, Maltz, Maxwell, 1960.

[3] Proverbs 23:7

[4] This idea was advocated by psychologist, Carl Jung, who said, *"What you resist persists."*

[5] These attributes for each level are based loosely on descriptions provided by my friend and colleague, psychologist, Dr. George Catlin, author of the book, *The Way to Happiness.*

[6] As reported in the book, *A Whack on the Side of the Head*, by Roger von Oech.

[7] www.mitchwilliamsmagic.com/MagMind.html

[8] *Esoteric Psychology Vol. II*, Alice A. Bailey, Lucis Trust, 1942, quoted with the permission of Lucis Trust, the publisher & copyright holder.

[9] *Think and Grow Rich*, Napoleon Hill, The Ralston Society, (Meriden), 1937.

[10] *Joy of Sports, Revised: Endzones, Bases, Baskets, Balls, and the Consecration of the American Spirit*, Michael Novak, Madison Books, 1976, 1994; used with permission.

[11] *The Hero with a Thousand Faces*, Joseph Campbell, Bollingen Foundation, 1949.

[12] *A Course in Miracles*, Foundation for Inner Peace, 1975.

[13] www.otherworldsarepossible.org/alternatives/defending-global-commons

[14] *A Course in Miracles*, Foundation for Inner Peace, 1975.

[15] *Liberating the Corporate Soul: Building a Visionary Organization*, Richard Barrett, Butterworth-Heinemann, 1998.

[16] *Windows into Waldorf: An Introduction to Waldorf Education*, David Mitchell, © AWSNA Publications, quoted with permission of the author.

[17] From the following website documents:
www.theatlantic.com/past/docs/issues/99sep/9909waldorf.htm
www.ibe.unesco.org/publications/ThinkersPdf/steinere.pdf

[18] From: www.en.wikipedia.org/wiki/Siege_of_Sarajevo

[19] See: www.en.wikipedia.org/wiki/File:Evstafiev-bosnia-cello.jpg

[20] *Paris France*. Gertrude Stein, New York: Liveright, 1970. (p. 12)

[21] As reported on:
www.aep-arts.org/files/AEPWireDoingWell.pdf

NOTES:

[22] *Arts & Economic Prosperity III: The Economic Impact of Nonprofit Arts and Culture Organizations and Their Audiences*, Americans for the Arts, 2007.

[23] www.en.wikipedia.org/wiki/Citizen_journalism

[24] www.theamericanscholar.org/solitude-and-leadership/

[25] From:
www.ori.org/Media/pressreleases/TaiChiNEJM_02_08_12.html

[26] As quoted by Agnes de Mille in *The Life and Work of Martha Graham*, Agnes de Mille, 1991, p. 264, ISBN 0-394-55643-7.

[27] As quoted in *Journal of France and Germany* (1942 - 1944) by Gilbert Fowler White, in an excerpt published in *Living with Nature's Extremes: The Life of Gilbert Fowler White* (2006) by Robert E. Hinshaw, p. 62. There is apparently some disagreement as to whether Einstein actually said this.

[28] Paraphrased from *Share International* magazine, Sept. 2011.

CPSIA information can be obtained
at www.ICGtesting.com
Printed in the USA
BVHW041302161220
595859BV00018B/189

9 781479 320349